THE NEW HAMPSHIRE CENTURY

The

NEW HAMPSHIRE

Century

Concord Monitor Profiles of

One Hundred People Who Shaped It

Felice Belman and Mike Pride, editors

University Press of New England

HANOVER AND LONDON

University Press of New England,

Hanover, NH 03755

5 4 3 2 1

Library of Congress Cataloging-in-Publication Data

The New Hampshire century : Concord monitor profiles of one hundred
people who shaped it / Felice Belman and Mike Pride, editors.

    p. cm.

  ISBN 1–58465–087-7

  1. New Hampshire—Biography. I. Belman, Felice. II. Pride, Mike,
1946–   III. Concord monitor (Concord, N.H. : 1970) IV. Title.

  CT248 .N47 2001

  920.0742—dc21   00-012462

Contents

Acknowledgments

This book would not have been possible without the hard work of the *Concord Monitor*'s photography editor and sleuth extraordinaire, Dan Habib, who arranged for portraits of the subjects who were still alive and hunted down images of those long dead.

We would also like to thank *Concord Monitor* photographer Ken Williams, who turned out to be chief photographer for this project, shooting photos for more than two dozen stories.

In addition, several current and former *Monitor* writers contributed full-length profiles for the newspaper project, but their names do not appear above any of the stories in this book. Their work is the basis for many of the fifty shorter biographies that follow. Christopher Cheney, now an editor at the *Boston Herald*, wrote about astronaut Alan Shepard. Jeffrey Y. Grappone, a Georgetown University student, wrote about the first women in the New Hampshire Legislature. Matthew T. Hall, a business reporter in San Diego, wrote about filmmaker Ken Burns. Copy editor Nancy Hendryx profiled two children's authors: Tomie dePaola and Elizabeth Yates. Technology writer Ed Hurley profiled the Hubbard brothers and their giant poultry operation. Medical researcher Yuri Pride profiled baseball great Red Rolfe. And Ann E. Marimow, now a reporter at the *San Jose Mercury-News,* wrote about public health pioneer Lilian Streeter of Concord, Franco-American leader Theophile Biron of Manchester, and several New Hampshire education reformers: Andru Volinsky, Charles Holmes Pettee, John Sloan Dickey, and Robert Rines.

Introduction

At the dawn of the twentieth century there were just 410,000 people and thirteen moose living in New Hampshire. At the century's end, the human population had nearly tripled and the number of moose had exploded, to more than 9,000. On the other hand, dairy cows (115,000) and farm horses (54,500) were doing well in 1900 but dramatically less so in 1999: The populations had plummeted to 20,000 and 4,700.

At the start of the century, there were just 414 lawyers in New Hampshire; by 1999 there were 5,006. Progress? Perhaps.

By the century's close, traffic fatalities were up, up, up—as were the number of black bears, wild turkeys, and prison inmates.

Statistics, of course, can't begin to tell the complicated, contradictory, confounding story of New Hampshire in the 1900s.

It was a century in which environmentalists struggled mightily to protect the state's precious resources from the excesses of industry. Often they succeeded, as in the creation of the White Mountain National Forest and the defeat of plans to construct a giant oil refinery on the Seacoast. Sometimes they failed, as in the fight against the Seabrook nuclear plant.

It was a century that began with suffragists like Marilla Ricker fighting for women's right to vote and ended with a woman as governor (not to mention women as speaker of the House and president of the Senate).

It was a time in which a small state enjoyed a spot on the national political stage far out of proportion to its size. If Richard Upton hadn't cooked up the first-in-the-nation primary, Sherman Adams and John Sununu might never have become presidential chiefs of staff—and David Souter might not have landed on the U.S. Supreme Court.

It was an era in which artists of all types sought out New Hampshire's peace and quiet. Most recently, Lotte Jacobi, Donald Hall, and Ken Burns. Before them, Amy Beach, Augustus Saint-Gaudens, and Thornton Wilder.

It was an era in which the nation's social movements were reflected here, too. But activists fighting for the rights of war resisters, black people, women, the poor, gays, and religious minorities in New Hampshire had not just public opinion but also *William Loeb* to contend with.

It was an era in which first tourism and then computers became the industries we relied on most. It was a time in which Hannes Schneider taught the state to ski—and Bob Bahre taught us to love auto racing!

It was an era in which politicians spent nearly 100 years debating the necessity of a statewide income tax—without coming to a decision.

And it was a period that began with reformers like Frank Streeter pushing to improve New Hampshire's public schools and ended with reformers like Andru Volinsky pushing to do the very same thing.

In the fall of 1998, the editors of the *Concord Monitor* were struggling to find a project that would capture the important moments, overlooked heroes, and interesting trends in New Hampshire in the last hundred years. The result was the biggest project the small news staff had ever undertaken: profiles of 100 people who shaped the century. The first story, about the old man who looks after the Old Man of the Mountain, ran in the *Monitor* on January 1, 1999. The hundredth story, about a crusading federal judge, ran on December 31 that year.

Between the two was a quirky series that included stories about politics and music, tourism and UFOs, wartime and baseball. We created a list not of the 100 most important people in the state but of 100 people with interesting stories to tell. Some (like David Souter and Warren Rudman) were big shots in their own right. Some (like the contra-dance composer and the anti-nuke protester) were part of movements bigger than themselves.

In a state full of politicians and lawyers and judges, we tried not to profile too many politicians or lawyers or judges. On the other hand, we may have gone overboard on writers and artists (seventeen of 'em!). Our list was about two-thirds men and one-third women. About half of the subjects were alive and half were dead. There were twelve business people, two religious leaders, three musicians, and seven athletes. We wrote about seven governors and five people who had served time in jail. There were people working hard to preserve the state's past (a stone wall builder, for instance, and the founder of the League of New Hampshire Craftsmen) and those who looked steadily forward (astronaut Alan Shepard and computer guru Patricia Gallup).

Many subjects were well-known—like Robert Frost and J. D. Salinger. Others we chose because they were not known publicly at all. Instead of profiling the head of the Berlin paper mills, we told the story of Dennis Theriault, one of thousands of North Country residents who have made their livings there.

Throughout the series, we heard regularly from readers. Some suggested subjects we never would have come up with ourselves—like William Butterfield, an architect from the early part of the century who designed many public buildings still in use today. Others had suggestions we chose not to take. Gov. Hugh Gallen didn't make the list. Neither did state Supreme Court Justice Frank Kenison. Sen. Styles Bridges, as it turns out, has something of a local fan club in Concord, but, alas, he didn't make the list either.

What amazed us most about the series was how "ancient history" no longer felt remote, once we learned about it. Some things, in fact, haven't changed much at all. Betty Hill, who made headlines in 1961 with her tales of alien encounters in the White Mountains, turned out to be alive and well—and still being visited by mysterious guests. Robert Bass, a reformer governor from the turn of the *last* century, worried about the corrupting influence of big money in politics much the way we do today. And Jessie Doe, one of the first women in the legislature, used the 1921 session to push for (what else?) a statewide income tax.

In this book we present our fifty favorite stories in full – and the second fifty in condensed form. They are presented not chronologically but in a deliberately random order intended to highlight the quirky diversity of the state: Mary Baker Eddy followed by Steven Tyler of Aerosmith, Grace Metalious next to Mel Thomson. To read them is to understand much of New Hampshire in the twentieth century: how it started, how it ended, and what happened in between.

FELICE BELMAN

THE NEW HAMPSHIRE CENTURY

Christa McAuliffe

Her selection as the teacher in space was a triumph for every ordinary person who nurtured dreams.

BY MARK TRAVIS

Nothing in her life prepared Christa McAuliffe for the instant when the Vice-President announced that she had been named the nation's teacher in space. But in following George Bush to the podium, McAuliffe rose to stardom as if she had been born for it.

"It's not often a teacher is at a loss for words," she said, a wobble in her voice as she faced the cameras. "I know my students wouldn't think so." Then she addressed the other finalists standing with her in the Roosevelt Room: "I've made nine wonderful friends over the last two weeks, and when that shuttle goes, there might be one body"—she sobbed once, put her fingers to her lips, then continued—"but there's gonna be ten souls I'm taking with me."

Outside on the White House lawn, McAuliffe posed for pictures and answered questions—no longer a Concord, New Hampshire, teacher, but a national celebrity. What did she expect to see from space? someone asked. "A

Christa McAuliffe and her children ride in a celebratory parade through Concord after she was chosen for the Challenger mission.
Concord Monitor.

world with no boundaries," she answered. Would she count down from ten for the cameras? Sure, she said. "Then what do I do? Blast off?"

Finally one reporter threw a hardball: Why no black teachers among the finalists? What message did that send? "Oh, goodness," McAuliffe answered. "There was no place on the application for race, sex, or age. It was totally color-blind."

CNN had broadcast the ceremony, and *People* magazine liked what it saw. "Cut! Print!" its next edition said. "You can hear America thinking, 'Christa, this could be the beginning of a beautiful friendship.'" It would have been so much easier if McAuliffe's story had ended in this spirit, full of hope and excitement. It ended, of course, in tragedy instead. But the notion of sending an ordinary person into space was an inspiring one, and McAuliffe was an inspired choice for the role.

When the *Challenger* exploded, the shock of her death immediately eclipsed the glory of her moment. It is still hard to see the moment for what it was. But it is possible.

In 1969, NASA put Americans on the moon. On the moon! It was, to state it mildly, a tough act to follow. Subsequent Apollo flights somehow fell short, and Skylab seemed a big step down. NASA focused its energy on developing the space shuttle, a reusable space vehicle.

The *Columbia,* the first shuttle, flew in April 1981, and soon NASA had four shuttles in operation. Public interest spiked but, just as quickly, began to wane again.

Though the shuttle program fell far short of its goals—sixty flights a year and financial self-sufficiency—it also managed to seem boringly routine. "Astronauts aren't so famous anymore," a *Concord Monitor* editorial said. "They go up, they come down, they train for their next flight, and America hardly notices them. The days of throwing confetti are gone."

But this curse contained the seed of a charm: If space flight itself had become routine, perhaps it was time for regular people to take their turn in orbit. NASA's interest was in finding someone who could communicate the excitement of space travel, something most astronauts—engineers, scientists, and military men—were not naturally inclined to do. Some thought that a journalist might be the first to blast off; Walter Cronkite seemed a logical choice. But in August 1984, President Reagan announced that the first ordinary citizen in space would be a teacher. Anyone with five years' experience and good health could apply.

Interest ran high, so NASA's first challenge was separating those who were serious. A 25-page application form did the trick; it could take 150 hours to complete. Forty-four thousand teachers requested the form, but only 11,500 submitted it.

McAuliffe almost fell on the wrong side of the line. She got her application just after Thanksgiving 1984, stuck it in a drawer until Christmas, and didn't mail it until deadline day: February 1, 1985.

Then she began to advance, as surely as a good student rising through the grades. Seventy-nine New Hampshire teachers had applied; McAuliffe was one of two who were named state nominees, joining a crowd of 114 nationwide. That brought a trip to Washington for briefings and a new interview by a panel of prominent judges. The judges' job was producing the ten national finalists. McAuliffe was the first one they picked.

It wasn't her resume that set her apart. McAuliffe had graduated seventy-fifth in a high school class of 176, and she had attended Framingham State College in Massachusetts. Her answers to the essay questions had been straightforward: "I watched the Space Age being born and I would like to participate." Her centerpiece project was straightforward, too: a journal of her experience, to humanize space travel and serve as a resource for future historians.

What really separated McAuliffe from the pack was her manner. "She had an infectious enthusiasm," said Alan Ladwig, the NASA official who ran the Teacher in Space program. "She showed she was not going to shy away from being a communicator."

The final selection would be made after a week of testing and talking in Houston. Now the competition was really tough. Kathleen Beres of Baltimore had crossed the Atlantic in a thirty-one-foot boat. Richard Methia of New Bedford, Massachusetts, had written poetry, short stories, and award-winning plays.

Even in this company, McAuliffe stood out. "Something about Christa was very comforting," finalist Peggy Lathlaen told Bob Hohler, then a *Concord Monitor* reporter. "Her eyes said peace and calm."

Dr. Terrence McGuire was a NASA psychiatrist who had screened every astronaut since Alan Shepard. One thing he assessed was the ability to tolerate high stress; McAuliffe had the highest score among the finalists.

"In my opinion, she was the most broad-based, best-balanced person of the ten," he told *New Woman* magazine. "I know this doesn't sound very scientific, but I think she's neat."

Investigative reporter Dave Olinger was in the *Concord Monitor* newsroom when McAuliffe's selection as teacher in space was announced. To his embarrassment, he began to cry with pride. It was such a triumph for Concord— and a triumph for every ordinary person who nurtured grand dreams. "We took our measure of excitement from her," Olinger said.

Like every community, Concord had its circles of companionship: the educators, the lawyers, the lunchtime basketball crowd. But Concord was small enough for many circles to overlap. Olinger hadn't met McAuliffe, but he knew her husband. "He was a pretty good basketball player, nothing special," said Olinger, who was nothing special on the court himself.

Christa McAuliffe's selection gave every circle in Concord something to strut about—in part because there seemed to be few she had not touched. She taught Sunday school. She played coed volleyball on a team called the Court Jesters. She led a Girl Scout troop and volunteered as a receptionist at a family planning clinic. She had even played Granny Greenthumb in a production of *Little Red Riding Hood and the Monkey Flower Wolf*.

To know the McAuliffes was to like them. She and her husband, Steve, had been high school sweethearts. They lived in Concord's best neighborhood but put on no airs. Her tastes ran toward BLTs and cold beer, the music of Carly Simon, hiking, and jogging. They had two children, a boy and a girl.

McAuliffe had an infectious giggle and bouncy energy, but there was steel in her, too. While her husband had studied law in Washington, she had taught at a primarily black school in Lanham, Maryland. A feminist, McAuliffe had insisted on being called the "chairperson" of a faculty advisory committee there. A Democrat, she had pitched into union politics, leading an unsuccessful campaign for a new bargaining agent at the school.

After moving to New Hampshire, McAuliffe taught first at Bow Memorial School and then at Concord High. Her field was social studies; she pioneered a course called "The American Woman," which is still taught at the high school. She had a tendency to arrive at school later than she should have, with her hair still wet. Her fondness for field trips sometimes made her students late for other classes. She was, without question, overcommitted.

But Principal Charles Foley found no fault with her work in the classroom, and many of her students loved her. She reached out to them in ways other teachers did not, and her enthusiasm for learning was contagious. Andy Violette, one former student, long remembered the day she waved his paper on the Panama Canal over her head, holding it out as a model to the class. More remarkable still was the night he joined the McAuliffes for supper. "No other teacher ever invited me to dinner," he told a reporter, "but it was really cool."

The day after McAuliffe's selection as the teacher in space, she was the guest of honor at a Lions Club parade in Concord. The McAuliffe family rode in a Mercedes convertible. She wore her blue NASA uniform and greeted well-wishers by name as she passed. "It was a pleasure to be just a little part of it—even if it was just directing traffic," said Stephen Holdsworth, then a Concord police officer. Like so many others in Concord, Holdsworth had his own stories to tell of this sudden celebrity. His wife had worked in Steve McAuliffe's law firm, and he had been a guest in one of Christa's classes.

NASA officials were delighted with McAuliffe's debut, but no one knew how she would respond to the kind of continued attention usually reserved for movie stars. "One day she's a teacher and mother in Concord," said Ladwig, the NASA executive. "The next minute she's on the cover of *People* magazine. That's a lot of pressure to put on anyone."

One morning alone McAuliffe made appearances on *Good Morning, America,* the *CBS Morning News,* and *Today.* On another day came a trip to California for Johnny Carson. "I think NASA has made a very good choice," Carson said after interviewing her, "because I think you can communicate this to most of us who really can't understand all of it." At the end of the show, Carson called her Christy.

McAuliffe was under affectionate pressure in Concord, too. August 6 was officially declared her day in the capital. "Johnny Carson has had you!" Mayor David Coeyman shouted to a crowd gathered outside the State House at dusk. "NASA has had you and Ronald Reagan has had you. Now your hometown has you!"

McAuliffe signed autographs on everything from cash register tape to a pocketbook. After she spoke, Coeyman surprised her by announcing that she would lead the local Nevers' Band in "Stars and Stripes Forever." McAuliffe was game; she picked up the baton as the crowd stood and clapped in rhythm.

There were deeper tensions in the weeks that followed. Contract negotiations with NASA proved disturbingly difficult, and McAuliffe enlisted the help of a lawyer in her husband's firm.

Concord leaders, meanwhile, planned a welcome-home gala that was far grander than the city, costing up to $173,000 and bordering on exploitation of McAuliffe's fame. She put a stop to that in a press conference. "I'm hoping it's a very simple celebration," she said, "because that's what Concord's all about."

In early September, McAuliffe headed to Houston for several months of training. It would take 114 hours, far less than full-fledged astronauts received. McAuliffe rehearsed for emergencies in a space shuttle simulator, flew in a supersonic jet, and learned the fundamentals of working and living in space.

There was also the challenge of developing her mission. The plans called for her to teach two lessons while floating in the shuttle's mid-deck; they would be televised live into classrooms across the country. The first, "The Ultimate Field Trip," was to focus on daily life in space. The second, "Where We've Been, Where We're Going and Why," was to explore the history and prospects of space exploration.

NASA wanted these lessons scripted; McAuliffe said that wasn't how she taught. In this clash between a teacher and her administrators, the teacher prevailed.

In retrospect, what impressed NASA's Ladwig about McAuliffe's performance in those weeks was her ability to balance a variety of intense and competing pressures. It would have been easy for her to lose her focus, he said; she did not.

When Richard Scobee, the commander of the *Challenger* mission, met McAuliffe, he wanted to make sure she understood what she was in for. "This is serious business," he told her. "This ain't no firecracker you're sitting on." Many of the questions she faced from reporters had to do with the risks and her fears.

Even so, neither McAuliffe nor the public at large seemed to see a disaster as anything but the remotest of possibilities. "Have you ever gone through the intersection at Centre and Liberty streets?" she asked the *Monitor's* Hohler. "I've put my life on the line every time I've gone through it. The shuttle can't be much worse than that."

The *Challenger's* launch was scheduled for January 1986, and as the date drew near, excitement in Concord built to a fever pitch.

With NASA's help, McAuliffe's mission was built into the curriculum of every school in the city. Students made shuttles and conducted rocket experiments. Rundlett Junior High School featured a space shuttle made from seventy gallons of ice cream. The *Monitor* produced a special supplement for children. It featured McAuliffe's answers to questions from Concord kids.

Why did you apply to be a teacher in space? one asked. "As a history teacher," she answered, "I couldn't pass up the chance to be a part of the history I teach."

What are your fears? "I truly do not have any fears. I'm excited about the trip and am thrilled to have the opportunity."

What did you like least about your training? "There's nothing that I don't like. Everything is new and fun, and remember that I'm getting ready for the ride of a lifetime!"

McAuliffe's presence on the shuttle had, as NASA hoped, generated a surge of interest. The launch itself was expected to draw nearly twice the usual crowd.

That made the delays that followed a particular embarrassment. Six times the *Challenger's* launch was postponed, due to everything from high wind to a frozen bolt in a hatch. The Florida weather was unseasonably cold, and the family members and friends who had gathered to cheer McAuliffe found themselves wearing stadium coats instead of T-shirts.

Time ran out for Gov. John Sununu, who was among those forced to return to New Hampshire before the launch. An engineer, he said it was better to get things right than to make a deadline. "There really is no rush to get it up," he said.

It was still cold enough to worry some officials on the morning of January 28, but the shuttle crew woke up at 6:20 and headed for the launch pad just the same. On McAuliffe's way into the shuttle, a technician gave her a Red Delicious apple. An apple for the teacher in space.

One legacy of the *Challenger* disaster is pain, and it is still felt deeply in Concord. To ask people who knew McAuliffe to talk about her is to invite tears to flow, and they often do. Her loss is felt in personal ways because so many knew her, and in abstract ways, too, because everyone identified with her.

Compounding the grief is anger—at NASA, at fate, and at the journalists who descended on the city hours after McAuliffe's death. Their presence was a measure of how she had come to personify the *Challenger* mission—just as NASA had hoped.

The attention, by and large, was not welcome, and even when the journalists kept their distance they seemed intrusive. Bob Cowan, a Concord High teacher, remembers standing in a school window with a colleague after the ac-

McAuliffe is buried in Concord, where she is remembered as a wife, mother, teacher, and pioneer woman.
Concord Monitor.

cident, "engulfed in sorrow." Soon he sensed a camera with a telephoto lens being aimed his way from the grounds outside; the two teachers had to move.

But the attention was not all bad. Thousands of cards, gifts, and expressions of grief were mailed to Concord High, filling dozens of boxes. One quilt sent by students at Chesterfield Elementary School is among the most touching. "Remember the smiles and how happy they were," one panel says.

There are thirty-five schools named for McAuliffe, five of them outside the country. Concord is home to the Christa McAuliffe Planetarium, and the auditorium at Concord High has been renamed in her honor. Each year a distinguished New Hampshire teacher receives the Christa McAuliffe Sabbatical Award.

Cowan, the Concord High teacher, wants very much to see McAuliffe and her spirit remembered in such ways—for the sake of his students and adults alike. Being selected the teacher in space didn't make McAuliffe great, Cowan said; instead, it revealed greatness that was there all along. So many celebrities are hollow figures who rise for the wrong reasons. McAuliffe was different, whether a celebrity or not.

One day not too long after her White House breakthrough, Cowan encountered Christa and Steve McAuliffe walking down a Concord street. The teacher in space flashed that familiar smile and embraced her old colleague. "It was one of the friendliest greetings I'd ever had," Cowan said. "I always picture her giving me that hug."

Ruel Colby

He told the stories of World War II.

BY MIKE PRIDE

War is not a game. Those names chiseled in granite down on Main Street are sons of Concord who left home young, robust, and confident. As they saw it, a dirty job had to be done before they could come home again. The dirty job was World War II. Although it ended more than half a century ago, if their names were not in granite, you might still see these men around town, happy to be alive.

Ruel Colby knew most of them personally. War is not a game, but for nearly three years Colby, the *Concord Monitor's* sports editor, covered it as though it were. When the boys—and some of the girls—went to war and Concord's summer fields and winter rinks fell mostly idle, Colby turned his

Colby told the story of World War II through the lives of Concord's young men and women.

Concord Monitor.

column over to the letters and stories of men and women in uniform. His beat became global. He still fondly referred to some of the soldiers he wrote about as "divot diggers" and "puck pecans," but their fields of action now were islands and deserts, jungles and mountains, oceans and continents. North Africa, Attu, Sicily, New Guinea, the Philippines, Bastogne, Guadalcanal, Tarawa, the Rhine—to read Colby's "The Sport Galley," world geography was a prerequisite.

For a city of just over 27,000 people and the towns around it, "The Sport Galley" was a community gathering place in a world gone mad. If a man in the Pacific wanted to know what had happened to his old Concord High teammate, last heard from fighting Rommel in North Africa, he wrote Ruel Colby. If a soldier had been in the jungle too long and developed a craving for Tootsie Rolls, a mention in "The Sport Galley" would bring some in the mail.

Colby had a nickname—"The Old Scout"—and he was true to it. If he hadn't heard from one of his pals for a while, he visited the boy's family, borrowed a letter or two, and told the boy's story in his column. When soldiers and sailors came home on leave, they dropped by Colby's desk, and their stories soon appeared in "The Sport Galley."

No matter how gloomy the headlines on page one, the underlying message of Colby's column was this: The war will be won. It is only a matter of time. The boys will come home. In the meantime, here's what came in the mailbag today.

As the war ground on, the mailbag grew. Most of Colby's correspondents managed to find copies of the *Monitor*, sometimes secondhand, and others received regular clippings from mothers or wives. "I have followed the Galley ever since I left home—through N. Africa, the invasions of Sicily and Italy and even on the not-so-romantic Isle of Capri," Lieutenant Guy Gowen wrote Colby in early 1944.

The men and women in uniform did not want to be forgotten, and they trusted the Old Scout to see to it that they weren't. "When we read of a buddy and think back on some of the good old times, it gives out with a good feeling," Corporal Tommy Michael wrote from a California airfield. "I have received several letters from fellers from overseas, and they all tell how swell it is to read about their friends from home. They think of a fellow and how he may be, and then all of a sudden read about him in the *Monitor*."

Colby saw sports as a community bond. When the young men he had lionized on fields of play went off to war, he preserved the bond by writing about them in the same way. As a contemporary said of "The Sport Galley," Colby "could make a corporal sound like an admiral."

After Pearl Harbor, the number of Concord area men and women who joined the military quickly climbed into the hundreds. By 1943, there were more than 2,000. Military censors were heavy-handed about locations and engagements, but Colby's correspondents mailed in reports from all corners of the globe. Army Staff Sergeant Walter Burtt, whom Colby knew as a marathoner and tennis player, also proved to be a keen observer. In a letter from New Guinea that his sister shared with *Monitor* readers through Colby's column, Burtt wrote: "The natives' garment, where they're around white settlements, is a bright-colored calico waist cloth. Women's wear is the same, and either with or without top coverings. Tattoo marks, hair-dos and nose-plugs show where the natives come from."

Burtt was taking atrabrine and sleeping under nets to prevent disease. "The mosquito is more dangerous than Nippie slant-eyes," he wrote. "One hundred percent of the natives have malaria. Other mosquitoes carry dengue fever (love buster) and filariasis."

> As for animal life, there are many marsupials, as in Australia— several types of kangaroos, none more than three feet high. . . . There are many types of bats, including a giant flying fox. A fruit-eater with a four-foot wingspread. Rats are plentiful, too, some over two feet long.
>
> The most striking creatures are the birds. Their voices in the early morning sound like a jazz band. They range from the big, black flightless casowary (similar to an emu or ostrich) to the beautiful yellow and red-plumed birds of paradise.

In 1943, Captain Worthen Muzzey, a tank commander, wrote to Colby from the other side of the world. He was among the first Americans to enter Bizerte, Tunisia, after that Axis stronghold fell. In his letter, he recalled how he and his men had carried their own livestock during the campaign. In the long desert caravan, he had seen hens bobbing from the turrets of Sherman tanks and cows tethered behind half-tracks.

Later that year, Muzzey was campaigning in Italy. He and his men had slept in the wet and cold several nights in a row before bivouacking in a Naples cemetery, where Muzzey at last found shelter for a good night's rest. "There were six of us in the tomb," he wrote his wife in Concord. "Five of us had been there for twenty years. It was really a beautiful place, up in the hills, with marble floors and walls and a little altar. Pictures of the dead, with their names and biographical data, were on each tombstone."

Nearly all the men in combat zones missed the company of women. In their letters, they recorded, if only in lament, their impressions of the few they did encounter.

Hugo Hermanson had been island-hopping in the Pacific with the Navy's Construction Battalion, better known as Seabees. "The beauty and charm of these islands that one reads about in books is quite contrary to reality," he wrote to his friends at Concord's Moose Lodge from a location that was snipped by a censor. "It seems the lizards and flies are never mentioned, nor the interminable heat.

"As for the beautiful island maidens—that tale is also a fallacy. The gals seem to be blacker and blacker at every new location. And words cannot describe their hideousness!"

When men saw women who appealed to them, something told them not to believe their eyes. After he was wounded on Iwo Jima, Marine Private First Class Ed Atwood wrote that one consolation was the staff in the hospital in the Marianas. "All the nurses are beautiful, or else I've probably lost my taste," he wrote. "Probably the latter." Writing from New Caledonia, John Mortimer expressed similar doubts about his judgment. "The few French girls that I saw lived up to their reputation admirably, but it may be their extreme scarcity that caused my enthusiasm," he wrote.

Although soldiers and sailors were always willing to talk openly about such matters, many kept to themselves when the subject turned to combat. Late in the winter of 1944–45, Navy Lt. Louis Clarner returned home on leave two months after the Japanese had sunk his landing craft in the Philippines. Clarner went to see Colby, who knew instantly that Clarner had a tale to tell. When the two men sat down to talk, however, Colby quickly sensed that Clarner didn't want to discuss the sinking of his LST.

This reticence was something the Old Scout had seen many times before. When he reported his conversation with Clarner a few days later in his column, Colby wrote:

> We didn't press him, because long since we have learned that veterans of "contact with the enemy," in whatever theater they may have been stationed, do not care to discuss matters that only shipmates and buddies can possibly understand. . . . Men who have had close calls and lost good friends should not be urged to relate experiences they simply want to forget.

But this was a world war, and Colby could do only so much to keep the horrors of war from his readers' doorsteps. He might defer to soldiers who wanted to forget, but he faithfully recounted the combat stories that showed up in his mailbag.

Bob Byron Jr.'s job was to record images of war on camera. A Marine private first class, he entered the battlefields when the shooting had stopped and the smell of death mingled with the smell of the unwashed. In November 1943, he wrote to his mother in Concord from Tarawa Atoll, and she gave the letter to Colby.

"To me the most horrible sensation of the whole thing was the ever-present smell! The dead and dying and men like all of us who haven't had a chance to wash or even take off their clothes for days—it adds up to a disagreeable aroma," Byron wrote.

> The other day we were out taking "horror" pictures and wandered up on top of a tremendous blockhouse. We stayed up there with dead Japs all around us for quite a while "shooting." Just when we came down, we ran into a group of men coming up with dynamite and hand grenades.
>
> They told us all to clear away because there was still a bunch of snipers in the blockhouse and they were going to blast 'em out. Those Japs have a trick of living in among their own dead, just to fool us and take some pot shots. I've been shot at so much by snipers that I instinctively hit the deck at the slightest noise. It's not so good a feeling.

Experience had taught Byron to view his gruesome duty through the lens of humor. After the Marines stormed one beach and moved inland, he walked alone amid the carnage. "With bodies all around me, it looks as though I took the beach-head single-handed," he wrote his mother.

Byron's description of the dead Japanese as props reflected the common opinion of the enemy in the Pacific. Japan had carried out a sneak attack on Pearl Harbor. In battle, Japanese soldiers were known for suicidal tenacity and deadly deceit. American GIs routinely saw examples of their cruelty toward prisoners of war. These factors, combined with their Oriental appearance, made the Japanese easy to stereotype as sneaky, inhuman, and robotic.

"The first thing I saw when I hit the beach in our second invasion was one of Hirohito's high-ranking officers with his skull crushed in and his thinking apparatus spilled over the nearby ground," Army Lt. Edward O'Toole wrote to his family in Contoocook.

In early 1945 in the Philippines, John Whicher, an infantry major from Concord, witnessed a caravan of 510 American prisoners of war who had been liberated after nearly three years in captivity. They were all skin and bones. "Many of them had been in the infamous 'March of Death' conducted by the Japs from Bataan," Whicher wrote his wife. "Many were litter cases and had to be carried a long, long way through the jungle trails. I talked to several of them. And any Japs I meet sure are to be dead men after what I saw today."

Eric Andrews, a lieutenant in an anti-aircraft battalion, wrote home with a complaint shared by many GIs in the Pacific theater. They believed—with some justification, since U.S. war policy focused on Europe first—that their efforts were underappreciated. "Germany is the big cheese, but the Japs are twice as tricky and a lot harder to dig out," he wrote. "They're like rats in a corner when they're trapped."

Possibly because Germans were thoroughly assimilated into American society, the enemy in Europe was harder to hate—at least in such demonic terms as GIs applied to the Japanese. The Nazi SS was an exception. Infantry Corporal Walter Lafford, who fought in the Battle of the Bulge, wrote home:

> As hardened as we of this division are to the bitter scenes of war, we saw things on the snow and ice-covered hills of Belgium and Luxembourg that made us realize more fully than ever the treacherous, murdering nature of the horde of Hitler's SS troops. We had faced these troops before, at Orleans, St. Lo and other places in France, but never before had they murdered American boys in cold blood. They did in Belgium! Let me assure you that they paid a dreadful toll for their actions there, as I personally saw German dead everywhere.

Lieutenant Andrews and Guy Gowen had played sports as members of Concord High's Class of 1937. One year behind them, Bob Mullen and Chet Wheeler were star athletes. By mid-1943, Mullen had been shot and killed at El Guettar, Tunisia, and a severe wound had knocked Wheeler out of action. For Lieutenant Gowen, the death of Mullen and the wounding of Wheeler were sobering events. A veteran of campaigns in North Africa, Sicily, and Italy, Gowen was training in Northern Ireland by early 1944. He already knew his mission. After landing behind German lines by glider, he was to lead his rifle platoon as part of the Allied invasion of Normandy. He found a helpful analogy in his experience as an athlete.

"Decisions in combat are the same kind as any football coach is called upon to make, except possibly the results are a little different," Gowen wrote Colby.

But there is one parallel. The success of decisions, in either field, is weighed by the ground gained, or lost.

The sickening feeling in the stomach, the worry as to whether or not each man knows his job and will carry it out—every coach gets it before a game—also hits an officer when "H-hour" approaches and a last-minute check is made of a platoon. The feeling of relief, once the action has started, and the pride in the outfit after the final whistle has blown and the old bacon is ours—is the very same, in both cases.

One night in Naples, Gowen heard of Mullen's death and Wheeler's wound. "It gave me that 'What to H—— is the use?' feeling," he wrote.

I remember doing some heavy thinking that night about this whole mess. Yet any man who visited Naples at the time I did, and had a firsthand view of what a nation can sink to, and what bombs can do to a city, can realize what a "high-test" place the States really is and he also soon becomes thankful that it has happened over here and not on the corner of Main and Pleasant streets.

Gowen never made it home. He was killed leading his platoon in Normandy shortly after D-Day. His name is engraved not far from Mullen's on the granite wall on Main Street in front of the State House.

As winter turned to spring in 1945, victory was near, but the nation lost its leader. Colby's mail reflected this bittersweet churning of events.

Many warriors long for a joyous welcome in a liberated land, but this was not Navy Lt. Raymond Rawcliffe's dream—until he lived it in the Philippines. "When we arrived, the children cried, 'Americanos, Victory' and sang 'God Bless America,'" Rawcliffe wrote Colby. "They gave us the V sign with their fingers and are as happy a people as I've ever seen. Somehow this sort of thing was never very significant to me until I had actually seen it."

Americans owed much of their confidence about their place in the world to President Franklin D. Roosevelt. Victory in Europe was just weeks away when Roosevelt died on April 14, 1945. Even as the nation mourned him, the seeds of hope he had planted were evident.

Nineteen-year-old Patricia Fairfield caught this optimism in a letter to her mother back home on Concord's Eastman Street. Fairfield had graduated from Concord High the previous June and was now a cadet nurse in Troy, New York. "Doubtless you, mother, have been listening to the radio this morning," Fairfield began.

You, too, must have felt as humble, as grateful as I do. Just the little things: the absence of commercials, of light music, the presence of grave, sincere, heartfelt mourning have made me feel how close each man is to his neighbor; those on the same street and those thousands of miles away. I knelt down during the minute of silent prayer on The Breakfast Club program.

Those who think they should pity my generation are so very wrong. True, we are becoming adults in a changing world not because we want to but because we are forced to. We are growing into adults in a world of sorrow, death, and cruelty; the meanest, poorest side of man is all around us. But we are also, and more important, growing up in a time when we can see also the best of man brought out. We are surrounded by bravery, courage, and determination; man accomplishing that which even he thought was impossible.

This lesson of greatness we shall carry through life. That is why I say those who are sorry for us are wrong. We are learning at the beginning of our lives what many go to the grave without learning.

Colby's wartime columns conveyed to local men and women in uniform that all the good things they remembered about home would be waiting for them when they returned. Certainly, the Old Scout was one institution they could count on.

When the war ended, he gladly resumed his coverage of local sports and remained a colorful figure in Concord for decades. He loved to play poker

During the war, Colby's newspaper column was read around the globe.
Concord Monitor.

and seemed to live on chocolate frappes from Davis's drugstore, conveniently located half a block from the *Monitor* building.

Colby remained sports editor until 1971—forty-one years in all. He was still writing his column on a part-time basis when he was diagnosed with throat cancer. In 1977, at the age of seventy-one, he took his own life. To the end of his days, he was proudest of the columns he had written during the war. On August 16, 1945, the day after V-J Day, he summed up this phase of his community's life and cast his eye to the future.

The tumult and the shouting have subsided in our beloved capital on the banks of the Merrimack, in the tranquil New Hampshire valley that outwardly has been so little touched by the past 3½ years of world warfare. In the hearts of all of us is a deep and abiding thankfulness that the fighting is over. For the thousands who have loved ones in the armed forces here and overseas, the end of combat means the end of dread, anxious hours. . . .

V-J Day spells the return to the baseball and football fields, to the tennis courts and hockey rinks, of thousands of young men who for more than three long years have had to forego those simple pleasures while they took up arms for a nation in need of their great young strength. Victory and peace mean that Concord's host of athletes in uniform will be coming home, back to the games, the friendly rivalries that lent spice and zest to their way of life. . . .

Today we're a little tired, but still eager—for the resumption of the old ways of peace.

It seems to the Galley's aging Scout that his work is done. But in the weeks to come he may discover that there still is a place for the column in the glorious new existence that we all so fervently pray will eventually be built in the wake of war.

William Loeb

From his pulpit on the front page of the Union Leader, *he left an indelible mark on New Hampshire.*

BY SCOTT CALVERT

On September 14, 1981, a black border framed the front page of the *Union Leader* of Manchester. For thirty-five years, publisher William Loeb had amazed and amused, annoyed and angered readers in New Hampshire and beyond. Now his paper mourned. Loeb was dead, his voice silenced by cancer, and an era was over.

Perhaps not since William Randolph Hearst had a publisher used his paper so forcefully and colorfully to get his way. His front-page editorials decrying Communists and shredding political enemies often employed capital letters, as if he was screaming. And he didn't hesitate to mold the front page to suit his views.

William Loeb's newspapers have recorded—and created—controversies for generations.

Ken Williams/Concord Monitor.

Without Loeb, it's fair to say that conservative Meldrim "Ax the Tax" Thomson never would have become governor in the 1970s. And who knows? Ronald Reagan might not have reached the White House in 1980, and Democrat Edmund Muskie's 1972 presidential hopes might not have skidded away in the snows of New Hampshire.

Without Loeb, today's political discourse might not be so rough-and-tumble, either. Loeb made everything personal. Angry at President Dwight Eisenhower, who had helped save the free world a decade earlier, Loeb labeled him "Dopey Dwight." He once called President Gerald Ford "a jerk" in an editorial printed the very day Ford visited New Hampshire.

And in a famous episode in 1969, his newspaper gave days of coverage to Meg Peterson, the fifteen-year-old daughter of Gov. Walter Peterson, after she declared she didn't see anything wrong with smoking marijuana. The episode provoked a war of words between Loeb and the Republican governor, his politically moderate enemy. It also, she says, changed her life forever.

Twenty years later, Loeb's ghost still inhabited the state. The "bankerly" moderate wing of the state Republican Party never recovered from his constant clobbering; and some trace to him the caution exhibited by Democrats like Gov. Jeanne Shaheen.

But Loeb's biggest legacy by far is the state's refusal to enact a sales or income tax, a stubbornness at the heart of the school funding crisis that dominated state politics at the end of the twentieth century. Loeb so effectively vilified broad-based tax proposals and their supporters that candidates from both parties still regularly took the anti-tax "Pledge" popularized by the *Union Leader*.

"It's part of his inheritance that they are the words—'income tax' and 'sales tax'—that the average politician, particularly if he is of any prominence, dares not speak," said Jim Finnegan, the paper's long-time chief editorial writer under Loeb.

Susan McLane, a former state senator from Concord known to *Union Leader* readers as Simpering Sue and "the chief dingbat of the dingbat brigade," rues the day Loeb bought the paper in 1946. Her husband's politically moderate family thought the newspaper was theirs and was celebrating when word came that Loeb and a partner had cobbled together the necessary cash at the last minute and beaten them out.

"That was the worst moment in New Hampshire history," she said. "Seriously. Because the tax structure—all of these things—have fallen into place because of the *Union Leader*."

Indeed, not everyone mourned Loeb's passing. In one New Hampshire home, a cake was baked as part of a macabre celebration. Shaped like a gravestone, it was covered in black frosting.

Bill Loeb saw the world in terms of black and white, right and wrong. He showered praise on hard-line cold warriors and his favored conservatives—as long as they didn't stray. (When President Richard Nixon went to China, Loeb turned abruptly on his old ally.) He spat venom at Communists, liberals, university intellectuals, and big-government types. And like the loaded sidearm he frequently carried, his paper could inflict pain: Anyone with the gall to criticize Loeb risked winding up in the paper's sights.

In 1974, Brad Cook, a young University of New Hampshire graduate, returned to his alma mater to give a speech. He lashed out at Loeb, saying his "power must be diluted and what he stands for must be destroyed."

Loeb replied on page one. He said Cook's "spewing" of hate "would have done credit to one of Hitler's 'Brown Shirt' youth goons trying to stir up fellow Nazis to hate some German publisher who didn't go along with their totalitarian views."

Despite his love of absolutes, Loeb himself was a man of many contradictions:

- He wielded his editorial power like a sword, skewering governors and presidents alike with personal attacks. But in person, he was kind and gentlemanly, never raising his voice, so guests sometimes watched his thick eyebrows for signs of what was going on inside his bald head.
- He kept the broad-based tax wolf at bay and boosted Thomson into the governor's office, but more often than not he backed political losers, partly because few candidates shared his extreme views. Some of his candidates have long since faded from the public's memory. Remember John Ashbrook for president? Gen. Harry Thyng for governor?
- He thought of himself as a man of the people but led a privileged life. His father was Teddy Roosevelt's private secretary, and Loeb attended private schools, graduating from Williams College and attending Harvard Law School for two years. After two unsuccessful marriages, Loeb wed Nackey Scripps Gallowhur, an heir to the Scripps Howard publishing fortune.
- He touted his friendship to labor and his enmity for big business, but he once shamelessly lobbied for a corporate titan. When Aristotle Onassis wanted to build an oil refinery in Durham in the mid-1970s, Loeb wrote a front-page editorial likening the shipping tycoon to Santa Claus and utterly dismissing residents' concerns about pollution and noise.
- He became one of the most powerful men in New Hampshire but wasn't from here and never lived here. He grew up in Washington and New York, and as owner of the newspaper, split time between Reno, Nevada, and a thirty-room mansion in Prides Crossing, Massachusetts, patrolled by a German shepherd and a Doberman pinscher. "Be careful when you get out of the car," he once told Andrew Merton, a University of New Hampshire English professor who had an appointment to interview him in Massachusetts. "The dogs, you know."

The source of Loeb's power was no mystery. The *Union Leader* was—and is—New Hampshire's only statewide newspaper, and for years it was the only morning paper. It long enjoyed a monopoly as the only statewide news source. Moreover, until the 1980s the state's lone Sunday paper was Loeb's *New Hampshire Sunday News*.

As a result, Loeb and his minions could largely define the news. As Peterson, the former governor, put it, "It was the word." And rarely did Loeb leave it at just one word. He embarked on editorial crusades, massing editorials and stories into a journalistic armada for battles that could last for days on end.

"Like a dog on a bone" is how Dayton Duncan, chief of staff to former Democratic governor Hugh Gallen, thought of Loeb. "He just kept chewing and chewing and chewing, particularly when it had to do with any of his political enemies," he said.

In the early 1970s, New Hampshire House Speaker Marshall Cobleigh backed an income tax proposal that went down to major defeat. He was asked whether he feared his support would cost him his House seat. Maybe if the election were tomorrow, he said, but people will forget.

It was an unwise comment. Loeb did his best to ensure that no one forgot by running frequent editorials with the same message: "Cobleigh thinks you'll forget."

"At election time, he went cuckoo," recalled Cobleigh, whose Nashua constituents reelected him anyway.

To some critics, Loeb seemed largely concerned with expanding his influence. "I think he was obsessed with power, and he used the paper to create that power," said Jim Ewing, former publisher and owner of *The Keene Sentinel*.

But those who knew him well say Loeb was no megalomaniac. "He couldn't be less interested in the power," Nackey Loeb said in 1999. "Certainly more interested in the future of the country."

Cobleigh also believed Loeb was genuinely worried about communism and the counterculture. "He thought the country was going to hell," Cobleigh said, "and he was going to do his best to stop that."

In 1969, for example, Loeb's paper served notice to Moratorium Day marchers protesting the Vietnam War that they were not welcome in Manchester. "ATTENTION ALL PEACE MARCHERS: Hippies, Yippies, Beatniks, Peaceniks, yellow-bellies, Commies, and their agents and DUPES—HELP KEEP OUR CITY CLEAN! . . . Just By Staying Out of It!—The Editors."

Below was a photo showing *Union Leader* employees standing on top of the newspaper building holding a banner that read: "AMERICA love it or leave it! VICTORY IN VIETNAM." Loeb, whose front-page editorial that day was called "Hanoi's Little Helpers," once claimed to have infiltrated the Communist Party in the 1930s and seen the danger firsthand.

Shortly after acquiring the newspaper in 1946, Loeb permanently added to the masthead a lofty quote from storied nineteenth-century legislator and orator Daniel Webster: "There is nothing so powerful as truth."

Of course, not everyone agreed with Loeb's version of the truth, and several attempts were made to diminish or eliminate his power. His closest call occurred in the late 1950s, after he started a bruising newspaper fight in Haverhill, Massachusetts, and his opponents moved to dry up his credit. Strapped, Loeb borrowed $2 million from the Teamsters' pension funds, which explains his later efforts to free jailed Teamsters boss Jimmy Hoffa.

While Loeb could not be silenced, he could be answered, and a few brave souls took him on.

In 1957, when U.S. Sen. Joseph McCarthy died, Loeb erupted with fury. "MURDERED!" was the headline over his front-page editorial, bordered in black. "MCCARTHY WAS MURDERED BY THE COMMUNISTS BECAUSE HE WAS EXPOSING

THEM," Loeb raged. In an extraordinary response, the state Senate considered censuring Loeb but rejected the idea.

The day before the 1960 election, Sen. John F. Kennedy visited New Hampshire and accused Loeb of running the most irresponsible newspaper in the country. Loeb denounced him as "a liar and a spoiled brat."

In 1962, while running for Congress, moderate Republican James Cleveland lambasted Loeb after a slashing editorial attacked him for representing a Communist in court. "I did not crawl out of a foxhole in the Pacific Theater," Cleveland said caustically, "to come back home and crawl on my belly before a junior grade Goebbels whose combat experience has been chiefly confined to lawsuits and character assassinations."

Above a story about Cleveland's remarks was a Loeb editorial titled: "Not a Communist, Not an Atheist—Just Confused." Cleveland won the election and enjoyed a long career in Congress.

The same year, a group calling itself the New Hampshire Committee for an Informed Electorate placed an ad in newspapers around the state to protest what it considered biased coverage of the U.S. Senate race. The group, led by Susan McLane, claimed Loeb was tilting news coverage to help Doloris Bridges win the seat formerly held by her husband, Styles, who had died in office.

"BEWARE!" the ad warned. "Loeb likes to think he runs the State of New Hampshire. Does he?" The ad then listed "typical Loeb attacks," consisting of his nicknames for various politicians. Former governor Sherman Adams, who went on to work in the White House for "that stinking hypocrite" Eisenhower, was "Shermy Wermy," for example.

Though he did not print the ad, Loeb often allowed space for unkind words about himself and even considered criticism a victory of sorts, Nackey Loeb remembered. "He had a tough skin and always felt if people criticized him, he probably was making an impression (and) that in itself was worth doing."

Loeb's defenders note that he even printed unflattering news about himself. In 1949, readers learned that he had been arrested in Vermont after a man named George Gallowhur filed an "alienation of affections" lawsuit against Loeb, accusing him of an affair with Gallowhur's then wife, Nackey. Unable to post $150,000 bail, Loeb spent a night in jail.

Loeb never regretted anything he said or published, according to Nackey Loeb, except for an editorial praising the Boston Red Sox. After the editorial ran, the team fell into one of its famous tailspins. Loeb wished he had waited.

Nor, apparently, did he feel a need to edit his statements. In 1971 he told *The New York Times Magazine* that everyone should be trained in the use of guns. "It might lead to a few more wife killings and that sort of thing," he conceded, "but it would lead to a great diminution in armed crime."

Sometimes Loeb gave his critics ink unwittingly. A woman named Lillian Watson from Connecticut had a twelve-line poem printed as a letter to the editor. It seemed harmless, with lines like, "When hours seem long and somewhat blue, / You never should forget the view." But when the first letters of each line were strung together, a different meaning emerged: "SCREW YOU LOEB."

Edmund Muskie, a senator from Maine and leading Democratic presidential candidate in 1972, chose the head-on approach, and it may have ended his political career. It was about ten days before the primary, and Muskie was irate at Loeb, mainly because he published the infamous "canuck" letter purporting to expose Muskie as bigoted toward Franco-Americans.

The letter was allegedly authored by Paul Morrison of Deerfield, Florida. It described a conversation Morrison supposedly overheard while Muskie campaigned in Florida in which a Muskie aide said there were no blacks in Maine, but there were "Cannocks." Asked what he meant, Muskie supposedly laughed and said, "Come to New England and see."

"WE HAVE ALWAYS KNOWN THAT SENATOR MUSKIE WAS A HYPOCRITE," Loeb wrote in a front-page editorial. "BUT WE NEVER EXPECTED TO HAVE IT SO CLEARLY REVEALED AS IN THIS LETTER SENT TO US FROM FLORIDA."

Muskie's advisers in New Hampshire advised against attacking Loeb, recalled Norman Abelson, Muskie's state communications director. Nevertheless, in a driving snowstorm Muskie jumped on a flatbed trailer in front of the newspaper's Manchester office and lit into Loeb.

To some observers Muskie appeared to cry; whether he did or not, that was how it was played. *The Union Leader* sub-headline read, "Senator Rants Emotionally at Publisher." The story quoted Muskie saying of Loeb, "This man doesn't walk, he crawls." One paragraph later, Loeb was quoted as saying the speech was "an excited, near hysterical performance."

This was the beginning of the end for Muskie's campaign. Later, *The Washington Post* reported that the "canuck" letter was a fraud, the work of Nixon aide Ken Clawson.

In 1968, a Georgia native named Meldrim Thomson ran for governor. The conservative Republican had been an obscure law book publisher from Orford, an Upper Valley town near Hanover, but with Loeb's help he rose to prominence.

Thomson did not win overnight, a reminder of the limits to Loeb's power. In both 1968 and 1970, Thomson lost to Peterson, the choice of old guard New Hampshire Republicans. Irate that Peterson was reelected in 1970, Loeb printed names of Manchester residents who failed to vote, blaming them for the outcome.

Peterson represented a grave danger in Loeb's view, exemplified by his desire to implement a sales tax. "My theory is if you give politicians money, they'll find a way to spend it," Loeb once said. Defending the state's meager aid to local communities, he once explained, "The more burden you put on the community, the better it is."

In late 1969, the Loeb-Peterson antipathy spilled over to Peterson's fifteen-year-old daughter, Meg, who said at a conference on drugs that she did not see "anything wrong" with smoking marijuana. In the flurry of coverage, Loeb implied the Petersons were not good parents and crowned Peterson "the high priest of permissiveness."

Loeb's newspapers found numerous ways to punish enemies. Cobleigh felt the repeated sting of *Union Leader* cartoons, one of which assailed his prochoice views on abortion. He was depicted hitting a woman on the head with his speaker's gavel and sawing into her stomach. The caption said, "My mother murdered me with the help of Speaker Cobleigh."

And, of course, there were the nicknames. In one of his anti-Ford columns, Loeb wrote: "TO PUT IT BLUNTLY AND PERHAPS A BIT HARSHLY, BUT WE THINK AC-CURATELY, JERRY IS A JERK AND WE CAN'T STAND ANY MORE JERKS IN THE WHITE HOUSE IF WE ARE TO SURVIVE AS A FREE NATION."

Joe McQuaid, who succeeded Nackey Loeb as publisher in 1999, said Loeb liked to call "a spade a spade and rile people up. I think he went over the top deliberately to get people to pay attention to his editorials." Loeb himself once said that if his attacks could scare people from running for political office, "they've got no business running."

But Dayton Duncan said Loeb went too far and coarsened the political dialogue. "His refusal to know any bounds in his lust to destroy people could chew up innocent people along the way."

Despite Thomson's back-to-back losses, Loeb stuck with him, and in 1972 Thomson wrestled the Republican nomination from Peterson and soon became governor, a job he kept for six years. Thomson's ascendancy marked the zenith of Loeb Republicanism.

Finnegan, the former *Union Leader* editorial writer, agrees Thomson probably would not have been elected without Loeb's assistance, which was hardly relegated to editorials. During the campaign, an article on taxes written by Thomson appeared above the front-page flag.

Once in office, Thomson kept in close touch with Loeb. Reporter Rod Paul documented in the *Concord Monitor* that Thomson called Loeb from the State House hundreds of times in 1973 and 1974. The implication was that Loeb was helping Thomson run the state, or worse.

But Cobleigh disagrees. By then he was working for Thomson and claims to have overheard Thomson's end of about two-thirds of those calls. He said

William Loeb in federal court.

Ken Williams/Concord Monitor.

Thomson, far from taking orders, usually just wanted to give Loeb advance word of his latest move in a bid for favorable coverage.

In 1973, the New England Daily Newspaper Survey analyzed *The Union Leader* and found most of its political and government coverage unbiased. But it also discerned a philosophy that the news should support the editorial policy. For example, Loeb was so angry at Muhammad Ali for not serving in the armed forces that he allowed no coverage of Ali's 1971 prizefight against Joe Frazier.

"The paper is remarkably thorough and lively," the survey said. "It also is less objective and less fair than most other papers."

Duncan pointed to another case where Loeb's political goals came before journalistic fairness. In 1980, he supported Reagan for president while an unknown congressman from Illinois named Phil Crane was emerging as a younger arch-conservative.

But Crane was dogged by rumors that he was a womanizer. Before long, *The Union Leader* dispatched reporters to Washington and Illinois to write about those rumors, Duncan said. "From the very start," he said, "one of their missions was to derail the Crane campaign."

After Loeb's death, *The Union Leader* became a different newspaper in many respects. Nackey Loeb, who died in 2000, was in charge for nearly twenty years but wrote fewer editorials and mostly kept herself out of the news. Her husband used a sword, she once said, but she preferred a needle.

Even people who disagree with its editorial stance say the paper is much improved journalistically. They say the once-pronounced news slant on some issues has basically disappeared. So has the paper's dominance: Channel Nine probably has as much influence as *The Union Leader*, and several daily newspapers—most now publishing in the morning—have added Sunday editions. All these factors have led *Union Leader* circulation to dip.

Nonetheless, William Loeb's legacy endures.

Duncan says that by the time Loeb died, the moderate wing of the Republican Party "had almost been extinguished" and has yet to revive in any meaningful way. Abelson thinks Loeb gave Democrats too many excuses for failure and kept good candidates from running while prompting those who did run to use extreme caution. "That's given us the Jeanne Shaheen syndrome," he said.

Abelson also thinks Loeb made the state a hostile place for black people. Before the Civil Rights Act of 1964 passed, Loeb wrote: "UNDER THE CIVIL RIGHTS BILL NO INNKEEPER WOULD BE ABLE TO REFUSE TO SERVE NEGROES, EVEN THOUGH HE MAY NOT WANT TO DO SO OR EVEN THOUGH HIS GUESTS MAY NOT WANT HIM TO DO SO. THIS IS THE FORCED ASSOCIATION OF A TOTALITARIAN STATE WITH A VENGEANCE."

At the same time, Rod Paul believes Loeb's staunch support for the first-in-the-nation primary has enabled today's leaders from both parties to warn those with a mind to steal it, "You can't take this away from us, and if you do, we're going to kill you."

And there is near unanimity that without Loeb's steady drumbeat, a broad-based tax might have passed as early as the 1950s, under Gov. Sherman Adams. At the end of the twentieth century, that opposition to a broad-based tax, still a cornerstone of *The Union Leader's* editorial policy, faced its biggest test yet. Legislators were considering such a tax to finance public schools, a development that would surely have Bill Loeb turning in his grave.

"If they pass one, we're bringing him back," quipped McQuaid. "That's our ace in the hole."

Thornton Wilder

His play turned Peterborough into Our Town.

BY MARY ALLEN

You come up here, on a fine afternoon and you can see range on range of hills—awful blue they are—up there by Lake Sunapee and Lake Winnipesaukee . . . and way up, if you've got a glass, you can see the White Mountains and Mt. Washington—where North Conway and Conway is. And, of course, our favorite mountain, Mt. Monadnock, 's right here—and all these towns that lie around it: Jaffrey, 'n East Jaffrey, 'n Peterborough, 'n Dublin and (then pointing down in the audience) there, quite a ways down, is Grover's Corners.

—Stage Manager, Act III

Thornton Wilder rehearses *Our Town* with director Bert Mitchell and cast members Jennifer Holt and John Stearns in 1940.
Collection of the Peterborough Historical Society.

When Thornton Wilder wrote *Our Town* in the late 1930s, he did more than put the mythical town of Grover's Corners on the map. Wilder's quiet little play shook up the world of stagecraft, bending rules and setting new standards in American theater.

Gone was the invisible fourth wall of the stage, the so-called box set that separated actors from the audience. Gone too were most of the scenery and props. In their place was an intimate look at the simple truths of everyday living, set in a place where the Stage Manager is a main character and talks directly to the audience about life, death, and almost everything in between.

For America at the end of the Great Depression, Grover's Corners, New Hampshire, became an idealized place where honest, straightforward people lived, loved, and died. For Peterborough, the play was a source of pride—the beginning of its long-running image as *Our Town.*

Wilder is believed to have written at least part of the play, which won a Pulitzer Prize in 1938, when he was a guest artist at the MacDowell Colony in Peterborough. He was a frequent visitor at the colony during the 1920s and 1930s and returned to Peterborough in 1940, when the Peterborough Players staged their first production of *Our Town.*

He did a great deal of walking during that period of his life. While staying at the colony, Wilder was in the habit of strolling down the hill into town almost every day. According to local legend, his stops included a brick house on High Street, Moulton's drug store, and other downtown shops, with the route ending at what's now the Peterboro Diner.

Wilder took pains to say that Grover's Corners was a fictional place, drawn in bits and pieces from his memories of several New England towns. Only the character Howie Newsome, the milkman, was based on a real person, he said—Fletcher Dole, the town's real-life milkman.

As for the rest: "Lots of observations in Peterborough, which has no cemetery on a hill (that I saw once in Vermont) and has no 'Polish Town' across the tracks—I forget now where I picked that up—maybe Keene or one of those mill towns on the way to Keene," Wilder told the critic Malcolm Cowley.

"*Our Town* is not offered as a picture of life in a New Hampshire village; or as a speculation about the conditions of life after death (that element I merely took from Dante's Purgatory). It is an attempt to find a value above all price for the smaller events in our daily life. I have made the claim as preposterous as possible, for I have set the village against the largest dimensions of time and place," Wilder wrote.

Fine statements—but few folks in Peterborough believe them. And others around the world don't either.

I think if you hold your breath you can hear the train all the way to
Contoocook. Hear it? —Emily Webb, Act I

Generations after its debut on February 4, 1938, at Henry Miller's Theatre in New York, it would seem *Our Town* is being performed somewhere on some stage at any given moment. The conventional wisdom is that every high school in America has produced it at least once, and there could be some truth to the claim that *Our Town* is the most frequently produced American play in history.

Confronted with the New England dialogue and a sparse set, directors and producers are often puzzled about how to proceed. So they call, write, or e-mail the place they think is the real Grover's Corners.

The Peterborough Historical Society gets so many pleas for information about the fictional town that the members have prepared a twenty-page packet to fill these requests. It contains information about the real Peterborough and its link to Thornton Wilder and *Our Town*.

Theatrical groups want to know what Peterborough looks like, how big it is, what Wilder would have seen on his daily walk down the hill. They also want to know how to pronounce Contoocook, Winnipesaukee, and some other tongue-twisting words in the play's dialogue. Occasionally they are hoping to find the fictional town they grew to love in the play.

"One day last spring, a man from London stopped looking for information he could use in a travel brochure for vacationers," said Michelle Stahl of the historical society. "He seemed a little disappointed that we had all the modern conveniences here. 'It's changed quite a bit,' he said."

Bessie's all mixed up about the route ever since the Lockharts stopped takin' their quart of milk every day. She wants to leave 'em a quart just the same—keeps scolding me the hull trip.

—Howie Newsome, Act I

Peterborough has grown over the years. The town is proud of its connection with the play but not obsessed with it.

A few Peterborough businesses have made a commercial tie-in. There's Our Town Realty, Inc., Our Town Kennels, and Our Town Landscaping (actually, it's in neighboring Hancock). A defunct restaurant in Peterborough was called Grover's Corners.

It's been a good-natured pastime over the past six decades to try to figure out whether Wilder was talking about a particular spot in town or person he may have known when he wrote the play.

"My grandfather was the editor of the newspaper at the time when Wilder was at the Colony," said Joe Cummings, publisher of the *Peterborough Transcript*. "Our family has always figured that the character of Editor Webb was based on my grandfather."

Maybe and maybe not. *The Peterborough Transcript* has been publishing since 1846, and Paul Cummings Sr. was the editor when Wilder was at MacDowell, but Webb's paper in the play was called the *Sentinel*—the name of Keene's paper, which is even older.

Even the Howie Newsome character, the only one Wilder says was based on a Peterborough native, can't be pinned down. In 1978, when Fletcher Dole was eighty-seven, he was interviewed for an article in *The Boston Globe* about his character in the play.

"I never met him (Wilder), but I used to see him walking up and down the street. I had two or three cows then and delivered milk on foot. I was only a symbol, you see. He didn't try to picture me in the book—I was just a symbol, and I don't know why people took me to be the man in the play, but I didn't care to stop them," Dole said.

Others have said their aunts or grandmothers were the basis for either Mrs. Gibbs or Mrs. Webb, the mothers of the two main characters.

But most amateurs and experts agree that two pivotal characters, Emily Webb and George Gibbs—the young couple that grows up next door to each other—were creations of Wilder's mind.

And yet, some *Our Town* buffs note that there is a grave in a Peterborough cemetery that bears the name Emily Webb. Did Wilder walk in that cemetery and see the name?

And so the parlor talk in town continues.

The population, at the moment, is 2,642. The Postal District bring in 507 more, making a total of 3,149.—Mortality and birth rates: constant—By MacPherson's gauge: 6.032.

—Professor Willard, Act I

Wilder was born in Madison, Wisconsin, and educated in Shanghai and Hong Kong. His father was consul general in those cities, and the family traveled widely.

Wilder's formal education was far-flung and varied. He studied at Oberlin, Yale, the American Academy in Rome, and Princeton. He earned his living as a writer and taught at Harvard, the University of Chicago, and universities in Europe.

According to Jill Lawler, who teaches English at Con-Val Regional High School in Peterborough, and who based her college thesis on Wilder, the writer may have had an epiphany of sorts while visiting an archaeological dig. As he stood peering down into the ruins of a home he realized he was looking into a family's kitchen, Lawler says. This is where they ate, prepared food and cleaned up—the most mundane and simple of daily tasks—and ones that have gone on for centuries. In *Our Town,* much of the dialogue is held in the minimalist kitchens occupied by the Gibbs and Webb families.

Eventually Wilder settled in New Haven, Connecticut, and spent frequent summers at the MacDowell Colony. He taught at a camp on Lake Sunapee and walked to New London often.

He died in 1975. During his long writing career he won the Pulitzer Prize three times, twice for plays—*Our Town* and *The Skin of Our Teeth*—and for his novel, *The Bridge of San Luis Rey.*

What was Wilder like? Lawler says he was not as simple as his characters. After his death, it was revealed that Wilder was a homosexual, a fact he kept hidden during his life. He was extremely liberal politically. He had enlisted in the service and was active after the war in the American Veteran Committee in Connecticut, an organization that was considered a left-wing group at the time.

> Maybe letters from Grover's Corners wouldn't be so interesting after a while. Grover's Corners isn't a very important place when you think of all-New Hampshire; but I think it's a very nice town.
>
> —Emily Webb, Act II

What is it about *Our Town* that endures?

Tim Clark, former editor of *Yankee* magazine in Dublin, played Sam Craig in a production of *Our Town* staged by the Peterborough Players. Clark says the play's success is found in the tension created by the minimal staging, the straightforwardness of the characters, and the profoundly simple message of the savoring life every single day.

"The thing about this play is that it always works on stage," says Clark.

Our Town is on the tenth-grade curriculum at Con-Val High School, and Lawler still chokes up every time the class reads the last act. So do most of her students.

Other actors have had some of the same reactions. The Peterborough Players, a professional summer stock company, mounted productions of *Our Town* in 1940, 1960, 1976, 1983, and 1993. During the actors' first read-through for the 1993 production, cast members wept openly during the graveyard scene.

"But it isn't a maudlin play," Lawler says. "It's about living life to the very fullest."

In 1998, Con-Val decided to join the list of schools mounting a spring production of *Our Town*. Vanessa Muskie, a seventeen-year-old junior at the time, played the lead role of Emily Webb.

"I think that some people think that *Our Town* is dull or outdated," Muskie says. "It's anything but. It's so moving in its simplicity."

Was Muskie, who lives in Peterborough, nervous about her role in staging *Our Town* in Our Town?

"Oh, no. I loved playing the character of Emily. I could really get into her head. She was struggling with the same things as all teenagers are."

Clark says there are stories about how New York actors are taken by their directors out to a Peterborough graveyard and told to sit down on the grass, lean back against a tombstone and close their eyes. This is what eternity in a New Hampshire cemetery is like, the actors are told. This is the sense Wilder wanted to convey. This is how it feels. This is how simple life and death are.

"You can stage a play like Shakespeare's *Much Ado About Nothing* in a Southwest setting and it's still the same play," Clark says. "*Our Town* has to be set in New England. That's what makes it."

Marilla Ricker

For fifty years, she fought for women's right to vote.

BY FELICE BELMAN

When high school kids learn about the Nineteenth Amendment, the one granting American women the right to vote, a few big-name feminists are likely to show up on the final exam:

- Susan B. Anthony, who founded the American women's movement in the nineteenth century
- Alice Paul, who once burned President Woodrow Wilson in effigy
- Carrie Chapman Catt, Paul's more ladylike counterpart, who conferred politely with the president and ran the National American Suffrage Association

Ricker spent decades fighting for women's suffrage.

New Hampshire Historical Society.

But when the New Hampshire legislature finally voted in 1919 to ratify the amendment, it was a local woman, Marilla Marks Ricker, who deserved much of the credit. She had devoted a full fifty years to the cause of voting rights for women—in speeches, in writings, and in persistent annual attempts to vote. And in 1920, just two months before her death, her fiftieth and final attempt to mark a ballot met with success.

"I think we should all work for equal suffrage, and I trust the time is not far distant when no man or woman will even admit that it was ever opposed in New Hampshire," Ricker said in 1907. "I want New Hampshire to be the banner state of the East on the equal suffrage question."

By the end of the twentieth century, New Hampshire boasted a female governor, a female speaker of the House, a female president of the Senate, and selectwomen galore. Ricker's prediction, it seems, had come true: Surely no modern politician speaks proudly of the state's long, stubborn refusal to grant women's votes—practically no one even remembers it. But Ricker's work in smashing that tradition is worth recalling.

Marilla Marks was born in New Durham, graduated from Colby Academy in New London in 1861, and quickly found work as a teacher. In 1863, at the age of twenty-three, she married John Ricker and moved to Dover, where he had a real estate business. It was John's sudden death just five years later that ended Ricker's brief taste of conventional domestic life. Widowhood left her the money and the independence to do whatever she wanted—and she did, embarking on a life of political and social activism.

Her first test came in 1870. Having inherited some property from her husband, Ricker made her way to Dover City Hall, paid her property taxes, and then asked permission to vote in a local election. After all, she figured, she'd paid her taxes—she ought to receive something in return. Hadn't they ever heard about taxation without representation? Besides, just because the laws didn't specifically say women could vote didn't necessarily mean they couldn't.

"No woman was ever known to escape a criminal statute because its language ignored her sex. . . . Shall the word 'he' include woman in one set of laws and exclude her in another?" she wrote.

Ricker was the first woman in New Hampshire to try to vote—and she flopped. The next year, Ricker returned, paid her taxes, and filled out a voting form. Again, city officials refused to accept it. And again and again. Ricker paid her property taxes under protest for the next half century.

Fortunately for New Hampshire's women, Ricker decided suffrage was a bigger issue than just her annual spat with Dover election officials. For the rest of her life, Ricker tried any and all arguments to convince the people of New Hampshire—particularly those in the legislature—that women deserved the right to vote. And although they seem obvious now, her arguments were radical in their day. For example:

- Women deserve the same rights as blacks. "Her zeal in the cause of freedom has not been sated in the emancipation and enfranchisement of the black man and will not be, so long as white women and all women remain without voice or vote in the government under which they live," wrote the *Granite Monthly* magazine in a 1910 profile.

- Just because all women weren't agitating for the right to vote didn't mean they deserved it any less. "There is the contentment of ignorance and the contentment of indolence. In the old slave days when Lincoln was told that the slaves did not want their freedom, he replied, 'If they are so ignorant as that, they certainly need it,'" she wrote.
- Without the vote, women would never have equal economic power. In 1909, the average female teacher's salary was $970; the average male teacher made $1,542. "So long as woman has no political status, she will be the underdog as a wage-earner," Ricker wrote that year.
- Men don't vote with the same interests in mind as women. "Grave questions, such as the death rate of children, the waste of child life, the employment of married women and the care of the aged cannot be satisfactorily settled if the woman's point of view is left out," she wrote.

Ricker even tried some distinctly nonfeminist approaches. Rather than expanding the role of women in society, she said, voting rights might simply improve them in their current role. "Women need to have some interests outside the home and will be better comrades to their husbands, better mothers to their children, and better homemakers when they have the balance," she wrote.

Of course, she also argued the opposite: "When I was a girl, the field of woman's work was limited. Now see what she can do! The cause: the agitation of woman suffrage."

Ricker gave speeches on women's suffrage all over the state—and all over the country. She hounded newspaper editors to print her essays on the subject. She buttonholed lawmakers. Year in and year out, she made a fuss where others were content to leave things the way they were.

The residents of New Hampshire, many of whom heard Ricker speeches or read Ricker essays over the years, weren't quite sure what to make of her. Many seemed unable to get beyond her physical appearance, which, truth be told, was weird.

"As to her attire, Mrs. Ricker dresses for comfort rather than as a votress of Dame Fashion. Her dresses are simply made, without big sleeves or too long skirts. . . . She always wears a frill of soft lace at her throat, which lessens the effect of plainness and gives a womanly setting to her strong, intellectual face," wrote a turn-of-the-century biographer.

A 1910 photograph shows Ricker's curly hair cropped close to her head, like a man's. She wears a rose pinned over her heart and, oddly, a man's pocket-watch at her waist.

And while an 1895 volume called *New Hampshire Women* described Ricker as "frank, generous, and open-hearted," she could also be difficult and intemperate. Here's what she had to say about men who opposed suffrage: "No honest man, doing a legitimate business, need be afraid of a woman's vote. But some men scare easy." And *here's* what she had to say about women who opposed her: "Any woman who opposes equal suffrage has no more sense than the billy-goat that butted the hornet's nest."

The voters, meanwhile, took a long, long time to come around. In 1902, for example, the state constitutional convention engaged in a lengthy debate about whether women deserved the right to vote.

Delegate Edgar Aldrich of Littleton, who later became a federal judge, argued it would "disturb the serene security of motherhood."

Delegate Rosecrans Pillsbury of Londonderry suggested women had enough to do without worrying about the vote. "We all admire the motherly woman and the woman who raises her family, directs the feet of her children in the directions they should go, takes an interest in their pleasures and their tasks, educates them and watches over them," he said. "In the past we have had those women in New Hampshire, and I hope the women of our state will remain on the pedestal where we have always worshipped them."

Delegate Arthur Thompson, a hotel keeper from Warner, however, spoke up on behalf of women, even arranging for Catt, the national suffrage leader, to speak in Concord. Briefly, his efforts paid off.

The convention, on a vote of 143–94, agreed to give women the right to vote. But when the question was put to the state's (all-male) voters, it failed miserably: 13,809 in favor and 21,788 against.

Ricker had other interests too. She traveled to Europe and learned to speak German. She studied law and in 1890 became the first woman admitted to the New Hampshire Bar—and for a long time, remained the only one. "Her petition opened the way to women in the field of legal practice in the Granite State, although there seems little inclination on the part of the sex to follow therein," wrote the *Granite Monthly* in 1910.

Ricker lived for several years in Washington, D.C., where she became known as "the prisoner's friend" for her regular visits with inmates. Back home, she instigated legislation giving New Hampshire inmates the right to send sealed letters to the governor without interception by the warden.

Ricker was deeply interested in the fortunes and future of the New Hampshire Republican Party. So in 1910, when Robert Bass of Peterborough looked like a shoo-in for the gubernatorial nomination, Ricker stepped forward. Bass's progressive wing of the party, she reasoned, did not speak for her and other "stalwart" Republicans. Bass, she said, was a "mercerized" Republican.

Now, this was still ten years before women had the right to vote, but Ricker reasoned that she met the only two qualifications to run for governor listed in the state constitution: She had lived here more than seven years and she was more than thirty years old—in fact, she was seventy!

The Granite Monthly called her effort "the most unique candidacy ever known in New Hampshire political life." The magazine wrote: "She retains the strength, vigor and enthusiasm of youth, and her devotion to the principles she has espoused is as determined and unyielding as ever."

Ricker's campaign focused on two issues: property tax reform (she hoped to make churches start paying) and (what else?) voting rights for women. And so, in a sloppy, handwritten note, Ricker penned a declaration of candidacy in the spring of 1910: "I hereby request that my name be printed on the official ballot of the Republican Party as a candidate (for governor). I further declare that if nominated as a candidate for said office, I will not withdraw. And if elected, I will qualify and assume the duties of said office."

Secretary of State Edward Pearson heartily disagreed. Ricker wasn't a voter, he said, and therefore could not be governor. Her name never appeared on the ballot, and Bass won the nomination and the general election.

Ricker had won attention for her cause but lost the chance to put it into action.

By now, Marilla Ricker was old. But other suffragists took up her cause and, nine years later, the national suffrage movement finally caught on in New Hampshire. In 1919 the legislature met in special session to ratify the 19th Amendment to the U.S. Constitution, granting women the right to vote. The tally: 212–143 in the House, 14–10 in the Senate.

The very next year, women voted in force. Some even got elected. The political atmosphere changed. Suddenly, it was as if everyone had always been on the side of women. Savvy about the sheer force of numbers, political bosses who had once bitterly fought women's enfranchisement now made a concerted effort to win their support. Susan Bancroft of Concord was quickly named vice-chairwoman of the Republican State Committee, Alice Harriman of Laconia became vice-chairwoman of the Democratic Party, and Jennie Roby of Concord was named assistant treasurer.

For Ricker, who would die a year later, the work of a lifetime had paid off. She was proud of herself—and proud of her state. "The vote placed the state of New Hampshire on the right side of one of the great questions of the day," she wrote. "It gave her action an influence comparable in import with that vote of hers which ratified finally the first constitution of the United States of America."

Jessie Doe and Mary Louise Rolfe Farnum

They were the first women elected to the New Hampshire legislature.

Jessie Doe and Mary Louise Rolfe Farnum managed to do in 1920 what is difficult for politicians even today: wage a successful write-in campaign. These two, however, had no choice: By the time women actually won the right to vote (and therefore run for office), it was too late to get their names on the ballot.

Doe, a Republican from Rollinsford, and Farnum, a Democrat from Boscawen, were elected to the New Hampshire House just months after women's suffrage became a reality. They sat next to each other in Representatives Hall and worked hard on a variety of issues—everything from movie censorship (Doe was for it) to a statewide income tax (she liked that too) to plans to build a teachers' college in Manchester (Farnum hated that idea). And at the

Mary Louise Rolfe Farnum, a Democrat from Boscawen, was among the first two women in the legislature.

New Hampshire Historical Society.

Jessie Doe, a Republican from Rollinsford, was elected in 1920. She championed a statewide income tax.

New Hampshire Historical Society.

end of the year, they received their well-earned pay: $100, the same wage then as now.

Doe and Farnum set the stage for hundreds of female lawmakers to come. For many years, New Hampshire had the highest percentage of women legislators in the country. Feminism? Not necessarily. Donna Sytek, who served as speaker in the late 1990s, once explained the phenomenon this way: You can always find women in the world's lowest-paying jobs.

John Sununu

A three-term governor, he served as chief of staff to President George Bush.

When John Sununu saved George Bush from the brink of defeat in the 1988 New Hampshire primary, Bush owed him big. But Sununu's appointment as White House chief of staff was no mere reward for a job well done. Bush knew Sununu would lend needed toughness to his administration.

He did. Sununu torpedoed several too-moderate Department of Justice candidates. He pushed for the Star Wars missile defense program. He promoted New Hampshire Justice David Souter for a seat on the U.S. Supreme Court. And he was at Bush's side when the president reneged on his "read my lips" no-tax pledge of 1988.

John Sununu with President George Bush in New Hampshire.

New Hampshire Historical Society.

Trouble was, his bullying manner made him enemies galore. And when revelations surfaced about Sununu's heavy use of Air Force jets for personal trips, no one rallied to his defense. By late 1991, he was gone.

Sound familiar? Sununu's rise and fall bore an eerie resemblance to that of Sherman Adams, the governor who became Dwight Eisenhower's chief of staff, only to be driven from office for accepting gifts from corporate bigwigs.

"Both were no-nonsense guys, with a disdain for the social intricacies of Washington," said Republican strategist David Carney, who worked for Sununu in Concord and Washington. "Sununu wasn't a guy to pal around, and that undid him. He'd built a defense for Bush, not for John Sununu."

Frederic Dumaine

He shut down Manchester's mills.

At its peak, the Amoskeag Manufacturing Company was the world's largest cotton textile firm. It employed 17,000 workers in Manchester, providing steady jobs and housing for mothers and daughters, fathers and sons. That is, until 1936, the year Frederic Dumaine shut down the mills.

"It was a truly devastating time," said Betty Lessard, librarian for the Manchester Historic Association. "Generations of people had made a living from Amoskeag. It was their life, their home, their identity. But all of the sudden it was gone."

Among the factors leading to the Amoskeag's demise: competition from

Dumaine's legacy in Manchester remains controversial.

Courtesy of the Manchester Historic Association.

In 1914, Amoskeag work-
ers pose proudly with a
giant American flag.
*Courtesy of the Manchester
Historic Association.*

the South, antiquated machinery, high labor costs, and disastrous strikes in
1922 and 1933. Some historians say Dumaine, the company's treasurer, actually held on too long, expanding the Manchester mills when elsewhere in
New England similar factories were closing down.

But to the thousands of laid-off workers, Dumaine was to blame, abandon-
ing his employees—and the city that made him rich—in the midst of the Depression. "For God's sake, he exploited us, took our money, and never returned
to the city," said Mary McNamara.

Not surprisingly, his family disputes that view. "My grandfather was educated at Amoskeag," said Dudley Dumaine. "It was a part of him. He was not
an emotional kind of guy, but it really hurt him to hear his name was mud up
there."

At its peak in the early
years of the century,
Amoskeag employed
17,000 workers.
Manchester Historic Association.

Red Rolfe

He played for the New York Yankees and won five World Series.

When Red Rolfe left New Hampshire in 1931 to join the New York Yankees, he was already the pride of Penacook. "For the first time since the days of 'Young Cy' Young, more than twenty years ago, Concord is to have a 'home town' boy in the big leagues," a *Concord Monitor* writer boasted that year.

That pride was well placed.

Rolfe played alongside Babe Ruth and Lou Gehrig. He won five World Series with Joe DiMaggio. He was on the best team in the biggest town when baseball was the king of sports. "The luckiest thing I ever did was sign with the Yankees," Rolfe once said. "When you're with really great players, they pull you along."

But he was always a New England Yankee at heart. When his playing and managing career was over, he came home to be the athletic director at

Red Rolfe of Penacook won five World Series.

Courtesy of Don Randall.

Rolfe in the dugout.

Courtesy of Don Randall.

Dartmouth College, his alma mater. "Getting the New Hampshire kids into Dartmouth and having them succeed and do well, not necessarily in sports but just do well and graduate, was what he wanted," Rolfe's nephew Don Randall said in 1999.

Bill Morton, a Dartmouth athlete from Rolfe's day, said that attitude was apparent. "What I appreciated most was that here was a former big leaguer in every sense of the word, and he tried to get to know you."

Carlton Fisk

To Northern New England in the 1970s, he was a hometown hero.

BY ALEC MACGILLIS

To understand how an entire state fell in love with a man named Pudge, it helps to visit his hometown in midwinter.

The snowbanks seem to grow deeper as you wind west toward Charlestown in the Connecticut River valley, the boyhood home of Carlton Fisk. By the time they fully melt away, springtime will be well established in most other parts of the country. By the time the youngsters here take their baseball gloves out of the closet, their peers in Texas and California will have been on the diamond for weeks.

This state, it becomes obvious on the slush-covered road through Sunapee and Newport and Claremont, is not fertile country for baseball players. It produces great fans but few great practitioners: The growing season is just too short.

In this barren landscape, Carlton Fisk sprouted as improbably as ten-foot-high corn in a rock-strewn field. Those who watched his rise still shake their

On his first day in the Major Leagues, Carlton Fisk sits in the Red Sox dugout with his high school coach Ralph Silva.

Courtesy of Ralph Silva.

heads over it, like farmers reminiscing about a prize-winning oddity at the county fair.

"We played at most twelve games a season, that's it. How many guys from a little town like Charlestown with that short a season make it to be one of the best catchers of all time? It was mindboggling to me," said Ralph Silva, who coached Fisk in baseball and basketball at Charlestown High School in the 1960s.

There have been a few other major league players from the state, but they spent their careers with distant teams and never equaled Fisk in ability. And then there have been players who, through their exploits with the Red Sox, became synonymous with New England baseball, like Ted Williams and Roger Clemens. Yet Williams was forever a son of faraway San Diego, just as Clemens never let us forget that home to him was Katy, Texas.

Fisk was a rare convergence of the two groups, a local star on the local team. For one decade, the 1970s, northern New England had a favorite son. Every town that tuned in to the Red Sox for the thrilling and ultimately heartbreaking seasons of 1975 and 1978 could lay some claim to Fisk. If Bobby Thomson hit the Shot Heard Round the World in 1951 for the Giants, Fisk's twelfth-inning foul-pole-scraping home run in Game Six of the 1975 World Series was the Shot Heard Round New England. It was 12:33 in the morning when Fisk waved his game-winning blast fair, but that didn't stop Don Conant, a fan of Fisk's since the catcher's high school days, from ringing the church bells at St. Luke's in Charlestown to mark the moment. Local boy makes good, chimed the bells.

Boy, oh boy, does he make good.

In Fisk, there was someone the region could finally call its own, who wouldn't leave for warmer climes, like the farmers and factories before him. He even stayed in the state after he made it to the majors, choosing to live in Raymond and commute to Fenway Park rather than settle in the big city.

Charles Perkins, a volunteer firefighter in the town, recalls encountering the catcher on a call. "I went to respond to a chimney fire, and he was right up on the roof with me. I was there with the department, but he was just a neighbor come to help," Perkins said.

In the end, though, Fisk did leave. His strained relations with the Red Sox brass culminated in his filing for free agency and signing with the Chicago White Sox in 1981. In his first game back at Fenway with Chicago, his late-inning home run beat Boston. There would be many more avenging at-bats against his former employer during his Chicago career, which ended with his retirement in 1993.

Losing Fisk to Chicago, said Bart Giamatti, a diehard Red Sox fan from farther down the Connecticut River in South Hadley, Massachusetts, was "the worst moment for Red Sox fans since the team sold Babe Ruth."

After his retirement, there was talk of Fisk's returning to the state. He decided he'd rather not uproot his family again and remained in the Midwest, in a large country house outside Chicago. A grandfather, he spends his time at celebrity golf tournaments, in the weight room, and in the nursery with his orchids.

"I do a little bit of everything and a lot of nothing," he said in 1999.

That year, Fisk was back in the news after he narrowly missed making the Baseball Hall of Fame in his first year of eligibility. It was a tough year to be up for election, with three other stars from Fisk's generation on the ballot, and with the sportswriters who vote wary of inducting more than three players in any given year. Still, Fisk was sad to be overlooked.

"I have that old New England mentality of guarding my emotions well, of not getting all worked up so I'd be crushed if I didn't get it," Fisk said. "But I was disappointed. I feel as though I was as good at my position as the other guys were."

Fisk has the offensive numbers for the Hall of Fame: He hit 376 home runs, more than any other catcher, and batted a respectable .269 over his career despite several serious injuries. In 1972, he was unanimously elected American League Rookie of the Year.

If he is inducted, though, it will be for the intangibles not included in those figures. He is counted among the top five catchers of all time because he was one of the best ever at handling pitchers—the most important of a catcher's many duties—and because he embodied the virtues required in the ideal backstop: durability, leadership, and smarts. He ranks first in the number of games caught in a career, the result of having stayed in the game until age forty-five in the most physically grueling of positions.

Not surprisingly, commentators attributed Fisk's hardiness behind the plate to his Granite State origins. The catcher's sturdy build and proud bearing fit perfectly with sportswriters' portrayal of him as a cross between the Old Man of the Mountain and a crusty character in a Robert Frost poem.

Fisk doesn't dispute the stereotype. "My core was anchored in New Hampshire. Being stubborn and unwavering, never giving in, never giving up, keep going no matter what the obstacles, dig in, knuckle down, work harder, all that stuff," he said.

Those in Charlestown, though, knew the story behind Fisk's solidity lay even closer to home. Pitchers who were performing poorly had reason to fear Fisk's stern visits to the mound not because the catcher was a son of New Hampshire but because he was a son of Cecil and Leona Fisk, parents of a legendary brood of young athletes. Cecil, a machinist, part-time farmer, and former tennis and basketball great, and Leona, an accomplished softball player, raised six children, several of them as talented as Carlton.

"His father was quite a disciplinarian; he worked them hard," recalled Harold Ames, a longtime acquaintance of the family. "The kids were all the same, all athletes. It was a great family to know."

The Fisk parents, who still live in the big white house on Elm Street that Carlton and his siblings grew up in, had contrasting styles as instructors to budding athletes.

"When the kids were small, I used to take them out in the field in back and play catch with them. I figured, if they're interested in it you should go along with them," Leona Fisk said. "(Cecil) criticized them all the time; I praised them."

After a high school basketball playoff game in which Fisk scored forty points and pulled down thirty rebounds (setting a state record that still stands), his father criticized him for missing some foul shots.

Cecil Fisk doesn't apologize. The bar had to be set high so the kids wouldn't simply settle for what their inherited skill provided them, he explained. And, he said, "In a close game, it's often decided by foul shots. You've got to hit them, no matter what."

There was no weekly allowance for the Fisk kids. For spending money, Carlton and his siblings delivered newspapers and cleaned the local reservoir in the spring. One time Carlton complained about making only fifty cents an hour and considered quitting. His father set him straight. "I asked him what he would be getting if he wasn't working there and said until you make more doing something else you better do it."

Eventually, Fisk would be making much more, but there would be other times in his difficult dealings with baseball team owners when he would feel undervalued. Both his bosses, Haywood Sullivan in Boston and Jerry Reinsdorf in Chicago, were reluctant to give the injury-prone catcher the money and respect he thought he deserved. As he grew older, there seemed always to be a young prospect the owners wanted to have replace Fisk—even as his offensive numbers held strong.

His parents knew little of his troubles with his bosses, other than that they made their son unhappy. They did not fight Fisk's departure for Chicago, though it meant they could no longer make weekend trips to see him play in Boston, a luxury they had enjoyed for a decade.

They were at Fenway for Game Six in 1975, in seats that gave them a perfect view of their son's deep drive as it hooked toward the foul pole but then stayed fair. "It was breathtaking. Everyone was hooting and hollering," his mother recalled.

Looking back, their son said he sometimes wishes that he'd been able to enjoy playing for the local team more than he did, that injuries and battles with owners hadn't so obscured his good fortune. This shortcoming, Fisk said, had both physical and emotional roots.

"All those injuries and having to deal with management didn't allow me to enjoy it all as much I should have," he said. "But there was also a little of that thing they say about New Englanders: Being from here doesn't prevent me from doing anything, it just prevents me from enjoying it."

This was not the case when it came to his own memory of Game Six, which hasn't melded into the televised images others associate with it. In fact, the at-bat is one of the only things that hasn't blurred in his recollection of the series.

"That particular moment is etched in my brain forever," he said.

I remember so vividly standing in the on-deck circle with Fred Lynn—I can't figure out why I was there with him, because I never batted ahead of him—and saying, "I feel like something good is going to happen." It wasn't boastful or bold, it was just said in this conversational way. I said, "I think I'm going to hit one off the wall. Drive me in." And he said, "Sounds good to me."

When I got to the plate it was like they say, I was in a zone. Everything was coming in slow-motion. I took the first pitch and the next
one came in slow-motion and I knew I crushed it. I knew it had plenty
to get up over the wall but it seemed to be curving foul and I'm yelling
at it and then all of a sudden it just went straight.

For Silva, the baseball and basketball coach at Charlestown High, the Fisk
family was a gift to be opened over and over again, from the parents on down
to Carlton. Despite Cecil Fisk's high expectations, he never got in the way. He
always sat quietly behind the bench and said, "Nice game," to Silva afterward.

Not that there was much coaching to be done with the gifted Fisks.
Though Silva's natural bent was toward baseball, not basketball, the Fisk sons
and several of their standout classmates made him look like a hoops genius,
Silva said. From Fisk's sophomore through senior years, the basketball team
went 49–3.

When Silva first laid eyes on Fisk in junior high, he had no way of knowing
what was to come. Still exhibiting some of the boyhood chubbiness which
gave him the nickname Pudge in grade school, Fisk had "feet that were falling
all over him."

When Fisk showed up at the start of basketball season a year later, he had
stretched to a chiseled six-foot-three. "He had lost all his gangliness. I could
not believe the transformation," Silva recalled.

Fisk spent more time at Charlestown High pitching than catching; it was
his older brother Calvin who graduated as a top catching prospect, only to find
himself labeled as too old after he returned from serving in Vietnam. Silva said
he sometimes wondered if, beyond his bad luck in being drafted, Calvin Fisk
was "too nice" to make it to the big leagues. Calvin's younger brother, on the
other hand, had a toughness that served him well. If there was anything he
had to coach Carlton Fisk on, Silva said, it was pointing his boundless energy
in the right direction.

While Fisk's tenacity extended his injury-ridden career, it also made his
final years difficult to bear at times, as he watched rookies who lacked his old-
fashioned ethic break into the big leagues. In one well-publicized incident, he
chewed out the flashy Deion Sanders for not running hard to first base—even
though Sanders was on the opposing team.

To those who knew him well, though, Fisk shed his toughness. Whenever
he returned to Charlestown in his early years with the Red Sox, he made sure
to stop at his coach's house to play Wiffle Ball with Silva's kids. Silva's son
Kenneth, who worked as a ball boy at Fisk's high school games, plans to send
Fisk a copy of a solo folk-rock album he just recorded.

Years later, Kenneth Silva still marvels at the way Fisk jumped so high that
he could hold the basketball between his elbows and drop it through the
hoop—an alternative to dunking, which wasn't allowed.

"There was that regal kind of way he walked, like he knew he was somebody. He inspired me in my own life with that walk," Silva said.

When Ralph Silva attended a ceremony honoring his coaching career a few
years ago in Concord, the moderator startled him by reading a letter Fisk had

written for the occasion. "Ever since I had him, I've looked for that special a guy, and I never found him," Silva said. "So I've had to live on his laurels my whole life. I was kind of lucky that I hit town when I did, when he and the others were growing up."

The wonder of making it to the doorstep of Cooperstown from his back yard in Charlestown is not lost on Fisk. He recalled how it was as a young major leaguer to come across players like Fred Lynn, who attended college in California and played more than 1,000 games before even arriving in the minors. Fisk, by contrast, had played fewer than 100 organized games in high school and in a brief stint at the University of New Hampshire before he was signed by the Red Sox.

It was partly the dominance of winter that led the young Fisk to fantasize more of Boston Garden than Fenway Park. "Everybody's boyhood dream was to play for the Celtics or the Red Sox. I wanted to be with the Celtics," he said. "But of course it turned out okay anyway."

Fisk's only explanation for bucking the geographic odds was this: "Maybe I expect more from myself than I do from others." It was this resolve that produced the workout regimen that allowed him to return from five knee operations over the course of his career. After spending nine innings in a crouch behind home plate, he would retire to several hours of lifting and stretches in the clubhouse. It was the sheer challenge of keeping himself in form all those years that made returning to baseball as a coach—something many think he'd excel at—seem so daunting, he said.

"The thing I looked forward to most when I retired was getting off that baseball schedule—everything revolves around it, for 365 days," he said. "I'm feeling a little bit of a stirring these days that makes me think about getting back into it, but that kind of commitment, even as a coach, is tough to make unless you have that burning passion."

A few years ago, Fisk came back to Charlestown for Old Home Day. He rode on the back of a tractor and waved to the crowds. He said it was enjoyable but somewhat unsettling.

"Maybe this is a New England thing too, but it's hard to think of myself as a celebrity. Coming home, I always just feel like I'm one of the Fisks. To be treated a little extra special like that was kind of embarrassing. I saw people I knew from school as I went by, and they all called me Pudgy. I hadn't been called that since grade school!"

If Fisk does become the first New Hampshirite to be inducted into the Hall of Fame, he will have to decide whether to enter the shrine as a Red Sox or a White Sox. Which team's cap will his likeness wear on the plaque? It's something he's been asked for the past ten years. It's a tough one to answer, as he spent roughly the same time with the two clubs and bad feelings linger over his treatment by the management of both teams.

Ralph Silva thinks he has the answer.

"Tell him I've got an old Charlestown High cap ready if he wants it," he said.

(Postscript: Carlton Fisk was elected to the Hall of Fame in 2000. On his plaque he wears the cap of the Boston Red Sox.)

William Butterfield

An architect who built a lasting legacy

BY ALEC MacGILLIS

William Butterfield, architect. If it weren't for this brief annual entry in Manchester's turn-of-the-century business registries, you'd wonder whether the man who changed the face of the state ever existed. That's because Butterfield, the architect whose designs dominate much of New Hampshire, is all but invisible in the written record. If anonymity is the curse of architecture, then William Butterfield epitomized his profession. To find him, you must go outside.

If you live in the southern or central part of the state, you probably won't have to go far. In most of the region's larger communities, chances are that the most interesting structure in town was one of Butterfield's creations.

Butterfield was among the most prolific architects of his day.

New Hampshire Historical Society.

The list seems endless. In Hillsboro, there is the elegant Gov. John Smith House, now the town library and town hall. Pittsfield's Main Street is a veritable Butterfield Row, with the town library, the old Academy building, and the former school building—now reincarnated as the town hall—all on the architect's resumé. In Franklin, there is the old Soldiers Memorial Hall; in Laconia, the courthouse; in Weare, the Stone Memorial Building. You'll find little mention of the architect in the archives of Concord's New Hampshire Historical Society or State Library. But you'll find his work in the city's old armory, now the Green Street Community Center, and in the Aquilla building, the stately yellow-brick building that anchors downtown's central crossing, the corner of Main and Pleasant streets.

Nowhere, however, was Butterfield as omnipresent as in his adopted hometown of Manchester. As the Queen City rose up around its mills, Butterfield became its Christopher Wren, the man who decided what form its newfound preeminence and prosperity should take.

By the same token, nowhere was the bewildering breadth of Butterfield's abilities more visible than in Manchester, where his works came to represent every stylistic strain of his era. If you seek to discover the man's character in his creations, then a tour of Manchester will leave you thinking him schizophrenic.

His work ranges from the durable Romantic brownstone look popularized by the giant of late nineteenth-century architecture, Henry Richardson, to the fanciful Queen Anne style, to the Colonial restraint that made a comeback around 1900.

"He just went through all the styles. He mirrored what was going on, and he did anything he was called upon to do," architectural historian Lisa Mausolf said.

He designed the biggest of the new commercial buildings on Manchester's bustling Elm Street, including the towering Kennard Block, which symbolized the city's boundless aspirations until the block was destroyed in a 1902 fire. He designed the school's palatial high school, deemed in its day—by locals and outsiders alike—to be the most impressive schoolhouse in New England.

More often than not, it was Butterfield whom the city's newly rich drafted to display their wealth for all to see. The Goulds hired him to build their daughter a neo-Romanesque mansion as a wedding present (what is today Notre Dame College, on northern Elm Street); a few blocks away on the corner of Walnut and Prospect streets, cigar czar Roger Sullivan hired him to build an exuberant late-Victorian extravaganza of five fireplaces, twenty rooms, and too many nooks and crannies to count.

Brian Lawrence, whose family now lives in the Sullivan house, recently renovated the building. While doing the work, he wondered often about the man who conceived of the 107-year-old fantasy, with its turrets and towers, its windows of every imaginable shape and position.

He asked around among local architects about Butterfield, with little luck. "I wish I knew more about him," Lawrence said, admiring the chimney covered in terra cotta, the large circular window in the library, the rock-faced porch, which Lawrence restored. "He really threw a little bit of everything in here."

This much is known: Butterfield was born in Sidney, Maine, on October 22, 1860, and moved to Waterville, Maine, at age eleven. His father, an accomplished local builder and architect, passed the trade on to his son, who, at the age of sixteen, went to work for a Massachusetts general contractor for six years. At nineteen, he supervised the construction of the first wing of New Castle's Wentworth Hotel.

Without any formal education in architecture, Butterfield opened up shop in Manchester in 1881, at the age of twenty-one. He could hardly have chosen a better time or place to get started. Manchester was booming and everything needed building: marketplaces, mansions, municipal buildings.

In a city with relatively few architects, Butterfield started winning commissions left and right, and carved out a niche in one of the areas of highest demand: schools. Not only did the rapidly growing city need classrooms for its kids, but it also wanted school buildings of a style and scale that would reflect the city's rising stature.

In this ambition, they were not alone. In the latter half of the nineteenth century, many saw public schools as temples of sorts where no expense should be spared.

The simple schoolhouses of the early republic no longer sufficed, as a Massachusetts minister explained in a speech to the New England Historical Society in 1858: "An ugly or incapacious schoolhouse is never a good investment. As an educational means, a well-built schoolroom is not without large capacity," said the Rev. N. H. Chamberlain, "for if the children of the rich find at home the decent furnishings of civilized life, it is yet necessary that the children of the poor, living often in uncomfortable or unfurnished homes, should find in the schoolroom that neatness, comfort, and elegance which might serve as a protest against scenes they are familiar with elsewhere."

This high-minded philosophy of public education produced Manchester's Central High School, one of a half-dozen local school buildings Butterfield would design. In its stature and elegance, the building looks more like a

Butterfield designed this neo-Romanesque mansion (what is today Notre Dame College) on Elm Street in Manchester.
Andrea Bruce Woodall/Concord Monitor.

Prussian palace in Potsdam than a schoolhouse. It was built to hold 600 students, a large number at the turn of the century, and equipped with an observatory beneath its high dome. The building exhibits many of Butterfield's pet details, writ large: tall, arched windows, rounded turrets at either end of the building, intricate indentations in its rear facade, elaborate brickwork and scrolls and frescoes everywhere, even on the roof's air vents.

Even today, students know they've got something special in the big, yellow-brick building, Central High junior Melissa Pfaff said. The building is so inspiring, she said, it's too bad that administrators chose to put the math classes inside it. Its grandeur might rub off better in social studies or English classes, she said.

"You always find something new in it. I especially like the little insignias on the windows," Pfaff said. "And the ceiling, it's all patterned and designed. It's actually beautiful."

Across town, older students now appreciate Butterfield's abilities in an entirely different sort of building, what is now Notre Dame College. The picturesque building exemplifies neo-Romanesque excess, with its asymmetrical yet well-proportioned facade, its numerous dormers, turrets, and spires. Inside, a visitor is greeted by a tiled fireplace and frescoes lining the staircase, whose back wall is made entirely of stained glass. A large fountain that used to stand in the middle of the front hall has been replaced by a statue of the Virgin.

The building was a wedding present from the Goulds to their daughter Mary upon her marriage to banker George Chandler. Her daughter—cleverly named Marigold, in honor of her mother—would attend the new high school, graduating in 1914. Like a good number of local children then, she had the good fortune to spend most of her childhood hours in Butterfield buildings.

It wasn't long before Butterfield's name traveled to all corners of New England. At one point, thirty buildings designed by him and his five assistants were under construction at the same time.

Today, touring Butterfield's buildings outside of Manchester and Concord makes for a somewhat sobering lesson in local history. That's because the mill towns that were wealthy enough to employ him around the turn of the century

Central High School in Manchester exhibits many of Butterfield's pet details, writ large: tall, arched windows, rounded turrets at either end of the building, intricate indentations in its rear facade, elaborate brickwork, and scrolls and frescoes everywhere, even on the roof's air vents.

Andrea Bruce Woodall/Concord Monitor.

now rank among the state's poorer communities. Coming upon them is a little like stumbling into a stone wall in an old-growth forest: It takes some historical imagination to make sense of their presence.

"They're relics of a lost golden age that often look out of place today," said state architectural historian Jim Garvin. "They almost mock the present age because they're so exemplary of an age of prosperity that hasn't been seen for decades."

That is not to say the buildings are not appreciated by the towns' current inhabitants. A long civic struggle earlier in the 1990s saved Pittsfield's old school building, another neo-Romanesque marvel. Town librarian Joan Wadleigh still cherishes the brightness and airiness of the library, whose design included a fireproofed room for the stacks, with sliding steel doors. The Academy building, resembling a medieval chapel with its stocky tower and belfry, now serves as the local Mason hall.

In Hillsboro, former governor Smith's 1891 mansion, built for an unheard-of $100,000, remains the pride of the town. With its colonial porch and Victorian embellishment, it is a case study in Butterfield's eclecticism, noted by G. A. Cheney in a 1903 *Granite Monthly* article as one of the most notable surviving tributes to the architect:

"Indeed it is because of this very faculty to make use of the best in all the different types and make from them a harmonious whole that gives Mr. Butterfield that strong personality he has impressed upon his work," Cheney wrote.

Smith used to watch locals stream to his mills in the morning through his stained-glass bathroom window, and dock the pay of those he saw arriving late. Now, residents profit from his personal profligacy whenever they read books beneath his gold-leaf ceiling or his Louis Quatorze chandelier.

Wealthy clients like Smith notwithstanding, Butterfield's work did not make him a rich man. He lived in a handsome house near Sullivan's mansion in Manchester but left little money to his children upon his death in 1932, according to city records.

For a final resting place, the man who designed some of the state's grandest homes took a modest plot in Pine Grove cemetery. Like every other personal clue about him, it's very hard to find.

Niels Nielsen

He was caretaker of the state's most famous profile.

BY SARAH M. EARLE

T he Old Man of the Mountain has always been old. Nature sculpted him old, man discovered him old, notion named him old. And as one era slips into the next, he'll cast that same knowing gaze over the restless world, a granite giant who knew no youth. But he'll always be Niels Nielsen's baby. "I've fallen in love with that pile of rocks," said Nielsen, the burly construction worker who has dangled from the Old Man's forehead, knelt on his nose, and scrubbed his cheeks countless times. "Every one of us, the sons and daughters of this country, owe it something. My something just happened to be the Old Man."

For years, Niels Nielsen gave the Old Man of the Mountain his annual checkup.

Lara Solt/Concord Monitor.

By the end of the twentieth century, Nielsen himself was old—too old to caress the craggy visage he loved. But his toils had preserved the treasured landmark, ensuring it a place in the coming century.

"He is certainly in better shape than he was found," said Nielsen, whose own health keeps him largely confined to his Laconia home. It does not, however, stifle his stories.

Sitting in his easy chair among Maalox and magazines, greeting cards and a favorite painting of the great profile, Nielsen, a husky, tattooed, born-again Christian, can recall cracks and crevices, close calls and accomplishments that have defined a huge chunk of his life.

"I'm the caretaker emeritus," he said. "That means over the hill."

Nielsen still makes it up the mountain. Every year since 1991, when he passed the guardianship of the Old Man to his son David, Nielsen has ridden by helicopter with the rest of the work crew to a ledge just behind the Old Man's perch, 4,000 feet high on Cannon Mountain. He also serves as consultant, helping determine what repairs need to be completed each year. But an era has passed.

Nielsen first ventured onto the old stone face in 1960, 150 years after the Old Man's first recorded discovery. By then, a number of repairs had been made to the landmark, and a team of state workers conducted annual maintenance, but no one carried official and ultimate responsibility for the old stone face's well-being.

Nielsen soon found himself drawn to that calling. A former seaman and World War II veteran, Nielsen first saw the Old Man in 1947, on a trip through New Hampshire with his fiancee. He remembers being awestruck. "I have made several trips around the world, but I have never seen anything that compares with our Old Man," he once wrote.

Nielsen never suspected he'd one day become guardian of the giant. In 1960, after moving to New Hampshire from New York, he went to work for the state highway department. "Almost immediately, the guys started talking about going up on the Old Man," Nielsen recalled. At first, he thought they were joking. He soon learned otherwise. That summer, Nielsen found himself riding the tramway up Cannon Mountain, then traversing the rocky terrain, carrying the engineers' equipment.

When at last he reached the jagged heap of stones that form the face, "I could just tell that I was in a special place," he said. "From then on, whenever I heard the rumors that they were going to go up on the Old Man, I made sure I was part of it."

In 1965, the leader of the work crew passed his responsibilities to Nielsen. It was a duty Nielsen never took lightly. Having seen the condition of the Old Man, he no longer took for granted its stability. Wind and rain had carved cracks in the face, vandals had chipped at the head and cut holes in a protective membrane, and nature posed incalculable threats. Besides that, maintenance of past repairs demanded attention. Over the years, Nielsen performed numerous nips and tucks and a couple of major surgeries. He set up a system of taking measurements of the face, to determine how much damage had been done each year between projects. He regularly tested and adjusted the turnbuckles that hold the forehead slab in place and put supports under several boulders.

In 1971, Nielsen became the first person to conduct repairs on the south face and one of the first to go over the Old Man's forehead. Dangling in a wooden seat over a 1,000-foot drop, he cleaned out a crack on the Old Man's face, removing seven yards of debris. The next year, he affixed a membrane over the crack to keep it free of debris.

It never occurred to Nielsen to feel fear as he worked from his precarious perch. Years before, as a sailor, "I was the one that got called to shimmy up the mast to change the lights," he said. Even after a faulty cable sent Nielsen slipping down past the Old Man's chin, he kept plugging away. A steadfast faith in God and a deep love for the Old Man kept him going.

And for that, Nielsen became a savior. For years, the state wouldn't allow the workers to lower themselves over the side of the face. "It seemed that people were afraid to do anything to the Old Man," he said. No one wanted to be responsible for destroying the landmark in an effort to repair it.

Niels Nielsen's son David on the nose of the Old Man.

Jim Cole/The Associated Press.

But Nielsen felt an inexplicable bond with the Old Man. He has said that he talks to the Old Man, and the Old Man talks back. Sometimes he gets permission from the Old Man to do a sensitive touch-up.

Finally, in 1987, the state recognized that special bond by naming Nielsen the official caretaker of the Old Man. The decision ensured that Nielsen would retain control of the Old Man, rather than the task falling to a state agency.

And in the end, it was the Old Man who told the old man it was time to quit.

Years before, Nielsen had dubbed a somewhat treacherous juncture along the path to the Old Man "decision rock." When the day came that he couldn't leap across the seven-foot divide, he would announce his retirement. That day came in 1990.

It's a day his son David will never forget. "He came to that point, and he stopped and he looked at it and he looked at me. And then he walked around it without saying anything . . . and I knew that was very difficult for him."

Today, Nielsen can relive his adventures by popping one of his many videotapes into the VCR. He has been featured on numerous documentaries and news programs and has appeared in *National Geographic* and *People*. But his greatest satisfaction comes, perhaps, from knowing that the Old Man will outlive him by a good many years.

Barring an earthquake or the Lord's return, he said in 1999, "My gut feeling is that any baby that's born on this date, today, will not see the Old Man come down."

Alan Shepard

He was the first American in space.

Alan Shepard's greatest moment lasted just five minutes, but it changed the course of world history. In those five minutes, spent strapped inside a cramped capsule atop a slender rocket hurtling above the earth at more than 5,000 miles per hour, Shepard proved that Americans could fly in space. In those five minutes, he erased the doubts of a nation discouraged by Sputnik and fearful for the future.

Shepard grew up in Derry (later known as Spacetown, U.S.A.) and was one of the Navy's best test pilots when he was recruited by NASA. His flight aboard the Redstone rocket and its Mercury space capsule occurred on May 5, 1961, earlier than planned. After Soviet air force Maj. Yuri Gagarin became

Alan Shepard poses in the pressure suit he wore during the Apollo 14 mission, the third manned mission to the moon.
Courtesy of NASA.

the first human in space and the first to orbit the earth, the Americans canceled a monkey-in-space test and sent Shepard as soon as possible. His flight—from Cape Canaveral to just past the Bahamas—went off without a hitch. And in one of the first mass events of the century, millions of Americans witnessed the daring mission on television.

"The naysayers and the doubters about our nation were getting very, very serious attention," recalled John Glenn, the backup pilot for the first two manned flights. "But Al brought us back."

William Chandler, Winston Churchill, and Robert Bass

Against long odds, they reformed New Hampshire politics.

If you think the lobbyists for big business hold sway at the State House these days, you should have been there at the turn of the *last* century. Back then, powerful railroad bosses held the state in their grip. With free rail passes they were able to buy favorable legislation, ease regulations, and win elections. It took three maverick Republicans—William Chandler, Winston Churchill, and Robert Bass—to break the machine. In doing so, they created a short-lived Progressive Party, improved life for farmers and factory workers, and defined a moderate wing of the Republican Party that controlled state politics for generations.

Chandler was a newspaper editor. Churchill was a novelist. Bass became governor. Their combined efforts led to a commission to regulate business, a workers' compensation program, and a ban on free rail passes for state officials.

Robert Bass.
New Hampshire Historical Society.

Winston Churchill.
New Hampshire Historical Society.

William Chandler.
New Hampshire Historical Society.

Other goals—direct primary elections, improved conditions in textile mills, limits on child labor—would take more time.

Just as important as legislative reform, the men believed, was reform to the two-party system. They hoped to take progressives from both major parties and create something new. "We shall no longer vote for a man at the polls just because he bears a party label," Bass said in 1912. "We are out in the open, working and battling shoulder to shoulder with those men who at heart believe as we believe."

William Chandler,
Winston Churchill,
Robert Bass

Patricia Gallup

She revolutionized the way people buy computers.

As recently as 1982, most Americans lived two-and-a-half hours away from a store selling computers. And in those days, stores were where computers came from. That is, until Patricia Gallup came along.

Gallup and her business partner David Hall started PC Connection, Inc., that year based on the notion that there must be a better way to match businesses and individuals with information about the latest personal computers and how to get their hands on them. "We thought," Gallup said with understatement, "a huge demand would develop around these computer products."

And how. Today, the concept of buying computers through the mail seems natural. Back then it was revolutionary—and it worked. In 1998, telephone, catalog, and Internet orders generated $732 million in sales for PC Connection and its 1,000 employees. Gallup figures the company's sales could soon

Gallup changed the way Americans buy computers.

Robin Shotola/Concord Monitor.

exceed $1 billion. And unlike today's mercurial Internet stars, PC Connection's balance sheet shows a profit.

Making big money, however, was never her primary goal. "What drives entrepreneurs is changing the way people think," Gallup said. "We wanted to change the way people buy computer products. That was the kick, changing the buying environment."

Patricia Gallup

Hannes Schneider

He was the father of downhill skiing.

W hen Hannes Schneider arrived at the Mount Cranmore ski area in North Conway in 1939, he was greeted with the cheers of an admiring crowd. It was, one historian noted, akin to Michael Jordan coming to coach basketball at Concord High School. For while skiing was still reserved for the wealthy and superathletic, Americans had heard of Schneider's skill in both skiing and teaching in his native Austria—and they were eager to learn.

Schneider taught America to love skiing.

New England Ski Museum.

Within weeks of his arrival, Schneider's ski school was thriving. On any given weekend, 500 students came to the slopes for lessons, where they were taught Schneider's own techniques: a crouched stance replacing the customary ramrod straight posture. He taught, laid out plans for new slopes, and transformed the very skiing population, popularizing the sport among regular people.

Americans, Schneider once told a reporter, made the best pupils. "They have courage and are not afraid of accident."

Dick and Mac McDonald

Two Manchester brothers found success under the golden arches.

BY STEVE VARNUM

The birth of McDonald's is usually attributed to an entrepreneur named Ray who, the legend goes, launched a fast-food empire from one humble burger shack in Illinois. What a Kroc.

The real story is that a couple of brothers from Manchester drove to California, felt America's first postwar cultural tremors, and founded one of the world's most successful businesses.

Dick and Maurice "Mac" McDonald fed the future with speedy service, fifteen-cent burgers, and skinny fries. They created the fast-food philosophy,

Dick McDonald enjoys a burger with the head of the McDonald's Corp.

AP/World Wide Photos.

the familiar golden arches, and the signs that read "Millions Served," then "Billions Served" and now "Billions and Billions Served."

They brought the assembly line to restaurants, emphasized quantity over quality, homogenized their product and dehumanized service. Their innovations transformed America, starting with restaurants, but spreading to education, medicine, travel, and even religion, according to George Ritzer, author of *The McDonaldization of Society.*

By the end of the twentieth century, there were nearly 25,000 McDonald's restaurants in 115 countries. One was on Manchester's Second Street, where the golden arches towered above a quarter-mile strip containing a half-dozen fast food joints. Dick McDonald was mighty proud to walk into that particular McDonald's. It stood barely a block from 500 South Main Street, where he, his brother, and three sisters were raised by Irish immigrant parents in a working-class neighborhood long since given over to vinyl siding.

It also stood on the very street where his father worked for G. P. Krafts Shoe for forty-two years before abruptly, cruelly being told he had outlived his usefulness to the company. No pension, just "We don't need you here anymore." The McDonald brothers never forgot. "We made up our minds that, one way or another, we'd be financially independent," Dick McDonald said years later.

In the 1930s, the textile and shoe industries that sustained New England's mill towns were withering. Mac McDonald had left for California after graduating from Manchester's Central High School, and Richard followed after graduating from West High School a couple of years later, in 1927. They were classmates of the three Revson brothers, who turned a nail polish business into the Revlon empire.

Hollywood was about as far from Manchester as they could get, in more ways than one. The brothers worked at Columbia studios but soon realized they weren't getting anywhere lugging lights and props around movie sets.

Maybe they were on the wrong end of the movie biz. They opened a theater in Glendora, but people didn't have a lot of spending money during the Depression. Across the way, though, a guy named Walt Wiley seemed to be doing good business selling hot dogs. The brothers opened a hamburger stand in 1937 near the Santa Anita racetrack and did okay, at least in racing season.

Mac McDonald suggested a different location. San Bernardino was a town of 100,000 people, and, like much of Southern California, growing quickly. With a $5,000 loan, they opened a barbecue drive-in three blocks from San Bernardino High School in 1940 with cute carhops who attracted teenagers and low prices that attracted families.

The restaurant was profitable, but the McDonalds weren't satisfied. Carhop service was slow, and teenage boys lingered and plugged the parking lot. "We had trouble finding efficient help. There were these drunken dishwashers and all sorts of breakage. Our restaurant was getting to be a headache," Dick McDonald said. They offered an extensive menu, but hamburgers comprised eighty percent of their sales.

In his book *The Fifties,* David Halberstam points out that the McDonalds recognized the changes that the rise in postwar wealth and the proliferation of the automobile were bringing to America. Americans who had lived in the shadow of the factory for generations moved to the suburbs. They lived farther from work than ever before, changing both the pace of their lives and institutions like dinner.

"Customers weren't demanding it, but our intuition told us they would like speed," Dick McDonald told Halberstam. "Everything was moving faster. The supermarkets and dime stores had already converted to self-service, and it was obvious the future of drive-ins was self-service."

In his personal and business lives, Dick McDonald liked things orderly, clean—and on time. "I think it's damned inefficient and discourteous to keep someone waiting," he told an interviewer years later. "If someone had an appointment for nine and showed up at ten after, I wouldn't see him. No way."

The fast-food restaurant was born in December 1948. San Bernardino. Fourteenth and E Streets. Halberstam called it "the perfect restaurant for a new America."

"We were told quite emphatically we were insane," Dick McDonald said.

The McDonalds fired the carhops and dishwashers, cut an unwieldy twenty-nine-item menu to nine, and replaced plates and silverware with paper wrappers, bags, and cups. They trashed the drippy condiment table. Customers would come to the counter to order food and get it in seconds, not the fifteen to twenty minutes they usually waited. Hamburgers cost fifteen cents, french fries a dime. A family could eat for $2.50.

The restaurant was mechanized and standardized far ahead of its time. Cast-iron grills that lost heat when loaded with beef were replaced by stainless-steel grills that were double the size and easier to clean and held heat better. Dick McDonald examined the machines candy companies used to make patties and found one that could punch out a perfect 1.6-ounce hamburger patty every time. Food was made in assembly lines and kept hot under infrared lamps.

With invaluable help from a friend who had a small machine-tool shop, the McDonalds looked for ways to produce their food better and faster, always faster.

A stainless steel pump squeezed exactly a tablespoon of ketchup or teaspoon of mustard atop each burger, to be topped by a quarter-ounce of onion and a one-inch pickle. A couple of dozen burgers could be prepared on a stainless steel lazy Susan and shoveled onto a wrapper with a bigger, stronger stainless-steel spatula. A machine called a Multimixer that spun five milk shakes at a time was cut down to accommodate the twelve-ounce cups the McDonalds used; that saved time pouring the drink from a metal cup to a paper one.

They opened the new restaurant the week before Christmas. "It was a disaster," Dick MacDonald said.

A freak Southern California snowstorm dropped three inches the day McDonald's opened. People didn't want to get out of their cars to get their food. They didn't want to throw away their own trash. Employees were told to park in front so it looked like the restaurant had customers.

"At the end of the first week it didn't look like McDonald's would last twenty-seven days," Dick McDonald said.

But within a year the McDonalds were raking it in. Their location near the school paid off. ("Kids just love going to McDonald's, and they always have, from the very beginning," Dick McDonald said.) They began to attract travelers, cab drivers, and families who didn't have to wait for food and didn't have to tip.

They were on the cover of *American Restaurant* magazine in 1952, a huge success story. They each bought a new Cadillac, the symbol of the rising wealthy class, and traded it in each year.

Dick McDonald came up with the idea of the golden arch in 1953, not long before the brothers opened their first franchise store in Phoenix, Arizona. "I'll put the damn things in, but don't tell anyone I was involved in it," his architect said. Photos of the store show a single arch holding a McDonald's Hamburgers sign, and an arch at each end of the shop. Much later, they would be combined into the famous golden M logo.

Halberstam reported that by the mid-1950s, Dick and Mac McDonald were profiting $100,000 a year. They had opened eight more shops in Arizona and California but spurned offers to expand nationally.

Mac McDonald told his brother, "We are going to be on the road all the time in motels, looking for locations, finding managers. I can just see one hell of a headache if we go into that kind of chain."

Instead, Ray Kroc did it. He was selling Multimixers and came west in 1954 to look at the restaurant that was using eight and had ordered two more. His usual customers, drugstore lunch counters, were dying off. Kroc liked what he saw and saw almost unlimited potential. He began by selling McDonald's franchises, and bought McDonald's in 1961 for $2.7 million. Each of the brothers walked away with a cool million. By 1961 the hamburger might have been cut down to size, but a million bucks was still a million bucks.

"We always said we were going to be millionaires by the time we were fifty. We may have been a little late, but we made it," said Dick McDonald.

Although he would make his investment back hundreds of times over, Kroc was bitter about the price the McDonalds demanded. He opened a McDonald's a block away from theirs in San Bernardino, and made them remove their own name from their restaurant.

Dick McDonald moved back to New Hampshire, married West High School sweetheart Dorothy Jones, and retired at about the same time Manchester's first McDonald's opened in 1964. Mac McDonald retired in Palm Springs and died in 1971. Neither had children.

Kroc later claimed to be the McDonald's founder, which always riled Dick McDonald. He carried a business card with just his name, the famous arches embossed in the center, and a single word: "Founder." But there was another part of him that enjoyed the secret celebrity status. He told of being introduced to a group of children as the man who started McDonald's and said, "They had the most disappointed look in their eyes that I'd even seen. They thought they were going to meet a clown." He had another story, this one of waiting in line at the Second Street McDonald's with his step-grandson.

"You have to wait in line, Grandpa? You have to pay for it?" the boy asked.

"I lost a lot of points with him that day."

Richard Upton

He was father of the first-in-the-nation presidential primary

BY ALEC MACGILLIS

T he New Hampshire primary, it could be argued, became what it is today one winter evening in 1952, at the Green Street Community Center in Concord. Ohio Sen. Robert Taft, running against Gen. Dwight Eisenhower for the Republican nomination, had just finished giving a speech to a couple of hundred potential voters. A local campaign aide, Fred Upton, took the mike and told the crowd, "Please, everyone, don't leave yet. The senator just told me he wants to shake hands with every last one of you before you leave!"

The notoriously aloof Taft pounced on Upton. "I never said any such thing!" he muttered under his breath.

Richard Upton in the late 1970s.

Ken Williams/Concord Monitor.

Taft's displeasure at having to descend into the crowd and press the flesh captured the presidential primary process at a defining moment. Three years before, a young Concord lawyer, Richard Upton—Fred Upton's brother—had changed the rules by which the primary was played. Worried the presidential nominating process had become an insiders' game, Upton drafted a law providing for a more populist primary. As Taft and other old-schoolers soon learned, American politics—and New Hampshire—would never be the same again.

Before 1952, presidential primaries were simply elections for local delegates who were pledged to a particular candidate; the delegates, in turn, fought for their man at smoke-filled nominating conventions. Voters rarely saw the actual presidential candidate, and the elections often amounted to popularity contests for those running as delegates.

Yes, political society took note of the outcomes in New Hampshire, for its primary had been the first in the nation since 1920. In fact, the state had been a bellwether of sorts since the mid-nineteenth century, because it held its elections on town meeting day in March, giving an early hint of where the national mood stood. But the indirect nature of the primary limited its national relevance—that is, until 1949.

That was when Richard Upton, speaker of the New Hampshire House, decided it was time to get voters more involved. He designed a new wrinkle in the state presidential primary: In addition to selecting delegates, voters would be able to check off their preferred presidential candidate. As Upton conceived it, this selection would have no formal weight; the nominations would still be decided by the elected delegates at conventions. For its apparent inconsequentiality, the new ballot item was nicknamed the "beauty contest" provision.

This was a legendary understatement. Candidates soon realized that winning a popular vote in the New Hampshire primary would give them as much of a boost as racking up a majority of delegates. As a result, the 1952 presidential primary, the first to follow Gov. Sherman Adams's signing of Upton's bill, was unlike any preceding it.

On the GOP side, Eisenhower supporters place him on the "beauty contest" ballot even though he was in Europe directing NATO troops and hadn't announced a campaign—much less which party he was in. When Eisenhower saw how much attention his name was getting, he declared himself a Republican and quit his NATO post to run.

Meanwhile, his lone opponent, Taft, grudgingly realized that to defeat the immensely popular Ike, he would have to go straight to the people. His primary campaign became a blueprint for the dozens that have followed: In the week before the vote, he went on a three-day, twenty-eight-town tour around the state.

Such intensive campaigning had never before been required of candidates at the primary stage. As Concord author Charles Brereton recounts, Taft had little use for it; at one stop, he refused to put on an Indian headdress someone handed him. Eisenhower, the World War II hero, would win the beauty contest handily, his first step to wrapping up the nomination.

On the Democratic side, Tennessee Sen. Estes Kefauver, initially the only challenger of President Truman, embraced the new style as strongly as Taft had resisted it. The tall, good-looking senator strode the streets of New Hampshire, wearing the coonskin cap he had adopted as his prop. His office sent follow-up letters on Senate stationery to passersby who had shaken hands with him.

Truman, meanwhile, didn't deign to campaign in the state (he called the primary "so much eyewash"), and as a result became the first candidate to feel the state's righteous wrath.

Here's what the *Concord Daily Monitor* made of his absence: "What the president was saying is that he is the boss of a national political machine, held together with the patronage and favors bought with taxpayers' money, and that this machine will do whatever he bids, regardless of what is best for the people, or of what the people themselves may think best. What the president was saying is that the sovereign state of New Hampshire can go to hell."

Truman would lose badly to Kefauver, forcing the incumbent out of the race. The lesson for future campaigns was clear: Don't dare spurn New Hampshire. Just three years after Upton drafted his bill, New Hampshire voters had helped bring down one president and create another one. And that was just the beginning: Still to come were Muskie and McGovern, Johnson and McCarthy, Carter and Clinton, Reagan and Dole, all the men who would be made or undone by the fickle Granite State.

"Little did my father know at the time what he was creating," said his son, William Upton.

One of the ironies of the primary is that the men who have brought such superegos as Nixon and Clinton to the state were so exceedingly modest themselves. This was as true of Upton as of those who succeeded him in guarding the institution, like Portsmouth Rep. Jim Splaine and Secretary of State Bill Gardner. Upton, who died in 1996 at eighty-one, was born into politics, but he wasn't wedded to it. The son of prominent state politician Robert Upton, he was elected to the legislature at age twenty-five and became speaker at thirty-four. When Adams announced he wouldn't run again for governor in 1952, Upton was considered an ideal replacement.

As it happened, Upton's father decided to run for the job, and Upton deferred to him, turning his attention instead to his young family and his law firm. His name surfaced again and again as a possible candidate for higher office, but one thing always stood in the way: Upton refused to sign the pledge against broad-based taxes, and had even fought for a sales or income tax while in the legislature in the late 1940s. His words on the subject recalled Henry Clay's famous line. "I'd rather not have the office than have to make the pledge. If I did take the pledge, I couldn't really mean it, and it would tear me apart."

As a result, the man who brought the political circus to the state remained largely aloof from it himself. Every four years, the national press corps would interview the small-city lawyer, calling him the "Father of the New Hampshire primary." Other than that, life went on as usual for the Uptons.

When it came down to it, his brother Fred Upton said, Upton's first love was probably neither politics nor the law, but history. As a Dartmouth undergraduate, Upton published a full-length history of New Hampshire during the

Revolutionary War. According to his son, Upton's interests in colonial history, constitutional law, and politics all came together in crafting the primary bill. Seeing how little voter interest there had been in the 1948 primary, Upton worried the democracy whose roots he had studied in college was at risk, his son said.

"It was his belief that good government can only come about when the voting public takes an interest in the candidates," William Upton said.

By that measure, Upton's law was an immediate success. Voter participation doubled in the 1952 primary; today, the state's residents are renowned for the active role they take in screening the candidates. As Upton himself noted in a column he published shortly before his death, though, the effects of his law would go far beyond voter behavior.

Even new residents to the state are aware of the primary's economic impact: The Center of New Hampshire, Manchester's grandly named Holiday Inn, was booked solid for the weeks leading up to the 2000 vote for two years; Robie's, a Hooksett general store that closed up in 1997, reopened in 1999 to serve the campaign caravans. And the economic boost goes beyond full motels and advertising airwaves, according to a 1999 study: The free publicity brings the state business long after campaigns fold up their tents.

Equally well established is the lift the primary has given local politicians with national aspirations. The list of beneficiaries includes Adams, who became Eisenhower's chief of staff after stepping down as governor, and John Sununu, who served the same function for George Bush.

These and other perks, Upton said in his column, were unintended.

"My principal objective was to make the primary more interesting and meaningful to the New Hampshire voters of each party, so there would be a greater turnout at the polls and the delegates would receive advice more truly representative of public sentiment," he wrote. All other benefits were "simply byproducts."

From the country's point of view, the enduring legacy of Upton's law has been the state's knack for picking future presidents and exposing failing ones. Jimmy Carter was a peanut-farming, small-state governor before he won here; George Bush, it could be argued, never recovered from the primary fright Pat Buchanan gave him in 1992.

Accounts of the dozen primaries since Upton's law read like an abridged history of postwar America. Every four years, the imperceptibly shifting tensions of the political landscape were raised in relief in the peaks and pitfalls of the Granite State.

Never was this truer than in the turbulent 1960s and 1970s, when the primary betrayed the depth of national opposition to the Vietnam War. In 1968, little-known Minnesota Sen. Eugene McCarthy, running against the war, came in a close second to incumbent Lyndon Johnson. The stunning showing forced Johnson out of the race and inspired Robert Kennedy to step into it, shaping one of the most memorable primary seasons ever.

Four years later, Democratic voters went for another obscure, anti-war Midwesterner, George McGovern, over the establishment favorite, Ed Muskie of Maine, who took a softer stance on Vietnam.

In both instances, the state's anti-war votes registered all the more considering where they were coming from. It was one thing for long-haired peaceniks to protest the war, but for a state that relied as heavily on the defense industry as New Hampshire to do so? The message was unmistakable.

"We saved lives over the long run by encouraging a change in attitude about the war," said Splaine, the Portsmouth lawmaker.

The state surprised the country in another election involving a near-favorite son. In 1992, many expected revelations of Bill Clinton's womanizing and draft record would doom him in a state known for its conservative values. Instead, the recession-racked state declared the economy the order of the day and voted Clinton second only to Paul Tsongas of Massachusetts.

Still, the primary has come under fire almost since the beginning. Every election cycle brings protests that the small state is too rural, too white, and too Republican to serve as a representative first hurdle for the country's candidates.

Loyalists counter by pointing to the state's intimate experience with the ballot box—with so many town and state elections, voters are smarter voters here, they argue. "We're election-ready, election-prone," said former governor Hugh Gregg. "That's why we do a good job with this thing."

Not surprisingly, some of the state's staunchest defenders are the outsiders who fared well here. Former Massachusetts governor Michael Dukakis, for one, fondly recalls his 1988 campaign.

"It was great fun for me. It was my meat and potatoes. The accent sounded very familiar to me," Dukakis said. In Iowa, he said, he had spun his third-place showing in an Olympic year as "winning a bronze"; then, "the next week I win New Hampshire and my dear wife puts a gold medal around my neck."

Not all the assaults on the state's status came from the outside. After the sordid sequence of the early 1970s—*Union Leader* publisher William Loeb's attacks on a weeping Muskie in 1972, followed by the Watergate saga—there was talk of scrapping the primary altogether. Politics seemed soiled, and by extension the primary did, too.

Coupled with a drop in local enthusiasm were bids by other New England states to replace the state's primary with a regional one. It took a concerted effort by a few remaining primary believers, like Splaine, to pass a law, in 1975, mandating that the state primary always be at least one week ahead of any other, effectively rebuffing the regional push.

At the end of the twentieth century, the targeting of the state continued, as a half-dozen rivals threatened to crowd their primaries into February 2000. Gardner, the secretary of state, repelled them one by one, saying he would set the primary as early as December 1999 to retain the state's primacy. If New Hampshire relinquished its role, he said, the country would be left with a one-day, multistate free-for-all dominated by advertising.

"The tradition is seven days," he said. "As soon as you let that tradition go, you'll never get it back again."

Missing from the chorus trying to save the institution, of course, is its founder. Even if Upton were still alive, his brother wonders if he'd be part of the fight. As the years went by, Richard Upton found he recognized the primary less and less.

Where he once saw Kefauver working the streets for hours on end, he instead saw movie stars flying in to stump for Hollywood's flavor of the day. Where candidates once fought for mention in the state's tiny weeklies, they instead made the Manchester television station rich with carpet-bombing ad campaigns. Where they once started their campaign the month before the vote, they now showed up two years early, like impolite guests.

"Now we're fighting for hell to hold onto the first-place position for all the money it brings us," Fred Upton said. "That's not what it's all about. I think he'd be horrified about what it turned into."

Mary Baker Eddy

Despite hounding by critics, her new religion spread across the world.

BY CHRIS MORRIS

oncord loved Mary Baker Eddy. In 1908, when the founder of Christian Science packed up and moved after nineteen years in town, local officials approved a resolution to thank her for two decades of generosity:

Whereas, her residence here has been the source of so much good to the city, and

Whereas, the most kindly and helpful relations have ever existed between Mrs. Eddy and Concord people,

Be it resolved, that the City of Concord, through its Board of Aldermen and Common Council, in joint convention, convey to Mrs. Eddy

Eddy was ridiculed in the national press but beloved in Concord.

New Hampshire Historical Society.

1. Its appreciation of her life in its midst,
2. Its regrets over her departure, and
3. The hope that though absent she will always cherish a loving regard for the city, near which she was born, and for its people, among whom she has lived for so many years.

Such a sticky-sweet declaration did not go to just any distinguished resident. Eddy was especially appreciated: When she left Concord, she had spent $1.5 million to benefit the city—$40 million in today's dollars. She donated 1,000 pairs of shoes to children so they could go to school in the winter. She paid to pave Main, State, and Warren streets for the first time. She gave generously to the YMCA, the New Hampshire Historical Society, and the Shaker Village. She helped build the First Congregational Church in Concord, where she was baptized, and paid for the Bow Bog Methodist Church bell.

The rest of the world, however, was not nearly so appreciative of Mary Baker Eddy. In her day, women were generally considered weak, frail, and inferior. For a woman to establish a widely practiced system of prayer-based healing, deliver lectures, and found a church, a teaching college, a publishing company, and a Pulitzer Prize-winning newspaper was unheard of. It was suspicious. And it drew criticism unparalleled in her day. Even the owner of the *Concord Monitor* at the time, William Eaton Chandler, acted as the lawyer for men trying to take control of Eddy's money on the basis that she was too crazy—"nearly worn out in body and mind"—to handle the fortune.

She drew criticism so strong and from people held in such great esteem, such as Mark Twain and Joseph Pulitzer, that she founded the *Christian Science Monitor* when she was eighty-eight to combat the tabloid journalism that labeled her a fraud and chased her until death.

Born Mary Morse Baker in Bow, she was weak and sickly from the start. She spent more time home from school than in class—and passed the time reading books her older brother Albert brought home for her from Dartmouth, much to their father's disapproval. Eddy began writing when she was twelve and had poems and prose published in local magazines and newspapers.

As a young woman, Eddy moved with her husband, George Washington Glover, to South Carolina, where he kept his business. She returned to New Hampshire a widow eight months later, six months pregnant. Childbirth and depression left her too weak to care for her son, Georgie, and she sent him to live with guardians in North Groton. Eddy's relationship with her son was strained all their lives, though they kept in touch. Later in life she adopted a son—a former student she found suited her spiritual liking more than Georgie.

In 1853, Eddy married again. She wed Daniel Patterson, a tall, handsome dentist from Franklin, but the marriage suffered from his infidelity, according to some accounts. Patterson, said to be Eddy's intellectual inferior, wandered too close to Confederate lines during a visit South and was taken as a prisoner of war. It was while her husband was captive that Eddy sought help for her chronic weakness and pain. She tried everything from dietetics and homeopathy to hygiene and hydropathy. Eventually, she entered Dr. William Veil's Water-Cure Sanitarium in Hill, where she heard about a man who would change her life.

Dr. Phineas Quimby of Portland, Maine, was a traveling mesmerist who believed health was all in the mind and used an early form of hypnotism to heal the sick. Eddy made her way to Maine, so weak she had to be carried from her carriage to her hotel room. But she met with Quimby and a week later professed a newfound health. With her husband still captive, she stayed on as Quimby's student.

When the war ended, Patterson returned north, and the couple moved to Massachusetts, where the dentist set up a new shop. That's where, in February 1866, Mrs. Mary Baker Patterson slipped on an icy sidewalk—a fall that would eventually draw the region's attention to her new faith.

The newspaper reported that she had suffered internal injuries, a concussion, and a partial spinal dislocation. The next day's *Lynn Reporter* said "she was taken up in an insensible condition and carried to the residence of S. M. Bubier, Esq., near by, where she was kindly cared for during the night. Dr. Cushing, who was called, found her injuries to be internal, and of a very serious nature, inducing spasms and intense suffering. She was removed to her home in Swampscott yesterday afternoon, though in a very critical condition." A clergyman was sent to her bedside to prepare her for death. She asked to be alone with her Bible.

The next morning Eddy met the doctor at the door. Cushing was so shocked by her newfound mobility, he thought he was seeing a ghost.

Mary Baker Eddy's written account of what happened that night is this: She read a New Testament account of Jesus's healing—and was healed herself.

> My immediate recovery from the effect of an injury caused by an accident—an injury that neither medicine nor surgery could reach— was the falling apple that led me to the discovery of how to well myself and how to make others so. Even to the homeopathic physician . . . I could not explain the motives of my relief. I could only assure him that it was in perfect scientific accord with divine law.

It was Mary Baker Eddy's religious coming out party—the moment she realized she did not need a man to heal her. Not Quimby. Not a doctor. Only God and herself. From that day on, there were reports of healing wherever Mary Baker Eddy went.

Following word of her healing powers, Eddy took out an ad in the *Lynn Reporter* offering her healing services. (She would take money only if a healing occurred.) Soon, she taught a course in what would become Christian Science. Its popularity grew into the need for a college, where she charged $300 per student per year.

She used Quimby's writings as the text for the course but soon decided she needed a textbook that more fully developed her own ideas. In 1875, she published *Science and Health,* a book she eventually revised 418 times. It is still used in conjunction with the Bible at Christian Science church services today. Its main tenet: You don't need doctors to be healthy, just faith in God. By the time of her death in 1910, she had sold 500,000 copies.

Business was so good she needed a bookkeeper. She met and married Asa

Eddy, a Singer sewing machine salesman, a year after he moved to Boston to study Christian Science. She was fifty-five. He was forty-four. Their wedding license listed them both as forty. In 1881, she got a state charter to start the Church of Christ Scientist and the Massachusetts Metaphysical College.

Of Mary Baker Eddy, suffragist Susan B. Anthony said, "No man obtained so large a fellowship in so short a time. For 1900 years since the dawn of Christianity, man has been much occupied establishing faiths and formulating creeds for woman to follow. . . . When woman does write her creed, it will be one of right actions, not of theological theories."

In 1889, at the height of her power, Mary Baker Eddy moved back to New Hampshire to live a quieter life and continue revising *Science and Health*. There, Eddy experienced a productivity explosion. The church was growing stronger than ever—in fact, she claimed to have 300,000 followers "obeying" her. She founded the *Christian Science Monitor* and authorized the German translation of *Science and Health*.

"When I removed from Boston in 1889 and came to Concord, New Hampshire, it was that I might find retirement from many years of incessant labor for the cause of Christian Science, and the opportunity in Concord's quiet to revise our textbook, *Science and Health with Key to the Scriptures,*" Eddy wrote in 1904.

"I have also received from the leading people in this pleasant city all and more than I anticipated. I love its people—love their scholarship, friendship and granite character. I respect their religious beliefs and thank their ancestors for helping form mine."

Eddy's daily rides through the city were so regular people could set their watches by them. And her money! Eddy had so much money she bought one of the first automobiles in the city. But not to use: Eddy didn't like the smell

Invited by Eddy, about 10,000 people showed up for a gathering of Christian Scientists at her home in Concord in 1903.

New Hampshire Historical Society.

cars gave off; she used her horses and carriage until she died. Instead, she wanted the car to be driven around the estate so that her horses could become acclimated to the sound.

On one of her daily rides, Eddy is said to have healed a Methodist minister, the Rev. E. N. Larmour, of the need to wear eyeglasses. And a *New York Times* reporter in town to investigate false rumors of Eddy's death was reportedly healed of throat cancer.

In June 1903, Eddy invited Christian Science followers to Concord for an inspirational address. On a rainy afternoon, 10,000 people showed up and stood beneath her balcony in awe of the woman they called "Mother," and later "Leader."

Of course, not everyone shared their reverence. Mark Twain wrote a whole book ridiculing Eddy, called *Christian Science*. In one passage, he described her as "famishing for everything she sees—money, power, glory—vain, un-truthful, jealous, despotic, arrogant, insolent, pitiless where thinkers and hyp-notists are concerned, illiterate, shallow, incapable of reasoning outside of commercial lines and immeasurably selfish."

But he also came to this conclusion: "In several ways, she is the most inter-esting woman that ever lived and the most extraordinary."

The church sold Eddy's Concord estate in 1975. Eventually, a retirement home was built in its place. The city's lovely Christian Science church holds 800 people, but by the end of the twentieth century, it attracted a far smaller crowd of worshippers.

Many of today's Christian Scientists are shy and private about their lives, stemming from the fear that their beliefs are misunderstood, and the religion is considered a cult by some people.

In 1996, for the first time, the U.S. Supreme Court ruled in a high-profile civil case against the church over the death of a diabetic eleven-year-old in Min-nesota whose mother was a Christian Scientist. The child's father sued four Christian Scientists for shunning the medical treatment of his son. Since then, an Iowa woman—a former Christian Scientist whose son died of treatable men-ingitis—has separated from the church and founded an organization called CHILD (Children's Healthcare Is a Legal Duty) to end legal protection for par-ents who withhold medical care from their children on religious grounds.

Practicing Christian Scientists admit to feeling "different," but spiritual healing is how most were raised—not with doctors and modern medical tech-niques. The belief is strong that God and the Bible are there when needed, during illness or emotionally trying times.

Cam Wagner, librarian at Concord's Christian Science reading room since 1981, openly tells of her experiences with faith healing. She was in a bad car ac-cident when her children, also Christian Scientists, were young. But in the split second before impact, Wagner asked God for help. She wasn't scared, she says. God guided her through it. And she and her children walked away.

Steven Tyler

The lead man for Aerosmith tours the world but calls New Hampshire home.

BY GWEN FILOSA

Over a scratchy phone connection from a car in Sunapee, Steven Tyler's love for New Hampshire sounded as heartfelt as his brand of rock 'n' roll.

"Is that the sun coming out?" he asked, taking in the sights of the stomping grounds that gave rise to one of the world's biggest bands—and one of the last of the full-blown rock stars.

"Oh my God," Tyler said in his famous rasp. "Otter Pond is like a mirror."

Tyler, the flamboyant front man who started Aerosmith in 1970 and never let go as the band stumbled, soared, collapsed, and resurrected itself as a

Steven Tyler at a 1997
performance.

AP/ Wide World Photos.

powerhouse hit-maker, may have been born in New York, but home is a place called Sunapee.

"I carved my childhood memories out of New Hampshire," he said. "It was probably one of the greatest gifts my parents could have given me, bringing me up here every summer. It was a gift from God, having both sides—the cement streets and the dirt between my toes."

Aerosmith, with twenty albums and three decades behind it, has a bloodline that traces back to the stately homes and shimmering harbor in Sunapee. Boston lays a big claim to America's ultimate party band, but New Hampshire is where the boys who would be rock stars cut their teeth in startup bands and where three of the original members got together in 1970 before moving to Commonwealth Avenue.

Rewind the history of the mighty band that launched a thousand imitators and a string of hit records, and you'll hear the names Steven Tallarico, Joe Perry, Tom Hamilton, and a teenage hangout called The Barn.

Tyler and guitarist Perry first laid eyes on each other at the Anchorage, a family-style restaurant in Sunapee where Perry once worked. Their families summered near the lake, and there they found a music scene, notably at a three-level barn in Georges Mills that hosted rock bands and drew hundreds of college students, townies, and summer kids.

Aerosmith bassist Tom Hamilton went to high school in New London and got together with Perry in bands, including the Jam Band. Tyler, like all the members of Aerosmith, had played in bands since he was a kid. A drummer first, he played with his father—the classically trained pianist Victor Tallarico—at the Sunapee Lodge. People around Lake Sunapee remember Tyler's grandmother, known as "Mrs. T," who taught piano to local kids.

By the late 1960s, Steven Tallarico (he switched to the nonethnic Tyler in 1972) was already a name around Sunapee. He formed his first serious band, The Strangeurs, there and acted like rock royalty even then, playing clubs in New York and New England.

"He really believed in himself more than anything," said Edward Malhoit of Claremont, who booked bands in New Hampshire in the late 1960s, including some of Tyler's. "He made believers out of everybody."

Tyler, who keeps a lakeside home in Sunapee (Perry has one, too), has a memo for anyone who dares discount his band's New Hampshire ties: "Tell them I said," and then he spat a raspberry. He laced the retort with a few lines from Bob Dylan, ending with, "Don't criticize what you don't understand."

He kept his place in Sunapee so his kids could have the outdoor experience he did, Tyler said. In every corner of Sunapee, the rocker also revisits his own youth.

"I had a relationship with the spirits of the woods," Tyler said, recalling days of running through the wilds of Sunapee. "I called them the children of the woods."

In New Hampshire, Tyler spent summers playing gigs and hanging out with friends. "It's where we smoked our first joints. It's where I had sex with my first girlfriend," Tyler said. "All those firsts."

Aerosmith's roots reach back to a summer day in 1969 when Tyler was out mowing the lawn at his parents' resort, Trow Rico, in Sunapee. Perry drove up in his MG and asked Tyler to come see his band, the Jam Band, play at The Barn.

The night Tyler saw the Jam Band play, something clicked inside his head. Sitting on the club's floor in front of the tiny stage, he turned to a buddy and said he had just found his next band. Soon, Tyler, Perry, and Hamilton hooked up and headed for Boston, where drummer Joey Kramer and rhythm guitarist Brad Whitford would complete the band.

"It's so storybook," Tyler said, "every bit of it."

The Aerosmith storybook, though, is for adults only. Their autobiography, *Walk This Way,* chronicles the band's life with all the conceivable details—booze, drugs, a whirlwind of women—fully intact. But it also goes back to a more innocent time measured out in the summers of the 1960s in a New Hampshire resort town. Back then, the state had a rollicking music scene all its own, with big dance bands and some scrappy rock groups.

Teenagedom was king on Lake Sunapee. Summer kids, townies, Colby-Sawyer girls and Dartmouth boys huddled around the harbor. Rock 'n' roll was their soundtrack, and The Barn was their source.

"After the Beatles hit, it was all over," the prologue of *Walk This Way* explains. "Lake Sunapee was the address where the world first encountered Aerosmith as a rough beast, slouching toward Bethlehem to be born."

Harold "Zunk" Buker watched the slouching begin. The New London native met Tyler when they were little kids and grew up in those same lake- and sun-filled summers. Later he and his father were Tyler's pilots, flying the band to gigs.

Buker's face lights up while taking a visitor to what used to be The Barn—it's now storage for the attached furniture store. Owned by the late John Conrad, The Barn rocked in the late 1960s, with live music on four nights a week in the summer. Wednesday was "Teen Night."

On a chilly day with a dusting of snow outside, Buker walked into the barn, packed with furniture. He pointed to where the dance floor used to be. It had a railing around it and booths were placed along the wall. Buker plodded up to the small stage where Tyler, Perry, and Hamilton, in different bands, once played. Upstairs is another floor, with a ladder leading into a cupola—its walls still lined with graffiti from the club's heyday.

Tyler's band packed The Barn's rafters. Hundreds of kids came, Buker said, with the line streaming out the door. "They charged $5—in 1966—and you would still have kids lined up because it was an event," he said.

The Barn jumped with music and teenage libidos. On hot summer nights when the music caught hold, the place smoldered.

"You can still smell what The Barn was like," said Tyler, who has one of the original booths as a keepsake. "The dance floor, the booths in the back where we'd go and suck face in."

Aerosmith has toyed with the idea of returning to that barn on Prospect Hill Road. "MTV, VH-1, they're all ready to bring cameras in at the drop of a hat," Tyler said. "We're not ready yet."

Aerosmith got its wings in 1970, playing its first official gig at Nipmuc

Regional High School in Mendon, Massachusetts. The band members shared an apartment at 1325 Commonwealth Avenue in Boston and, during lunchtime, set up their gear outside of Boston University and wailed away. Unsigned and dodging eviction notices, the band pressed on to land a record deal with Columbia and released a self-titled album that first introduced the radio warrior "Dream On."

The band peaked in 1976 as a solid headliner with "Sweet Emotion" and "Walk This Way." In simple terms, Aerosmith rocked, sharing the kind of fan swell that ZZ Top and KISS enjoyed, but the guys with the Sunapee roots had a success story all their own.

"We were America's band. We were the garage band that made it really big," Joe Perry said in Martin Huxley's 1995 book *Aerosmith: The Fall and Rise of Rock's Greatest Band.*

In 1999, Aerosmith meant dramatic power ballads and laughingly lewd music videos; those with longer memories—or the box set—are more likely to think bad-boy blues meets arena rock. Monster songs like their cover of "Train Kept A Rollin," "Lord of the Thighs," "Back in the Saddle," "Same Old Song and Dance."

The fact that Aerosmith survived its days of drugs and excess is a small miracle. Sober for more than a decade, the band turned around lives and careers that had once appeared doomed.

Money and privilege turned into the proverbial double-edged sword that has given VH-1 enough tragic tales to make a series out of (Behind the Music), and Aerosmith famously went down the well-worn rock star road that turns into a drain.

They reconciled at an Aerosmith show in 1984 and geared up for *Done With Mirrors*, which didn't cut it with radio or record store cash registers. Its gimmick—all the words on the album need a mirror to read straight—didn't help.

Aerosmith seemed on the road to kaput until some rappers scratched out a new version of "Walk This Way," and an album called *Permanent Vacation* unleashed the most unexpected—and perfect—rock return ever.

Run-DMC put Tyler and Perry on MTV in a different light: two music veterans who could smirk at their own reputations. When "Dude Looks Like a Lady" sent Aerosmith smack into 1987, a whole new band emerged. The ingredients for success included horn sections, Tyler's vocal chord workouts, and enough sexual double entendres to make a nation of high-schoolers' heads spin.

"Even critics liked them better the second time around," according to *Rolling Stone's Encyclopedia of Rock and Roll.*

Pump, in 1989, proved Aerosmith's comeback was no fluke. It got some of the best reviews the band ever saw and smashed the charts. "Love in an Elevator," "The Other Side" and "What It Takes" owned radio play lists. MTV couldn't get enough of the band's videos, especially the dramatic story line of "Janie's Got a Gun," a song about incest.

Thirty years later, Aerosmith has become a corporation as much as a band, expected to crank out the hits at a moment's notice. Their reported $30 million deal with Columbia (Sony's flagship label) is going strong. *Nine Lives,* the band's twelfth studio album, entered the chart at No. 1. The 1998 summer ballad, "I Don't Want to Miss a Thing," from the Armageddon soundtrack, was the band's first No. 1 single.

They write songs these days with hired guns of the industry (Glen Ballard, Desmond Child), and they remain on the awards show circuit, snapping up a Grammy and a Billboard honor in 1999. An Aerosmith tribute album came out in 1999, along with the Rock and Roll Hall of Fame's nomination for induction in 2000.

And although Tyler seems to sing dramatic love ballads more often than blues-borne swagger, his fans still marvel and he still has his moves and his brothers behind him.

"There is no substitute for arrogance," Tyler said. "We made something good come out of it."

Or, better yet, as his last words in the *Walk This Way* autobiography explain, "It's too late to stop now."

General Frank Streeter

His 1919 reforms brought public schools into the twentieth century.

BY ALEC MacGILLIS

As any student of the Claremont school crisis knows, necessity is the mother of education reform. If the state Supreme Court hadn't deemed the modern school funding structure unconstitutional in 1997, state lawmakers probably wouldn't have spent years trying to figure out a way to fix it.

The same was true in the early years of the twentieth century, when the legislature completely revamped the state's public school system and created a statewide property tax to pay for it. Only then, the driving force behind reform was more immediate and mundane than a court ruling from on high.

Frank Streeter modernized New Hampshire's education system.

The year was 1919. The state, like the rest of the country, was basking in the glow of victory over the Germans in World War I. But there was a shadow over the celebration in New Hampshire: The war had shed light on some glaring weaknesses in the state's public schools.

Simply put, many of the state's students could not read or write. Hundreds of local volunteers and draftees in the war effort were unable to read or sign their enlistment papers, and many had to be turned away as ineligible to serve. For a state that prided itself both on its strong schools and its willingness to join President Woodrow Wilson's defense of European democracies, it was a jarring discovery.

"There was a recognition coming out of the war and the standardized tests connected with the draft that maybe our citizens weren't that well educated after all," said Dartmouth College President and U.S. historian James Wright. Few were more alarmed by the rampant illiteracy than General Frank Streeter, a leading Concord lawyer and Republican Party power broker. And few were better suited to find a solution than Streeter, who immediately started working to pass what would become known as the Great School Law of 1919.

The law amounted to the most sweeping educational legislation the state has ever seen. By setting a minimum level of spending for school districts and a minimum number of school days per year, it essentially brought the state from the era of the one-room schoolhouse into the twentieth century. By appointing a state board of education and education commissioner to maintain standards for teachers and principals, it created the modern centralized education bureaucracy. Most notably, perhaps, by instituting the first-ever statewide property tax, the law challenged the inborn antipathy against statewide levies and foreshadowed the legislative battles over school funding of the late 1990s and beyond.

Streeter was able to push such an encompassing package through the legislature despite holding no elected office himself.

"He was cast in a larger mold than his immediate contemporaries," his friend and college classmate Judge Frank Parsons wrote after Streeter's death in 1922.

Streeter was not really a general. He received the title when the state appointed him judge advocate general some years before his school reform work. The name stuck, though, and with good reason. For the first two decades of the century, Streeter influenced state and city affairs much as a modern general commanded his troops: from well behind the front lines, but with unquestioned authority.

"The courtesy title had greater permanence than usually attends it, because it exactly fitted the man," Parsons recalled. "He was a general, skilled in strategy and tactics. He had vision and diplomacy. He could plan and command for others to execute. The plan once made, he had the force to carry it out over whatever obstacles stood in the way, ruthless perhaps at times of the consequences to others because of the importance, as it seemed to him, of the end aimed at."

To some, Streeter even looked like a general. Writing in the *Boston Herald* in 1949, journalist Bill Cunningham recalled encountering the general at

Dartmouth, where Streeter was a longtime trustee. Streeter, Cunningham wrote, "looked in the flesh like a portrait of Bismarck, with stern and craglike features and wore a set of eyebrows that made the current growths of (labor leader) John L. Lewis look like a bad case of falling hair."

Lonnie Gove, the Hanover Inn's head clerk, had asked Cunningham to watch over a bridge game that the general and other trustees were playing in the hotel's famous "Room No. 1." According to Cunningham, Streeter was a "bridge fiend" and

> smoked a pipe as big as a coal hod. He always seemed to have trouble keeping it lighted and he fired this impressive heater with old-fashioned kitchen matches that he seemed to carry by the bale. That part was all right with Lonnie but what followed wasn't.
>
> What happened was that he'd light a match, take a couple pulls that sounded like death rattles off it, and then merely throw the lighted torch back over his shoulder with apparently no care whatsoever as to where it landed, or what it did. By this quaint maneuver he generally set the room on fire, and Lonnie grabbed me that night and told me to stand behind the General with a dust pan and catch these flaming brands as they sailed back through space.

Streeter came a long way to get to the card table in Room No. 1. Born to Vermont farmers in 1853, he had to persuade his parents to let him go to college. He attended Bates College for a year before transferring to Dartmouth, where he paid his way by teaching school in the winter term. After graduating, he taught high school in Iowa for a year before deciding on a career in law. He returned to New Hampshire, where he clerked and practiced in Haverhill and Orford before landing in Concord.

There, the young Streeter built up what Parsons called one of the most powerful "law machines" the state had ever seen. Streeter was in the thick of all the major cases of the day. He represented the Concord Railroad in its bitter turf war with the Boston & Maine Railroad and became the New Hampshire general counsel for the Boston & Maine when it took over the smaller company.

Locally, Streeter successfully represented Christian Scientist philanthropist Mary Baker Eddy in two notorious actions: a challenge of her mental competency by a former senator, and an attempt by her sons to seize the money she left to the Church of Christian Science.

One of Streeter's first activist moments was not on behalf of good schools, but in defense of hard liquor. He vigorously opposed New Hampshire's prohibition law, finding it "unsound," and he lobbied successfully to replace it with a "local-option" system in 1903.

All the while, Streeter was making his way up the ranks of the Republican Party. For four years he was the state's representative to the party's National Committee. In those days of the party machine, his position meant everything: His collected papers describe closed-door meetings at Concord's Eagle Hotel where high-level appointments were made and blocked. Every week, aspirants for jobs from Hillsboro postal worker to assistant House clerk wrote him asking for his good word.

The general found his power in the party, but he found his purpose in World War I. Even before the United States mobilized, he was absorbed with the demands of "preparedness" and "Americanization." The latter was especially key: The need to make true Americans of the state's many immigrants had never seemed more pressing than now, with the country preparing to fight. Streeter started pressing to make English the official language of the state's schools. He met with the Catholic bishop in Manchester to work out a compromise for the state's parochial schools, which were filled with French and Polish immigrants who spoke little English.

When the Great School Law was passed after the war, it contained a strong English-language-only plank. But that wasn't all. What had started as a patriotic push had turned into a reform wave. The newly created state Board of Education was given the same power over local schools as "the directors of the ordinary business corporation have over the business of the corporation."

Schools would not only be required to be open 180 days a year but would also have to transport students who were more than two miles away from the schoolhouse. Every district with a high immigrant population would have to open evening schools for English instruction, and foreign-born students over sixteen would have to attend, even if it meant missing work.

How to pay for all the mandates? Every district was required to tax at least $3.50 per $1,000 of property to pay for education, creating a statewide property levy. Every district had to send $2 for every one of its students to Concord to pay for the "statewide supervision of the public schools." And every district that didn't spend what it raised with the minimum levy had to send the difference to the state, too. Most important in view of equalizing the state's schools, any district that lacked sufficient money to educate its students after taxing $5 per $1,000 of property was to receive supplementary state money.

In a speech to superintendents in 1919, Streeter explained that the new law would persuade bright young people to enter teaching, where the state was experiencing a dire shortage.

"We hope to see a body of teachers so well-trained and competent that New Hampshire will be regarded as the best educational training ground in the country," he said.

When the dust settled, General Streeter was named chairman of the first state Board of Education. Two years later, he and three other board members resigned after a new governor and legislature cut school funding, and in 1922 he died of cancer. But the structure he helped create remained.

Looking back, it may seem hard to believe that the legislature of New Hampshire—a state known even then for stodgy individualism—would have passed the centralizing Great School Law. The state's first education commissioner, Ernest Butterfield, conceded as much in a 1925 address to educators in Indianapolis. "The change from a district system to a town system and from a town system to a state system seems inexplicable in a section of the country which has always cherished local rights," he said. The fact was, Butterfield continued, circumstances of the moment left the state no other option. His descriptions of the state's schools, pre-1919, contains striking parallels to the scenario depicted by the five plaintiff towns in the Claremont lawsuit of the late 1990s.

"The majority of our children were living in cities and towns, rich, progressive, and prosperous. They had a full school year, in modern buildings, sanitary and well-equipped. They had trained teachers and effective superintendents," he said. "In the other townships, and these territorially were the larger half of the state, were few children. These children lived in scattered homes and attended for brief periods miserable schools."

Confronted with this situation, he said, the state acknowledged that educating children would have to be its responsibility. Education, after all, was the "national religion" of America, for it produced the sort of citizens a democracy required.

Thus, the revolutionary conclusion: "Whenever the welfare of the child is concerned, the state, and not the city or the township, must be the unit of taxation and administration," he stated. "The cities which had absorbed the wealth of the poor towns should so pay for schools in the poor towns that there should be for all children education without excessive taxation."

The dramatic shift produced results. Before the law, 924 schools were open fewer than 180 days, and after it all but nine schools were open 180. The graduation rate went up 25 percent, the attendance rate 3 percent. The teacher training schools were packed.

With such success, it was easy for Butterfield to overestimate the endurance of the Great School Law. "The work which we do today, if worthwhile, will be credited to our ancestors," he said. "Epochmaking or progressive laws are always the epitaph of those who have seen the vision and made ready the highway."

As it turned out, twelve years after that speech, the state abandoned the statewide property tax because it didn't raise enough revenue during the Depression. And yet, seven decades later, lawmakers, struggling with education funding once again, turned to the statewide property tax anew. "It's what you learn when you study history," Dartmouth President Wright said. "How to pay for education is never quite resolved for all time."

Annalee Thorndike

Her doll-making hobby spawned a giant business and nationwide collecting craze.

When Annalee Davis Thorndike was a teenager during the Depression, she sometimes made dolls as gifts for friends—and sometimes sold them to make extra cash. Years later, when her husband's chicken farm failed, she turned to doll-making again—this time with the whole family's help. The Thorndikes quickly had a growing concern: a factory in Meredith that employed neighbors galore and a product that grew in popularity decade after decade.

Annalee Mobilitee Dolls, Inc., made bunnies and mice, skiers and hockey players from felt and stuffing. Collectors kept track of the latest models in

Annalee Thorndike poses with her doll likeness, 1999.

Ken Williams/Concord Monitor.

magazines and, by the century's end, more than 26,000 people belonged to the Annalee Doll Society, which sponsored socials in Meredith and beyond. At a society auction in the mid-1990s, one rare doll fetched more than $6,000.

"Her dolls tell a story, and that was an important part of what she was selling," said Eleanor Ketcham, a longtime friend who recalled Thorndike painting doll faces by hand, squinting and smiling into a mirror to get each expression just right. Thorndike cared for each figure in explicit detail, Ketcham said. "It was more than just a doll; it was like they had a little soul."

Lou Smith

He built the Rockingham Park racetrack.

For three decades, Lou Smith was New Hampshire's ambassador to the sin tax.

Smith's creation, Rockingham Park in Salem, played host to everybody who was anybody and generated taxes for one-fifth of New Hampshire's annual budget between 1933 and 1969. Smith rubbed elbows with Judy Garland, Frank Sinatra, and just about every one of New Hampshire's governors.

Rockingham Park's reputation reached far beyond New England: Robert Redford is seen trying to place at bet at "The Rock" in the Academy Award-winning movie *The Sting*. At home, "The Rock" also symbolized New Hamp-

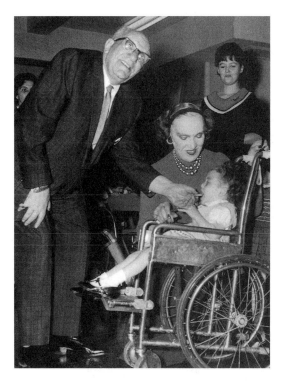

Lou and Lutza Smith gave generously to charities for disabled children.

Courtesy of Rockingham Park.

Rockingham Park, under
Lou Smith's ownership.
Courtesy of Rockingham Park.

shire's reliance on sin taxes to educate its children, pave its roads, and care for its needy.

Smith was a Russian-born Jew whose family fled the czarist regime. Before settling in Salem, he was a boxing promoter, circus hand, and whiskey salesman. Besides Rockingham Park, his business holdings included tracks around the country and Canada. None of this made him unpopular with the Yankee politicians he was trying to woo. New York City sportswriter Damon Runyon, for one, remarked on Smith's talent at charming suspicious lawmakers into taking a gamble on the track:

"Here was a man whose methods were so open and above board they were almost bewildering," he wrote. "The racing bill went through both houses of the legislature with astonishing speed. And it did not cost Lou Smith a dime over and above his traveling and living expenses. Not one dime."

Adam Sandler

From class clown he became one of Hollywood's biggest attractions.

In Manchester in the 1980s, Adam Sandler was the kid disrupting class at Central High. In Hollywood in the 1990s, he was a wealthy writer, producer, and star of some of the era's most mindless hits. He played the idiot golfer in *Happy Gilmore,* the simpleton in *The Waterboy,* and the shiftless bachelor with a heart in *Big Daddy.* His movies, his songs, his television skits on *Saturday Night Live* all rely on the seventh-grade humor that made him a hit back in . . . seventh grade.

Critics aren't fond of his work (one compares Sandler to Chef Boyardee: It's your favorite meal when you're fourteen, but you couldn't stomach it after age thirty), but his fans—most of whom are between thirteen and twenty—can't get enough. His five biggest movies grossed between $20 million and $80

Adam Sandler stars in the 1995 film *Billy Madison.*

million. Movie magazines included him among the most powerful people in Hollywood.

Sandler's secret?

"What he is today is what he was then," said Brian Allaire of Manchester, who knew Sandler in junior high. "He was annoying but funny."

J. E. Henry

He was a North Country lumber baron who fueled the economy—then created public support for conservation.

In J. E. Henry's day, wilderness was something to be tamed and exploited. His enormous turn-of-the-century lumber operation succeeded at that and more. He provided plentiful high-quality lumber to build a growing nation. He created thousands of dependable jobs when northern New Hampshire's farm-based economy went bust. He built entire communities, complete with schools, medical services, hotels, and general stores.

Before Henry came along, logging was practiced on a small scale in the White Mountains. Henry changed that dynamic entirely, building the region's first steam-powered sawmill on the Ammonoosuc River. And rather than dealing with separately controlled rail lines, sawmills, landowners, and logging operations, he realized huge profits by bringing the entire logging process under his control, from stump to market. Eventually, his empire stretched across 100,000 acres.

By the time he died in 1912, Henry had chopped down so many trees so quickly that environmentalists found public support for conservation in the White Mountains and beyond. Paul Bofinger, former president of the Society for the Protection of New Hampshire Forests, explains it this way: "He was so damn good at skinning trees off those mountains, he was bound to draw some notice."

Stephen Laurent

His work saved a native language.

BY SARAH KOENIG

If asked to tell the story of how he once stood up at a meeting in Conway and spoke Abenaki to the bewildered crowd, Stephen Laurent complies readily.

"Ni agua pasgueda wakaswak Wobankiak weskokogonozsa Maguak (Once upon a time a few Abenakis were intercepted by the Iroquois), kwahliwi Salonnaki Nbesek (not far from Saranac Lake). Maguak paamalozhanik ondaki agmiowo, ni mziwi Wobanakiak wmataoogwobanik chaga Maguak onda wzakpowlegwo. (The Iroquois were more numerous than they, and all the Abenakis would have been killed if the Iroquois hadn't been afraid.)"

Stephen Laurent inside a wigwam near his North Conway home, 1999.
Ben Garvin/Concord Monitor.

As if singing without a tune, he says the words smoothly, his eyes focused on some soft middle ground beyond the tiny Indian store in Intervale where he is standing, dressed in a fringed vest of caribou leather and a red tie beaded with a small blue bird.

The Abenaki words he spoke then, in 1988, were psychological ammunition; his testimony helped save the store—now a national historic site—from a Route 16 bypass that would have forced its removal. After finishing his story, he told the 500 people listening that he understood them as little as they understood him.

"Which would add more to the honor of New Hampshire," he asked, "the preservation of its culture or the construction of an eleven-mile toll road of doubtful effectiveness?"

Today he repeats the Abenaki words without pride, even though he is perhaps one of only five people in the world who can speak them.

Laurent, who turned ninety in 1999, is an Abenaki man whose red hair and glasses, he says, make him look "as if he came from East Boston rather than from the Indian Village of St. Francis" in Quebec, also known as Odanak, where his father was a famous chief.

He grew up hunting on a reservation but earned his living at the Jackson post office. He never finished seminary but knows Latin, Greek, Abenaki, French, and English; his bookshelf supports titles like *Cataracts* and *Iacocca* alongside little-known works of Nabokov, Solzhenitsyn, Plato, and Leonardo da Vinci.

And he is a man who says he does not particularly care if his native language dies with him but spent thirty years translating the first extensive published dictionary of Abenaki language in the world.

Asked if that was a paradox, he replies, "I don't know."

Laurent's modesty is as legendary as his linguistic work. "I don't know that I'll be able to tell you much," he tells an interviewer. Even the title of Laurent's red-covered book, of which only 500 copies were printed in 1995, defers credit to a Jesuit priest dead since 1755: "Father Aubery's French Abenaki Dictionary," it reads.

"Though I'm sure he will tell you he has not done anything, this is by far the oldest, intact complete Abenaki dictionary," said John Moody, an ethnohistorian who studies Native American cultures of the Northeast.

Laurent also has recorded his entire book on tape, so that scholars will know how to properly pronounce the odd-looking words.

For linguists, Laurent's achievement is not to be underestimated. "It's very rare," Moody said, adding that the language translated by Laurent is a middle dialect somewhere between Eastern Abenaki (extinct), Western Abenaki, and Penobscot. "It's crucial to have the kind of detail that this book provides, to get us beyond guessing. It's a snapshot of a very early period." Moody described Abenaki as "vast in its descriptive power. There's a tremendous amount of knowledge in the Abenaki language about Vermont and New Hampshire. It's crucial to maintain the integrity of these roots."

There are six words for moose, for example, depending on whether the animal in question is a male or cow moose, a yearling male or female, a two-year-old, and so on.

The value of such an extensive document—"Over 7,000 terms clearly defined and explained," the dictionary promises—reaches far beyond New England, said Ives Goddard, curator of the anthropology department at the Smithsonian Institution's Museum of Natural History.

"This contributes to our knowledge of human language in general," he said. "The catastrophic extinction of languages that is happening hand over fist is not just a linguistic tragedy, but a tragedy for our ability as human beings to understand how we speak and how we think."

Goddard cited predictions that the world's 6,000 languages now spoken will shrink by 50 to 90 percent in the twenty-first century. Even if an Indian language has a few hundred speakers today, he said, "all it takes is for the fourteen-year-olds to decide to talk English to each other, and it's gone. A whole community can lose its language in one generation." Laurent's dictionary, he said, "is one more brick in the wall" helping to stave off extinction.

Laurent describes it in less grandiose terms. "It makes me feel that I'm filling in a gap. Nobody is speaking it, but I am. That brings it to life," he said.

Laurent began translating Father Aubery's dictionary in the 1960s. Using copies of a handwritten manuscript that the French missionary meticulously compiled during the first half of the eighteenth century, Laurent worked three hours a day translating the French into English and explaining etymologies of many Abenaki words.

"It took me thirty years, because I didn't want to damage my eyesight," he said.

The dictionary lists entries in French, which can be found with an English index. To find a translation for the word "fool," for example, one must find "idiot" in French. The entry reads: Idiot: Niais—idiot, fool, simpleton: az8g8, nananbasamatt8 (ned-az8ghi: I am crazy; ne-nannanbazematt8: Il se comporte en niais—He acts like a nincompoop.)

The "8," a modernization of a Greek linguistic convention, signifies the letter "w" in English, which does not exist in French.

Laurent's fascination with the intricate language (which he characterizes from a borrowed quotation as "so soft and fluttery it would not disturb the birds") and the way Europeans came to understand and muddle it is evident in his writings.

"Most amazing, perhaps, in view of all the complexity is the fact that without written or verbal instruction, without academies or institutes to establish rules and prevent deterioration or alterations, the Indians managed to speak their language with grammatical correctness," he wrote in 1958.

For the white man, "Laying hold on a word was a little like trying to grasp a wriggling eel. Even the simple word 'hand' gave one missionary a great deal of trouble. The Jesuit, pointing to his own hand, looked inquiringly at the Indian. The latter grunted, 'Kelji,' meaning 'Your hand.' Later to verify his records, he repeated his question, pointing to the Indian's hand. This time the answer was, 'Nelji,' meaning 'My hand.'"

Finally, to isolate the noun, the missionary persuaded someone inside a wigwam to stick out his hand through a slit in the doorway. The answer was "Awanelji," "Someone's hand."

There are between 3,000 and 4,000 Abenakis living in Canada and New England—about 1,000 in New Hampshire. Of those, Moody believes a couple of hundred know the language. Other scholars subscribe to more conservative estimates. Goddard said he counted twenty speakers of Western Abenaki in 1974; that five remain, as some have suggested, would not surprise him.

Although Laurent may be the last of a handful of native speakers, Abenaki was not his native tongue. He was born in 1909 at the St. Francis reservation, a settlement of Abenakis whose ancestors had fled north to escape the diseases and wars brought by English colonizers.

His father, Joseph Laurent, spoke fluent Abenaki, but Laurent heard mostly French and some English from his parents. "You could explain more things that way," he said. Laurent was only eight when his father died but spent most of his life carrying on his work.

Joseph Laurent, a well-educated man, was elected chief four times between 1880 to 1892. But he became known internationally not for his political leadership, but for the primer he created of his own language. Titled *New Familiar Abenakis and English Dialogues,* the slim book, published in 1884, remains the standard for Abenaki grammar, and a wonder to modern scholars.

"This is a really remarkable case of native grammatical tradition emerging among native people. For a native to develop a way of describing his own language in a systematic fashion. . . . It's really hard to think of other examples for North America where that happened," said Goddard.

To supplement his village's hunting-based subsistence, Joseph Laurent set off south for the summer with a group of Abenaki and Sokoki Indians to sell baskets. In 1884 they settled on a permanent spot in Intervale. The seasonal journey continued until 1960.

The Indian shop there sold sweetgrass baskets and Indian "curios" to summer tourists. "For tourists, the presence of the 'noble savage' provided entertainment, a source of souvenirs, and an enhanced 'wilderness experience,'"

Stephen Laurent (Atian Lolo) Lexicographer of the Abenaki

Laurent, pictured in his Abenaki dictionary.

Ben Garvin/Concord Monitor.

Gary Hume, a state archaeologist, wrote. "For anthropologists, Intervale was an invaluable source of information."

Scholars of Indian language and culture began making annual pilgrimages to the encampment, continuing long after Joseph Laurent's death in 1917. The visits made a great impression on Stephen Laurent: A casual comment by University of Pennsylvania anthropology professor Frank Speck in 1944 inspired him to record Abenaki, a task he began systematically in 1960.

By that time he was living year-round in Intervale; in 1952 he married Margaret Pfister, a high school teacher of French and English who was of Abenaki decent, and who also had spent summers in Intervale.

Laurent still proudly recalls visiting his family in Odanak with her for the first time. On the street he heard two people talking about them: "Awani na? (Who is that?) Atianskwa (Stephen's wife)."

It was at Odanak that Laurent learned of the French-Abenaki dictionary that would occupy him for decades. "I was a Catholic," he explained. "On the reservation, a priest there told me they had the manuscript of Father Aubery." That copy was singed by fire and mostly unreadable, but a few years later a copy surfaced at the Maine Historical Society, and Laurent went to work.

When Stephen Laurent is mentioned to Conway residents now, their associations are as varied as his life. Some know him as the assistant postmaster in Jackson, where he worked for thirty years. Others remember him playing violin and cello in local chamber music groups; he learned the instruments from a summer resident who played with the Boston Symphony.

Still others identify him with the Intervale store, which he ran until well into his eighties. Struggling with the locks, Laurent recently opened the shop, where cheap leather wallets stamped with a picture of an Indian chief's head ($3.95) lie in the dust next to extremely rare books and papers about the Abenaki.

In the trees behind the store are the dilapidated remains of the six cabins his father built. Plastic hangs haphazardly in the broken windows of five, and one has collapsed completely. The totem pole that used to stand out front broke in half and was thrown away. Only a birch-bark wigwam he built in the 1970s still looks sturdy.

All of it—the store, the land, the rock with the plaque dedicated to his father—will be left to Laurent's nephew, who lives in Odanak but visits regularly.

"Oh, I loved coming here as a child," Laurent said as he made his way slowly to the wigwam with the help of a walking stick.

Laurent knows he assimilated and does not regret it. "Here I could earn my living. On the reservation, unless I went hunting, I couldn't earn my living," he said.

Asked if he worried that the Abenaki language could disappear with him, Laurent paused and said no. For him, culture does not live only in language, but in those Anglicized and Francofied Indians who make it into something else.

"It lives with the people if they follow some of the rituals," he said. As an example, he recalled how, as a child, he had watched relatives of recently buried kin sneak back and forth from the cemetery for weeks carrying lanterns. The

Indians believed the dead person needed help finding his or her way to heaven, a belief strongly discouraged by the Catholic missionaries at St. Francis.

Still, his greatest achievement, by his own admission, is a dictionary that translates a language he is calmly watching die.

A story he wrote helps explain why: The word Winnipesaukee has been understood by whites for more than a century to mean "the smile of the Great Spirit," a translation not even remotely connected to the Indian word (Joseph Laurent translated it as "lake region").

When Stephen Laurent looked into the erroneous etymology, he traced it back to a Penobscot named Lobal who acted as a guide for some missionaries in the 1860s. As they were paddling along the Penobscot River, the priest told a visiting missionary what Winnipesaukee meant, and looked for confirmation to Lobal, who nodded in agreement.

When upbraided by another Indian for reinforcing the nonsensical translation, Lobal

merely smiled and explained that it was such a beautiful afternoon . . . that he didn't want to spoil it all by starting an argument over something so inconsequential as the meaning of an Indian word. Lobal's viewpoint seemed to be: After all, if the white man liked to think that "Winnipesaukee" meant "the smile of the Great Spirit," what harm did it do? It wouldn't make or break the world whether "Winnipesaukee" meant that or something else more prosaic like, let us say, pork and beans.

Laurent wrote this in 1955; more than forty years later, his sentiment echoes Lobal's. "I think we are all human beings and the culture of this and the culture of that doesn't make much of a difference, so long as we all live decently," he said. "I think that so long as we communicate with each other, what language we use doesn't make too much difference."

Sherman Adams

A President Eisenhower's chief of staff, he wielded power but first and foremost did his boss's bidding.

BY MICHAEL J. BIRKNER

W hen the pressures and excitement of the presidential campaign concluded with Dwight Eisenhower's landslide victory over Adlai Stevenson in November 1952, Sherman Adams wondered what his own future held. Ike's triumph was deeply satisfying to his campaign team. But it was not self-evident what might be next for those, like Adams, the former New Hampshire governor, who helped engineer the victory that ended twenty years of Democratic dominance in Washington.

In hindsight, it seems inevitable that Adams would wind up on the White House staff, perhaps even as chief of staff, since he had performed admirably

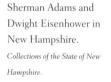

Sherman Adams and
Dwight Eisenhower in
New Hampshire.
*Collections of the State of New
Hampshire.*

in a comparable position during the campaign. But hindsight can mislead. The "great mentioners" in the press corps suggested that Adams might wind up as ambassador to Canada or Secretary of Labor, but nothing was assured.

Eisenhower offered the chief of staff job to New York lawyer Herbert Brownell, who had helped shape campaign strategy. Brownell demurred. He told Ike he preferred to be Attorney General and suggested Adams for chief of staff. Eisenhower also considered one of the architects of his campaign, Massachusetts Sen. Henry Cabot Lodge, for the job. Ultimately, he decided Lodge belonged at the United Nations and Adams was indeed the right man to be at his right hand.

On November 25, 1952, newspapers across America carried articles announcing Adams's appointment as assistant to the President. His duties were not spelled out, but as Adams recalled in his memoir, *First Hand Report,* Eisenhower wanted him to present the important cases and issues to him in a manageable form and to "keep as much work of secondary importance as possible off his desk."

That was his mission for five and a half years. And by the testimony of contemporaries in the White House, as well as journalists and historians, it is a mission he accomplished admirably.

Initially, Adams had to define the tasks and take the measure of members of his top staff, most of whom he had little voice in choosing. As events played out, the White House staff proved to be a cohesive and effective operation, in many respects a model unmatched in any administration since. Both Eisenhower and Adams had much to do with this success, because each proved to be, in a different way, an inspirational leader.

During their years in Washington, Sherman and Rachel Adams were constantly in motion. While not primarily interested in the social scene, they were much sought out by society mandarins, Sherman because of his clout and persona, Rachel because of her vivacity and quiet magnetism.

Just before the inauguration, the Adamses moved to C Street, on Capitol Hill, into a handsome Federal-style house once owned by President Andrew Jackson's Tennessee political confidant and secretary of war, John Eaton. Their early months were difficult beyond adjusting to new surroundings and an aggressive press corps.

Adams found it a demanding challenge to define his role and to assert his authority when his assessment of a situation clashed with those of Cabinet secretaries and congressional leaders. "It took a while for some members of the Cabinet and other high-ranking government executives to accept me as a spokesman of Eisenhower's viewpoints," Adams recalled. But by the winter of 1953–54 he had established himself and developed a harmonious working relationship with the President—so much so that when offered a position in industry at much higher pay, Adams stayed on at Ike's urging.

An underlying problem for the Adamses in Washington was financial stability. It was difficult to maintain two homes on a $20,000 annual salary. Unlike most others in the Eisenhower inner circle, the Adamses were not rich. They had lived well but frugally during the New Hampshire years, spending their discretionary income primarily on private schools for their children and regular vacations. There was no nest egg and no contingency fund like the one Adams had tapped while governor of New Hampshire. At the same time, the Adamses needed clothes, a car, and other accoutrements of high position in the nation's capital. There were no easy answers.

The solution Sherman Adams found was hardly unique to him or to that era. He accepted monetary gifts from a range of rich friends and associates whose motives varied widely. He assured himself that there was nothing wrong in accepting the money tendered, since no one was asking him to do anything in exchange. Ultimately, what started as a matter of expediency and was rationalized as normal came back to haunt Adams in the most humiliating fashion.

The Adamses defined their niche in Washington, enjoying a full and satisfying social life despite Sherman's grueling work schedule. By the end of 1953, they were ensconced in a handsome house on Tilden Street, where they enjoyed more privacy than they had near Capitol Hill.

Rachel soon earned her reputation as a popular hostess, especially with her regular soirées for Cabinet wives, focused on painting, crocheting, and other domestic activities. Mamie Eisenhower was not a part of this crowd—she preferred old Army friends—but Rachel occasionally visited the first lady in the White House and was deeply impressed by her "diligence and sincerity."

Sherman Adams was no more intimate socially with Dwight Eisenhower than Rachel was with Mamie. Their working partnership was strong, gradually moving beyond respect on Eisenhower's part to a deep admiration for Adams's commitment and competence. But as a rule, Ike socialized with his peers, people of his own generation, Army associates and business moguls. Adams was not in that circle.

Periodically, the President invited Adams to join him for golf, usually at Burning Tree Country Club in Bethesda, Maryland. Adams loved golf, so these were treasured occasions, even though the President took his golf so seriously that he rarely made small talk during a round.

Equally enjoyable were opportunities for the Adamses to attend state dinners or to share the President's box at Washington's Symphony Hall. Ike and Mamie were not particularly interested in classical music and frequently made their seats available to top aides. Adams was often first in line for the tickets.

Magazine profiles tended to portray Adams as a "taut" and "flinty" Yankee who worked hard and played little, usually getting to bed by 8 p.m., but the facts are more complicated. Although Adams put in long hours at work, the Adamses went out three nights a week on average to public receptions and parties. Less often, they attended or hosted private soirées with fellow staffers and Cabinet officers and their wives.

Rachel Adams's memoir, *On the Other Hand,* provides an intimate glimpse of social life in 1950s Washington, proving beyond doubt that the Adamses were not wallflowers. Rachel's modesty prevented her from saying so, but many a Washington hostess did not consider her party a success unless the Adamses made at least a brief appearance.

Americans tend to remember Eisenhower's Washington as a placid place in "the last fine time" before society turned topsy-turvy and good times were undone by assassinations, wars, and scandals. In the haze of memory, the 1950s were good times presided over by a genial golfer-President who smiled a lot and rarely frowned.

Memory lies. Eisenhower's Washington was a Cold War capital, focused on life-and-death issues, all stemming from geopolitical chess games with the Russians and the looming specter of the mushroom cloud.

The epicenter of hardball politics in the city—Capitol Hill—could be a roiling and even a treacherous place to operate. This was a world where one leading Republican senator, Styles Bridges of New Hampshire, kept secret files on friends and foes alike, in case he might need to call on them. It was a world where another GOP powerhouse, Wisconsin's Sen. Joseph McCarthy, saw communists infesting the executive branch and the military even after Eisenhower had reformed security policies.

Eisenhower's Washington was a city where the distrust between the two wings of the Republican Party was greater than the distrust between Republicans and Democrats on the Hill. It was a city that had become used to big government and was going to have to adjust to a more stringent fiscal regimen imposed by a moderate conservative chief executive. It was a city where money talked loudly.

In short, there was plenty of action in Washington, the stakes were high, and the game was not always played by Marquis of Queensbury Rules.

In playing this game, Sherman Adams had some distinct advantages. He had learned life's lessons the hard way, as a woods boss. His skin was tough. Each day, he somehow juggled "as many as two hundred phone calls, a score or more personal visitors and monosyllabic decisions beyond count" and took it as "all in a day's work," former Eisenhower speech-writer Emmet Hughes recalled. His decisions were usually consistent with the President's wishes, and he expressed them emphatically. This increased his influence—and his aura as Ike's right-hand man.

His schedule and his conviction that the work of the Presidency was critically important left him little time for pleasantries and no patience for lassitude. Up most mornings at 6:15 to scan half a dozen newspapers before work, Adams was in the office by 7:30 and expected the same of his staff. Maxwell Rabb, the Cabinet's secretary, overslept one day. When he arrived, Adams gave him a "look that could kill."

Adams was as curt as ever, typically opening a conversation by telling a scheduled visitor, "State your business." On the phone, he dispensed with hello and goodbye, not to mention pleasantries about the weather. When he thought the conversation was over, the caller often learned of it by the sound of the phone slamming down. "He even hung up once on me," Eisenhower said.

Coming upon staff members in the halls of the White House, Adams would neither smile nor make small talk, but ask, "What have you done for your country today?" and keep marching. Younger staffers found this inspirational rather than obnoxious. "We knew he was working as hard as we were, if not harder," said one of them, Bradley Patterson. "How could we not admire this man?"

To his subordinates, Adams's actions spoke louder than words. Once, Gordon Gray went to Adams's office after perceiving a problem that he thought would embarrass the President. Gray laid out the details for twenty minutes. Adams's full reply: "Well, what do you want me to do about it?" He motioned Gray out. "I got out of his office as quickly as I could," Gray recalled, "and I came back a couple of days later and had a proposed solution. It taught me a very good lesson. . . . He didn't want people going in and saying, 'Mr. President, you've got a problem,' without saying this is a possible way to handle it."

Sifting through thousands of papers about Adams's work as chief of staff, one cannot help but notice the inadequacy of the conventional wisdom about Adams's role in the Eisenhower administration. The core Adams was not so much a Svengali, as syndicated columnist Marquis Childs dubbed him in 1957, as he was a patriot doing his damnedest to help his President. He himself said he was in the White House "to save the President's time (and) take the burden as much as possible off the President's shoulders." Or as he would put it in his memoirs, to "scrub the backstairs of the White House."

Adams did not, in fact, scrub many stairs. But he did so many useful things and earned so much attention for the way he operated that it became all too easy to dub him, as *Newsweek* did in a cover story in 1957, "the second most powerful man in the White House."

Adams's perceived power derived in part from his station, his office being a chip shot from the President's, and the logical but incorrect assumption that Adams controlled access to Eisenhower. It also derived from Adams's ability to say, "The President wants this to happen." There's no evidence Adams ever substituted his own will for the President's—certainly Eisenhower never expressed any dissatisfaction with Adams's performance—but it is a mistake to assume that Eisenhower was delegating his power to a man who gave the appearance of knowing how to use it.

One of Adams's most important roles in the White House—one he understood and accepted—was that of "lightning rod" for criticism of executive decisions. It was Adams who kept out congressmen, GOP state officials, and lobbyists whom Eisenhower did not wish to see. Consequently, it was Adams who bore the brunt of their anger.

Because Adams said "no" so often, especially to those in the ranks of the Republican right, he was dubbed "the abominable No Man." The notion that he was at the head of a "Palace Guard" that kept conservatives from speaking to the President took hold early, and nothing Adams or Eisenhower ever said publicly could convince critics like former President Herbert Hoover and Sen. McCarthy that it wasn't true.

Adams was widely perceived as a "liberal" because he opposed the methods of McCarthy's anti-Communist crusade and helped orchestrate White House strategy to bring McCarthy down in 1954. Adams was an avowed supporter of black civil rights and was instrumental in bringing into the administration the first black man (Fred Morrow) ever to serve in an executive position in the White House. Finally, Adams made all too evident his impatience with those who felt the Eisenhower administration's first order of business should be to repeal much of the New Deal.

"The President," Adams said in a February 1954 speech, "is not trying to ex-punge the New Deal or (advance) it. He is taking off from the facts of life as they are in the U.S., A.D. 1954, going on from there to outline . . . a new course." In accord with Ike's notion of a "middle way" between ever more in-trusive government and the laissez-faire orientation of many GOP activists, Adams wanted to help Ike build a new Republican Party.

Adams could have been more tactful in dealing with the party's conservative wing, but there is little evidence that he slanted arguments to suit his own ideo-logical premises or denied information or perspectives to the president. Throughout his years in the White House, Adams did Eisenhower's bidding, first and foremost, and did it well. So well that the President frequently praised Adams, telling friends, "I sleep better knowing that little fellow is in that office."

Only Eisenhower fully grasped the many roles Adams played. It was Eisen-hower who saw Adams in action and conferred with him on the most sensitive issues that came before the President. Adams took responsibility for firing Air Force Secretary Harold Talbott when he learned Talbott was directing con-tracts to companies in which he had an interest. Adams knocked heads when federal agencies and Cabinet officers failed to compromise. Adams scruti-nized appointments to the most important positions in the executive branch and the diplomatic corps. Adams told lobbyists seeking White House inter-vention in their interests with regulatory agencies to forget about it (some-times, according to reporter Robert Donovan, in blunt and even "savage" terms). And Adams was in on virtually every White House political conclave.

For outsiders, who knew only the crusty public figure, Adams was hard to like, his power easy to overestimate. What they knew was that Adams spoke in Ike's name and had become famous for writing "OK SA" on important memos. Given that Eisenhower believed in delegating authority and tended not to advertise his political interests or his hands-on approach to policymak-ing, the assumption was too often made that Adams had the final say about key issues. In fact, Adams acted only when he was absolutely sure he knew the President's mind.

For White House insiders, Adams was the person to whom one could go for a fair hearing when no one else was listening, the man who got things done. One of Adams's real strengths was an open mind. When a Republican official or a staff member insisted that a particular viewpoint needed a hear-ing, Adams worked to assure it got one. When presented with evidence that contradicted his position, he was willing to stand corrected.

Adams did not put his finger to the wind when the going got tough. When junior colleagues like Maurice Stans, the assistant budget director, sought Adams's opinion about going public with his views against budget deficits, Adams did not say, "Look at the polls," or "Consider who you will offend if you do that." He told Stans, as he would tell others, "If you believe in it, do it. If you don't believe in it, don't do it, because you won't be convincing."

In the fall of 1955, Adams's influence reached a new peak as a result of the President's heart attack while vacationing in Denver. The negative public image of a "no man" or "frosty" gave way to a new image: that of Eisenhower's "almost indispensable man."

Adams was among the first to learn of the heart attack, which occurred while the Adamses were vacationing in Scotland. It took him barely a second to realize that he had to get the first plane home. Adams later recalled thinking about "how the President would expect his staff and Cabinet to act while he was disabled. He had never given me directives for such an emergency, but then he had never given me many directives of any kind and we had gotten along all right."

Backed by a formal Cabinet vote, Adams flew to Denver and established himself as the point man in the federal government. White House Press Secretary James Hagerty greeted Adams with relief, later observing, "I felt like kissing him, I was so glad he was there." Adams determined what documents and what people Eisenhower would see and framed the issues the President would have to decide. Nobody got access to Eisenhower without clearing it with Adams.

According to the reporter Robert Donovan, Adams's routine in Denver ran like this:

> Working in a plain office on the second floor of the administration building at Lowry (Air Force Base) overlooking a parking lot, Adams was on the phone to Washington from morning until night, giving instructions, and making innumerable administrative decisions. He would lay out areas of policy in which the President alone must make decisions and then see to it that decisions were reached on matters beyond these boundaries. In Denver, as in Washington, his authority was enhanced by his unique prerogative in speaking for the President as follows: "It is the President's wish that . . ." or "The President hopes you will," and so forth.

Each week Adams flew back to Washington to attend Cabinet and National Security Council meetings. There he reported the progress of Ike's recovery as well as Ike's wishes about such matters as preparation of the State of the Union message, farm policy, and relations with the Soviet Union.

From Washington, Adams remained in constant touch with the President by telephone and through the White House mail pouch that shuttled back and forth by courier plane. Whenever any significant matter was raised for presidential action, Ike offered a standard reply: "Take it up with Sherman."

The heart attack crisis cemented notions already in circulation about the disposition of power in the Eisenhower administration. Adams became the subject of numerous profiles, including a widely read cover story in *Time* magazine. That story quoted James Reston as saying that "there is a growing feeling here that Mr. Adams is now exercising more power than any man in America." *U.S. News and World Reports* suggested that even before the heart attack, Adams was "the only man in the White House authorized in the President's absence to direct a government agency to take action (and the) operating head of the government" during Ike's summer vacations. Such stories reinforced the commonplace, if erroneous, impression that Adams was the power behind the facade of an Eisenhower presidency.

The best reading of Adams's role in the Eisenhower's White House was that he did what needed doing, with Eisenhower's full approval. He never flinched from any responsibility. He cared not at all whether he was popular. He was serving his President, with whom he shared a vision for a better America.

Eisenhower and Adams were, at heart, moderate conservatives who could live with the welfare state. Both were determined to reduce the role of government where possible and encourage private initiative as the engine of American prosperity and creativity. Both were committed internationalists, convinced that the United States had a critical role to play in a postwar Pax Americana. Neither had much patience for the extreme right wing of their own party. Both were by temperament more pragmatic than ideological.

Sherman Adams was no paragon. He could be crude. He utterly lacked tact. And as the events of 1958 would prove, he came, little by little, to believe too much in the press clippings suggesting that he was "indispensable" to the Eisenhower White House when, in fact, he was only "almost indispensable."

The Bernard Goldfine scandal forced Adams out of his job, and later revelations about Adams's acceptance of gifts and money throughout his public career caused him problems with the IRS. Had these disclosures not tarnished his reputation, he might be remembered today in the words of the President he served so well. Adams, Ike once said, "is the rock on which I lean."

Sherman Adams

Freda Smith

Her fight helped revolutionize care for the disabled.

BY KATIE HELM

J anet Smith, dressed in a purple sweat suit with a white bib around her
neck, sits in her wheelchair at the kitchen table, her face frozen in a
blank stare, the outward expression of a severely damaged brain. It is only
when she sees her mother that a flicker of comprehension sparks in her eyes.

"Here you go, my darling," Freda Smith says tenderly, spoon-feeding lunch
to her thirty-seven-year-old daughter, who functions at the level of a nine-

Freda Smith fought for
the rights of her daughter
Janet—and all of New
Hampshire's disabled
children.

Ken Williams/Concord Monitor.

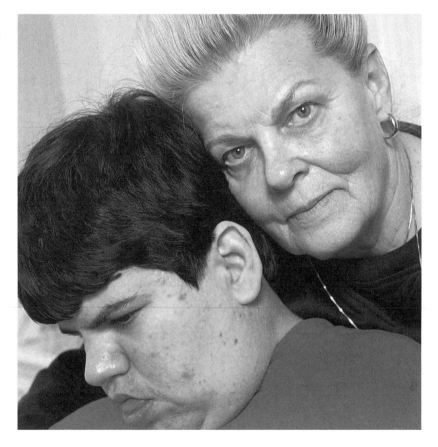

month-old. The dry toast, pureed carrots, finely diced meat, and applesauce are one of Janet's favorite meals, her mom says, wiping strawberry milk from her daughter's chin.

At first it feels like a terrible intrusion, being in Janet Smith's home, where she lives with Tom Valencourt, also severely retarded, under twenty-four-hour care supervised by a staff of fourteen. She cannot walk or talk. She is in diapers. Because of her brain damage, she is epileptic and blind in her right eye. She has no use of the left side of her body.

It is, at first, overwhelming to see her condition, to watch her respond to love and attention with noises only a devoted mother and staff comprehend.

It is only after hearing the extraordinary story of how Janet Smith came to live just a half-mile down the street from her mother that you understand how near-perfect her life is today.

She will go to bed tonight in her own room surrounded by pink curtains and plush carpeting, a scene drastically different from the Laconia State School, a former state institution where she grew up, sleeping on a hard bed—sometimes physically restrained—under barrack-like conditions.

It was the tireless determination of people like Freda Smith who brought the pressures to bear that eventually closed Laconia—changing the lives of her daughter and thousands like her for good.

The Laconia State School, founded in 1901 as the New Hampshire School for Feeble-Minded Children, was not so much a school as a warehouse, where for more than eight decades thousands of retarded and physically handicapped New Hampshire residents were dumped and sometimes forgotten.

"I literally had never seen anything so subhuman," said Richard Cohen, an attorney for New Hampshire Legal Assistance, which in 1978 sued the state on behalf of the Laconia State residents to improve conditions.

"In one building there were literally twenty-five males, severely disabled, sleeping in a tiny room, lined with cots," Cohen said. "Many were half-clothed or naked just staring into space. The residents displayed bizarre behavior that was due, in large part, to being institutionalized."

Janet Smith was one of six people chosen as plaintiffs to represent a cross-section of residents. The lawsuit, later joined by the U.S. Department of Justice, charged the state with systematically violating the rights of its residents, forcing them to live under inhumane conditions that induced institutional behavior, prevented development of normal behavior and skills, and caused their further deterioration.

Freda Smith, in addition to her maternal duties, served as a state representative, board member of the Association for Retarded Citizens, and president of the Laconia State School parents association. She is remembered for her dogmatic—at times bullish—efforts to give her daughter and the other residents better lives.

"She was the heart and soul of the movement," said Ron Cook, then a lawyer for the state Association for Retarded Citizens. "'No' was not in her vocabulary. She was an active participant through the whole legal process, refusing to surrender until she got what the residents deserved."

It wasn't easy being a named plaintiff, added Cohen. "Even though we knew we were right and the law was on our side, once you get into a litigation fray the other side takes potshots at you, and you become a lightning rod for criticism," he said. "Freda remained a strong leader."

The shutdown of Laconia State School took years of battles, including a ten-week civil trial wrought with emotional and angry testimony.

"The trial was intense, and the stories were heartbreaking—even from the staff," said Judge Shane Devine, who eventually ordered the state to shape up. "The school just didn't have the resources. They were terribly understaffed, and the burnout was very high. New Hampshire's legislature does not like to appropriate money."

In the fall of 1980 Devine ordered the state to educate every Laconia State School resident in the least restrictive setting possible. Devine did not specifically order the closing of the school, but he embraced a plan to develop alternatives to institutional care that became the cornerstone on which the current community service system was built.

"The state never appealed," Devine said. "It was clear from the beginning of the trial that it was time to give these residents some dignity, something better."

New Hampshire ultimately became the first state in the country to close its institution for the retarded, a feat that revolutionized the way retarded people were treated by the rest of society. The last of the Laconia State School residents left in 1991. They're living in apartments and homes all over the state, many working full-time jobs, supported by twelve area agencies that provide needed support.

For the relatively smooth transition, parents like Smith credit the leadership of Don Shumway, then the state's director of mental health and developmental services, who could cut through political wrangling, soothe the fears of resistant communities, and find homes suitable to individual needs.

"Don always did the right thing," Smith said. "Instead of drawing battle lines, he involved everyone. And he never stopped until the parents and the children were satisfied with their conditions."

Janet Smith was born on August 31, 1961. She was two and a half months old before there was any sign of trouble.

"I was giving her a morning bath, and she started making all these weird sounds," her mother said "Her arms and legs started to tremble, and her eye was going all over the place."

Freda Smith's husband, Harvey, was visiting his ailing father, so a neighbor drove them to a hospital near Haverhill, Massachusetts, where they lived at the time. That doctor sent them immediately to Children's Hospital in Boston.

"These are things you never forget," Smith said, crying as she remembered holding Janet in this uncertain state for eight hours before the hospital found a bed for her daughter. "The doctor came out a while later, and very coldly, like he was giving me the grocery list, he told me: 'Your daughter has brain damage. She has no use of her left side. The right side of her brain is damaged. Consequently she'll have no vision in her right eye. Your daughter's an epileptic. She'll always be a vegetable, so you might as well institutionalize her and forget about her.'"

Devastated by the news, the Smiths refused to turn Janet's care over to anyone. "It was out of the question," her mother said.

But at the time, physicians across the country told parents like Smith that institutions were the only answer. They believed nothing could be done to improve their children's condition. Since the end of the nineteenth century, the solution for people with "feeblemindedness" or "mental defects" was to segregate them from the "sane."

For nearly five years, the Smiths cared for their child as best they could. The couple and Freda Smith's two children from another marriage tried to teach Janet how to eat from a spoon and drink from a cup, simple tasks she has never mastered. "Children like Janet normally break families, but she strengthened ours," Smith said.

But the constant care required for Janet, who never slept, only napped, wore on her mother. "Janet was up morning, noon, and night," she said. "I knew nothing about mental retardation. There was no one to talk to. No support system. I used to get these excruciating headaches from the stress, and one day I just broke down."

While Smith was recovering from a nervous breakdown, five-year-old Janet was placed at Laconia State School.

"That was a very, very painful time," Smith said. "The guilt will never leave me. Besides closing Laconia State, the one great thing that came out of the lawsuit was that all the support systems were put in the community. Parents today will never have to experience the guilt of putting a child in an institution. There will always be something in the community to help them."

For six weeks, Smith was not allowed to see her daughter; she was told Janet needed to adjust to her new surroundings. After that period, the family made weekly drives to Laconia from Salem, where they had moved when Janet turned three.

Smith's visits increased as she found it necessary to do her daughter's laundry, buy her toys, and take her outside for fresh air—basic care she found lacking. The large brick buildings, some with bars on the windows, housed people who, Smith said, initially scared her.

"I knew my daughter, but I did not know the other residents—some of whom came on strong and were intimidating," she said. "That's why it is so important today for people to be educated about disabilities. So there isn't this fear of the unknown."

Other parents had concerns over the treatment of their children, and a parent association was formed. At first, they raised money for window screens and curtains. Their demands increased as the dormitories became crowded and conditions deteriorated. In 1962, there were 900 residents; in 1974, there were 1,000 with a waiting list of 400.

In 1975, the Laconia State School began releasing some higher functioning residents, but the state never came up with enough money to supervise them properly on the outside. The school's buildings were old, lacked privacy, and needed renovation. Staffing was inadequate; turnover was high. The school had poorly organized education and recreation programs, which did not serve all residents, and just one speech therapist.

At the same time public attention began to focus on the inadequacies at Laconia, Dr. Jack Melton became its superintendent and started to change the philosophy. Rather than a dumping ground, Melton said, the school would be a force to improve residents' lives.

"Without Jack Melton I'm not sure if this whole thing would have come about," said Smith. "He was vocal about how strapped the school was, and he always encouraged us to push and push because he knew things could change. He was a savior and one of our best allies."

In 1979, a year after the class-action lawsuit was filed, Melton urged state lawmakers to spend $5.5 million to resettle 600 residents in their home communities before a judge ordered it.

The legislature said no. One lawmaker said Melton's idea was "an awful squandering of state money for people who can't take care of themselves."

From 1974 to 1979, the state moved from forty-fourth in the nation in spending on services for the mentally retarded to fifth, but the conditions were still not optimal. On April 12, 1978, parents resorted to the power of the court to force change.

The lawsuit and 10,000 pages of depositions complained of wards that stank of urine, residents restrained in wheelchairs, excessive use of drugs, insufficient recreation facilities, physical and sexual abuse, and isolation of residents.

It was more than enough to convince Judge Devine.

Today the 400-acre Laconia State School campus is a medium security prison, its buildings used to segregate another population. But Freda Smith holds on to a collection of mementos from the bad old days: three massive scrapbooks filled with pictures, poems, letters, and hundreds of newspaper articles. The books sit on a table in her living room beneath a copy of Devine's ruling.

Janet Smith spends her days going on errands with the medical staff and eating meals with her mom. She's part of a group that puts on drama productions, goes on field trips, and bowls at least once a week—activities she has found ways to take part in. "She has more friends than I have," her mother said. "She has a very active life. I know when she's happy because the little corners of her mouth turn up slightly."

Janet has a personality all her own, her mom said; she hums when she's not happy.

"She still has lots of medical problems," Smith said. "The doctors told me she would not live past thirty, but here she is, and she's such a good patient. She's someplace where I know she'll always be safe."

Caroline Gardner Bartlett

She aided the wounded soldiers of World War I—until she was accused of treason.

BY FELICE BELMAN

The town of Warner first fell in love with Caroline Gardner Bartlett in 1904, the year she opened a music school in the Mink Hills and charmed residents with operatic classics and Negro spirituals. By the time she retired there for good, her neighbors weren't sure what to think: In the intervening years, she had become a soprano of international renown, a hero of the Great War, and an alleged German spy.

Caroline Gardner Bartlett was accused of spying during World War I.
New Hampshire Historical Society.

117

Sixty years after her death, Bartlett's life remains a puzzle, a story of early feminism and wartime paranoia. She was, for sure, a genuine hero. She dove into the war effort years before America formally joined the crusade. She dodged submarines and mines in the English Channel to ferry food and medicine to the conflict's earliest wounded troops. She created a hospital that tended to the black soldiers of France's colonies in Africa. And she convinced philanthropists and factory workers to dig deep, supplying the money and supplies that would ultimately help win the war.

But she also attracted deep jealousies and suspicions, both here and in Europe. She was accused of profiteering, thieving, spying for the enemy. The proof, according to the Justice Department, J. Edgar Hoover, and even Theodore Roosevelt and Calvin Coolidge, was scant. Yet Bartlett spent the last twenty years of her life in a frantic crusade to clear her name, an effort that eventually robbed her of her health and sight.

"Every possible scandal has been laid at my door," Bartlett wrote in 1917. "I have been followed and watched every moment by detectives. . . . But my motive was simply to alleviate the horrible suffering that I had seen."

It was an unlikely end to a life that started out quite differently.

Bartlett was born in Ohio in 1868. She was adopted by a Rochester, New York, family and soon showed a talent for singing. Her adoptive parents indulged her interest with voice lessons from well-regarded teachers in the United States and Europe.

When the family moved to Boston, she studied at the conservatory there, performing at several large churches and with the Boston Symphony Orchestra. Her fans came to recognize Bartlett's short, stout frame, her dramatic voice, and her old-fashioned monocle.

Eventually, Bartlett developed a scientific method of voice training all her own, made famous by the testimony of Madame Lillian Nordica, a New York prima donna who lost her voice and got it back with Bartlett's help. So curious was Thomas Edison that he invited Bartlett to his laboratory in New Jersey for experiments.

Bartlett didn't marry until the age of thirty, and her marriage was necessarily brief: Dr. James Bartlett was sixty-six years old. His death just twelve years later gave Caroline what she needed for her career: money, property—and a valid excuse for an independent and adventurous life. She never remarried, never had children, and never looked back.

Among the concrete things left to Caroline by James was a hundred-year-old farmhouse in Warner. At first it was a summer retreat for the couple, who came, with their horses, by train from Boston. "The pine woods, the trout brook, the deer which came to drink, the myriads of song birds, the lilacs by the wall, roses and wild strawberries in the grass made this lovely spot a veritable Eden," Bartlett wrote.

Eventually Caroline moved in full-time and established a summer singing school that attracted students from across the country.

The school, called Sunny Hill, took about fifty students a summer. Some stayed in "artistic bungalows"; others camped nearby. Bartlett and her students performed for local audiences and received positive reviews. "Mrs. Bartlett is one of New England's greatest sopranos, and her four numbers were a delight to the audience," wrote the *Kearsarge Independent* after one concert.

Bartlett loved New Hampshire, but she loved fame too. She embarked on a deliberate crusade for international acclaim—and succeeded briefly, singing concerts in New York, England, and beyond.

"You came to London unknown and unheralded, and one recital was sufficient to place you right in the front row of lyric artists," her booking agent wrote in 1910.

Bartlett was on tour in England in 1914 when the war broke out. When she couldn't get a boat back to the States, she fell into volunteer work that would change her life forever. Her talent for collecting and organizing supplies for the troops in France convinced officials to give her a major role in the war effort: collecting money, trucks, bed sheets, bandages—whatever was needed—to help the earliest wounded soldiers. Eventually, she was put in charge of an entire hospital for Belgian and French troops.

Bartlett adopted a new persona: Dressed in a nun's habit of deep purple cloth, she called herself Sister Beatrice. The idea, she said, was to be immediately recognizable in the war zone—and not to trade on the name she'd made famous through her singing.

It worked. Sister Beatrice was soon known to Allied soldiers throughout France as a savior of sorts—working tirelessly to supply medical equipment, food, nurses, and doctors. By her own reckoning, she crossed the English Channel more than eighty times, gathering supplies and bringing them back to France through dangerous waters. On both shores, she received unfettered access: Even the border guards recognized her dramatic purple cloak.

Each time she landed in France with supplies, she jumped aboard a two-wheeled horse cart and traveled the countryside, ministering to wounded troops. "We rode by night and day with hundreds of bandages, medical supplies, and greatly needed necessities," she wrote. In the early days, there were few formal relief organizations and volunteers. To some soldiers, Sister Beatrice meant the difference between life and death.

"You alone were here for us. You alone saw us through," one Belgian soldier wrote years later.

Bartlett's work at the Yvetot Hospital was brief but pivotal. In November 1914, the French military gave her an old seminary building about 60 miles from the front with orders to turn it into a hospital for 450 men by January. The building had no working plumbing, no electricity, no heat. She quickly set about renovating—and raising money.

She established a committee in London to handle the finances and hired doctors, nurses, and workmen. All the while, she continued her trips across the Channel, speaking to groups large and small, convincing them to send money and supplies to Yvetot.

Among the first patients were black soldiers from French colonies in Africa who appreciated Sister Beatrice's evenhanded care. They came from Madagascar and Tripoli. There were Senegalese troops who could speak only a jargon of French and their native tongue.

"They were brought in on stretchers, these wounded, after long awful days of hunger, of standing knee-deep in mud," *Concord Monitor* columnist Ruel Colby wrote years later. "They came caked with whitish clay from steel helmet to studded boots, almost unrecognizable as humans, these gallant infantrymen."

Bartlett said the first fifty soldiers who arrived at Yvetot had been in the trenches for 130 days, "freezing and thawing, famished and with lice propagating under the skin. And when I say trenches, I mean nothing more or less than cesspools. Most of these men lose either their foot or legs."

In the first year, Yvetot treated 1,380 such patients. Just sixteen died.

Once the hospital was up and running, Bartlett resigned as its president and concentrated on public speaking in Britain, Canada, and the United States on behalf of Allied hospitals.

Some audiences were small, like the one she addressed in February 1915 in Ascot, England. Her talk there yielded ten guineas from a Mrs. E. B. Wyatt, who encouraged Bartlett to "use it as you wish in buying some personal gifts for your soldiers."

Some audiences were enormous, like the 140,000 shipbuilders she addressed in Newcastle, England. That factory talk was among her most successful: The men's war relief fund raised 183,000 pounds for the war effort. To France they sent fifty beds, an ambulance, six operating tables, twelve wheelchairs, 900 blankets, one portable x-ray table, 150 hot water bottles, 3,000 towels, 4,000 surgical instruments, 12,000 bandages, 3,000 shirts, 4,000 socks, 6,000 games and puzzles, and 1.3 million cigarettes. The local press called Sister Beatrice "The Second Florence Nightingale."

It was on one of her speaking trips that Bartlett got her first inkling of the trouble that would follow her the rest of her life. In San Francisco in November 1915, she received a telegram from a friend in Montreal, where she had spoken two months before.

"Rumors persistent from highly connected person here you are German spy," wrote Mrs. Ryan Leduc.

At first, Bartlett ignored the warning. But on December 4, 1915, the front page of the *New York Times* included this damning headline: " 'Sister Beatrice' Accused; Mrs. Caroline Bartlett Called a German Spy."

"Neither she nor her friends can account for the circulation of the German spy story, but Mrs. Bartlett asserts that it has not the slightest foundation. There are said to be some reasons for believing that it is the work of the Germans or of people who sympathize with them," the *Times* reported.

The next day, the *Times* reported on Bartlett's earlier trip to Canada. "She called on Gen. Sir Sam Hughes, minister of the Militia, asking him for letters of introduction. It is understood that Gen. Hughes did not feel satisfied regarding her credentials and refused her request. While Mrs. Bartlett was in Ottawa, the Dominion police watched her movements closely, the impression having been created that she was a German spy. However, no information warranting her arrest was obtained."

The scandal worsened as other newspapers followed the *Times'* lead. "Right and left people fell away, even those whom I had counted as loyal friends in the past," Bartlett wrote. On a trip to England, she reported indignantly, she was held for "military inspection" and strip-searched.

Where had the charges come from? How could Sister Beatrice's reputation for wartime heroism turn so quickly into one for treason? The mystery became the obsession of her life. And while records from those years contain a tangle of conflicting stories, they also provide these clues:

In November 1915, Bartlett gave a speech in Massachusetts urging her audience to send supplies, particularly trucks, to France. One of her listeners, H. H. Willcox of Newtonville, promptly wrote to the War Relief Clearing House for France and Her Allies—the American organization channeling war supplies to Europe—asking officials there to vouch for Bartlett.

"I suppose you refer to the party known as 'Sister Beatrice,' in which event I cannot, consistently, vouch for the authenticity of the appeal," wrote one of them, Clyde Pratt.

While Bartlett was urging audiences to send supplies through Pratt's clearinghouse, she apparently had no formal relationship with the organization. She was a freelancer, speaking to audiences gathered by wealthy friends and music patrons around the country and relating her own experiences in France.

Pratt's skepticism was no doubt fueled by a letter from H. E. Beatty, his counterpart in France on the receiving end of the war relief supply line. Beatty's assessment: "She is not worthy of any assistance whatever, and it would not be safe to have any dealings with her." Beatty intimated that Bartlett's work at the Yvetot hospital had been unprofessional—and perhaps criminal. He suggested she had filched money from the hospital, and he raised doubts about her loyalty.

"Mrs. Bartlett is well known to us. . . . She is not persona grata in any respect with the government; in fact the government stated that the hospital at Yvetot could not continue so long as she remained its titular head. With considerable difficulty, she was prevailed upon to resign her office of president of the hospital."

There were other cautions too. When Canadian authorities checked up on her, they received the following report from Scotland Yard: "Her conduct is open to grave suspicion and she will bear watching." The British detectives said Bartlett did not represent any official organization—and had given an unsatisfactory account of the money she received on fund-raising trips in England.

Where was the truth?

On the matter of stealing, the record makes it seem unlikely—but unclear. Indeed, despite hobnobbing among wealthy arts patrons, Bartlett lived on the financial edge. Early in the war, she sold her jewelry to help make ends meet. And her personal papers are rife with IOUs written to rich friends. When Bartlett died in 1938, the Warner lawyer hired to settle her estate found just $59.60 in cash.

One rumor had Sister Beatrice stealing directly from the Yvetot hospital. Others had her profiteering from her collection work—diverting the money raised or selling the supplies that had been donated for free.

Bartlett's resignation from Yvetot is mysterious. Her version: French officials were uncomfortable with an American in charge—at a time when American soldiers had not yet joined the battle. And hospital workers were jealous of her power.

But others believed she had been forced out because of financial improprieties. Julia Cozzens, an Yvetot volunteer from America, said Bartlett had refused to submit to any auditing of her accounts or to travel with a companion. And, she said, by the time she arrived in France, the hospital was already $36,000 in debt—a claim Bartlett denied.

In a cryptic letter accepting her resignation, the board overseeing the Yvetot hospital wrote: "Regret was expressed by all present, but at the same time it was felt that under the circumstances there was nothing left to do but accept your resignation."

There were other complications too. For starters, Bartlett was an American in France—but her passport was British. (In those days, women took the nationality of their husbands. James Bartlett was born in Canada and therefore a British subject; though he'd been dead for years, that gave Caroline a British passport too.) All her trips between England and America were therefore complicated.

Her name, too, was suspicious. Her birth parents were called Gott—an Americanized Dutch name that, to those looking out for enemy sympathizers, sounded German.

Americans were willing to believe the spy story, even without proof. Anti-German sentiment ran so hot that spy plots were often the stuff of headlines. Once the United States actually joined the war, some accused traitors were rounded up, refused bail, and held for the duration of the conflict. The residents of Berlin, New Hampshire, changed the pronunciation of their town (from Ber-lin' to Ber'-lin), and many school districts stopped teaching German altogether.

If it was all just a misunderstanding, it didn't feel that way to Bartlett. She spent the rest of her life trying to clear her name—refusing at times to take yes for an answer.

Bartlett solicited letters of commendation from civic leaders to vouch for her character. A. Z. Conrad, pastor of Boston's Park Street Church, wrote: "In the interest of simple justice, I wish to emphasize the sterling worth and high character of Mrs. Bartlett, whom I have known well for more than twenty years." During the war, Conrad wrote, Bartlett "went to the war zone and plunged heart and soul into ministration to the multitude of wounded and suffering soldiers. . . . She deserves not the suspicion but the confidence and cooperation of all right-thinking people."

Bartlett contacted lawyers, judges, and members of Congress. She had the State Department investigate and got an audience with the President.

In October 1917, Mr. Charles Dewoody, a special agent for the Justice Department, summed up his investigation this way: "The general impression received is that she is a rather misguided individual, who, however, has been doing very good work and nothing very wrong; morally all right but methods perhaps slightly doubtful. Nothing in the record would indicate that she would be conniving at anything serious now."

Seven years later, U.S. Rep. Martin Davey of Ohio wrote that a Justice Department investigation had cleared Bartlett completely.

Still, Bartlett wasn't satisfied. In 1925, she pleaded with Myron Herrick, the U.S. ambassador to France, for a formal statement that she was no traitor, blaming him personally for the wartime newspaper reports, which he never publicly contradicted. "This whispering propaganda has continued until I can no longer exist in my profession," she wrote. "No one has the right to cause another such persecution as I have endured. . . . To be watched for years by the Secret Service of one's own country is a grave matter and must be corrected internationally."

Herrick's secretary wrote back, assuring Bartlett the ambassador "had no question in his mind that she was a spy." Realizing the statement could be read two ways, she persisted, hiring a string of lawyers to hound Herrick for a clarification.

By 1929, eleven years after the end of the war, all the American officials who investigated the Bartlett affair had come to the same conclusion: Caroline Gardner Bartlett was no spy.

"I am happy to say that there is not the slightest evidence that you were under suspicion for disloyalty," Wilbur Carr, assistant secretary of state, wrote that year.

It was nearly too late. Bartlett had returned to New Hampshire to calm her nerves and restore her health. But her frailty and growing blindness had rendered her nearly incapacitated. Her last years were spent writing a defensive memoir and collecting written praise from military and musical experts. She died at Warner's Austin Sanitarium in 1938, and in death received the acclaim and vindication she sought so desperately in life.

Her funeral included an American Legion color guard, a gun salute, and Taps. And in a memorial speech, retired Army colonel Arthur Edwards of Contoocook described Bartlett like this:

Madame Bartlett was a talented and noble woman who was faithful to the gifts God gave her. To a fine mind she added a heart rich in kindness for all humanity. She showed this by her sacrificial ministrations during the world war to the suffering soldiers in hospitals and elsewhere.

Bartlett, Edwards felt confident, would not soon be forgotten.

Philip Ayres and John Weeks

They saved the White Mountains.

At the turn of the last century, New Hampshire's White Mountains were ravaged by careless logging and devastating fires. Huge tracts of land—once called the "Switzerland of America"—were stripped bare, virgin woods turned into a wasteland. Hikers reached the summit of 4,000-foot peaks only to have their views obscured by smoke.

The situation was so dire that when Philip Ayres, the first forester for the Society for the Protection of New Hampshire Forests, and John Weeks, an environmentally minded lawmaker from Massachusetts, pleaded with Congress to open its purse strings in the name of conservation, they succeeded. The Weeks Act, signed in 1911, created the White Mountain National Forest and forty-eight others in the eastern United States.

The government bought up thousands of parcels from private New Hampshire landowners. At 780,000 acres, the White Mountain National Forest protects twelve percent of the state's land. By the century's end, 6 million people visited each year—more visitors than at Yellowstone and Yosemite national parks combined.

As early as 1920, the dramatic change was already apparent. In a letter that year to Ayres, Weeks marveled: "As he climbs through the hardwoods and hemlocks into the spruces and firs and through the gnome woods into the fir scrub towards the summits, he finds no more boundary posts. He realizes that as a citizen he is joint owner not only of the mountain but of the whole range."

Marian MacDowell

She created a world-famous artists' colony.

If Edward MacDowell was the inspiration for the Peterborough artists' colony that bears his name, Marian MacDowell gave it life.

Edward MacDowell, the most renowned American composer of his time, died in 1908 after the MacDowell Colony's first year. Marian MacDowell, his widow, devoted the rest of her life to buying land, building studios, and raising money to ensure its continuation.

"For fifty years Marian ran the show," said Joe Bills, the colony's publicity coordinator, in 1999. "She was an incredibly driven and focused and powerful woman."

The philosophy of the colony followed a practice that the MacDowells adopted when they first bought the abandoned farm in 1896: Edward needed seclusion to write. Marian made sure he got it.

At the century's end, the MacDowell Colony invited about 200 artists a year to spend their days in uninterrupted work amid idyllic surroundings. They included Leonard Bernstein, Thornton Wilder, James Baldwin, Willa Cather, and Studs Terkel. But many of those who came to the MacDowell Colony were not yet famous at all.

"It is more valuable for the emerging artist than an established artist," Bills said. "For people that have to exist in the nitty-gritty of the real world, this is a pretty impossible environment to approach."

Bob McQuillen

He kept old-fashioned music alive.

The popularity of traditional New England dance music waxed and waned over the course of the twentieth century, but like the steady piano beat he sent out across dance floors for more than fifty years, Bob McQuillen of Peterborough was a constant. A one-time high school shop teacher and bus driver, McQuillen composed more than 1,000 contra dance tunes and single-handedly preserved a deceptively simple style of traditional piano playing.

McQuillen first got hooked on old-timey music when he was sent overseas during World War II. When he returned, he played with bands and traveled all over New England, reproducing a style brought to America by the earliest colonial settlers and leaving his own mark on the movement.

Bob McQuillen has been a constant on the traditional music scene.
Robin Shotola/Concord Monitor.

"He's the pivotal figure in the music," said Laurie Andres, a Seattle-based contra dance accordion player, who recorded an album almost entirely of McQuillen tunes. "There was this gigantic revival in the 1960s and 1970s, and Mac was the musician who brought the traditional music into the revival. He was the genuine article."

John King

He created the nation's first state-run lottery.

John King was the only person in New Hampshire history to serve as a leader in all three branches of government: House minority leader in the 1950s, governor in the 1960s, and chief justice of the state Supreme Court in the 1980s—at a time when Democrats like him rarely made it big in state government. His most lasting act, however, appealed less to political big shots than to regular folks.

In 1963, despite bitter opposition from political conservatives and church groups, he signed into law the New Hampshire Sweepstakes, the first state-run lottery in the country. Other governors had vetoed similar legislation, but

King was a legislator, governor, and state Supreme Court justice.
New Hampshire Historical Society.

King refused "to deny the right of the people of the state to embark on a legitimate fiscal experiment."

That experiment grew from $5.7 million in 1964 to $187.1 million in 1998. For every dollar raised, about 30 cents goes toward education.

"He didn't think gambling was amoral and all that," Anna King, the governor's widow, recalled. "He analyzed the issue and he gave the people what they wanted."

John King

Elizabeth Flynn

A hero to American workers, she was considered a "red menace" by the FBI.

BY AMY McCONNELL

It was midwinter 1912. Night had fallen and striking workers had massed outside the woolen mills beside the snow-banked Merrimack River.

Furious mill workers had just opened paychecks of about $6, which bosses had cut by thirty cents that week, and more than 14,000 had shut off their looms and walked out. The crowd—leaderless at first—tried to picket the American Woolen Company's mills, but company officials sprayed them down with fire hoses.

Within a few days, nearly 1,500 state militiamen occupied Lawrence, Massachusetts, and troopers and strikers clashed daily. Cavalry rode into crowds, clubbing people on foot. A policeman's stray bullet killed an Italian woman. The next day, a sixteen-year-old Syrian boy was bayoneted in the back and died.

Labor leader Elizabeth Gurley Flynn, visiting her hometown of Concord and helping the strikes downriver, said their deaths helped steel her resolve to bring down capitalism.

"I spoke at the funerals of men and women shot down on the picket line, and the iron entered my soul," Flynn later wrote. "I became and I remain an enemy of capitalism. I will never rest contented until I see it replaced by a government of the people, led by the working class, where private ownership of the means of life and the profit system is abolished."

The ultimately successful Lawrence strike made Flynn, then twenty-two, a hero of the militant labor movement. It also solidified her career as a lifelong revolutionary, first as a leader of the Industrial Workers of the World, or "Wobblies," and later as head of the Communist Party of America.

Flynn, who was born in Concord and spent part of her childhood in Manchester, fomented rebellion from Midwest mining towns to East Coast textile mills for nearly sixty years. While workers usually struck industrial cities like Lawrence and Lowell, victories achieved there—shorter hours, higher pay, safer conditions—helped improve the lives of workers across the country. Americans may be afraid of Marxism, Flynn once wrote, but benefits many people prize—an eight-hour workday, Social Security, unemployment insurance, and aid to farmers—were made possible by militant socialists' early struggles.

Flynn, who served scattered jail terms and a two-year federal prison sentence, came by her rebelliousness honestly—it was part of her Irish birthright, she said. Her great-grandfather helped the French invade Ireland to attack the British. Her grandfather worked in New Hampshire granite quarries until—dissatisfied with poor working conditions and anti-Irish prejudice—he joined an expedition to overthrow the Canadian government and set up a republic there. Flynn's father, Tom, a civil engineer who lost an eye to a flying chip of granite while working in a quarry, read Marx's works to her and her sisters as children. Her mother, Annie, an early advocate of equal rights for women, was equally radical for her era.

From Concord, the family followed Tom Flynn's job with the railroad to "drab, bleak" Manchester. There Flynn first saw textile workers' deep poverty.

The mills of Manchester stretched along the banks of the Merrimack like prisons, she wrote in her memoirs. Half the workers were women, and they earned one dollar a day. The Flynns' neighbors, men and women alike, rushed to the mills before dawn and returned after dark. When business was slow, the mills shut down without warning. In hard times, children ate lard on their bread instead of butter, and many had no underwear even in the coldest weather.

The images took hold, and Flynn began planning to overthrow capitalism.

After the family moved to the South Bronx a few years later, Flynn gave her first public speech at the Harlem Socialist Club at age sixteen. The topic was "What Socialism Will Do For Women," a subject to which she returned when she organized strikes in the mines and mill towns.

By the time of the Lawrence strike, Flynn had stoked her rhetoric into fiery oratory. She had spent five years speaking at mass labor rallies of textile workers in the East and of miners and timber workers in Montana and Washington state. For the otherwise all-male Wobblies, Flynn's beauty and intelligence commanded attention and helped publicize the strike. Reporters gushed over Flynn's quick wit, black hair, and flashing blue eyes. Even negative attention—as when the *Los Angeles Times* dubbed her one of the "She-Dogs of Anarchy"—helped keep the Wobblies in the public eye.

Flynn and the Wobblies brought their knack for publicity with them to Lawrence in 1912. The original strike leaders called in by the local Wobbly chapter had been arrested January 29, threatening to destroy the walkout. But Flynn, "Big Bill" Haywood, and another Wobblies leader picked up the slack almost immediately. Forbidden to address crowds on the city common, Flynn and Haywood attended one small meeting after another followed by mounted militia. They sometimes made as many as ten speeches a day.

Flynn helped organize special meetings for the female workers to encourage them to join the strike for higher pay. If working conditions for men were bad at the Lawrence mills, the situation for women was worse. Pregnant women sometimes continued working for so long they gave birth in the mill, between the looms, Flynn wrote. Women were paid at least twenty-five percent less than men with the same experience.

In one of the first confrontations between strikers and authorities, a group of Italian women caught a policeman standing guard on a bridge and stripped him of his gun, club, and badge. They were trying to take off his trousers and throw him into the Merrimack River when troops arrived to rescue him, according to historian Helen Camp.

Soon after one of the female strikers, Anna LoPizzo, was shot to death, the strike committee decided to send workers' children out of town until the strike ended. The children would be safer elsewhere, and their parents could concentrate on the strike.

Sympathizers in New York and Philadelphia gave the children temporary homes. Big-city newspapers soon discovered Lawrence and its children, many of whom had also worked thirteen-hour days in the mills, and the strike soon landed on the front page of the *Boston Globe* and the *New York Times*. A cartoon in *Collier's Magazine* named Lawrence "The Hunger City."

On February 22, authorities tried to cut off the flow of publicity created by the children. Col. E. LeRoy Sweetser, who was commanding troops in Lawrence, announced that no more children would be allowed to leave the city. The police arrested seven children at the local railway station.

Two days later, Flynn—who was in charge of the evacuation—tried to put forty more children on a train to Philadelphia, and the police turned brutal. As mothers were saying goodbye to their children, troops moved in to arrest everyone in the crowd. Officers choked and beat the women and children to get them into the patrol wagons, as mothers tried to fight off officers by biting and stabbing them with hat pins. But instead of shutting down the pickets, the crackdown stiffened strikers' resolve, galvanized public opinion, and turned the country's sympathy toward the workers.

Congress began an investigation of working conditions at Lawrence, and President Taft called for an investigation of industrial conditions across the country. Quickly, the Lawrence mill owners surrendered to workers' demands for better pay and shorter workdays.

Strikes in Lowell, New Bedford, and Fall River, Massachusetts, followed quickly and successfully. That year, New England manufacturers increased the wages of more than 200,000 other textile workers to keep the peace.

In later years Flynn turned to the Communist Party, speaking to party gatherings from Madison Square Garden to the coal mines of West Virginia. She also wrote a regular column for the *Daily Worker,* the American Communist Party newspaper. Eileen LaPierre, a cousin from Concord, remembers Flynn sending a copy to her parents' home during the growing anti-Communist hysteria of the 1940s. Her father told the postman to take it away and not to bring any more.

"She just thought she was giving him something to help him follow her career, but he wasn't interested," LaPierre said. "He told the postman, 'Get rid of it. . . . I don't want anything to do with it.'"

No one in LaPierre's family ever openly discussed Flynn or her career as a Communist. But as a child, she overheard her parents talking about an impending visit by Flynn. Her mother mentioned "Elizabeth" was going to be in town, LaPierre recalled. Her father replied, "Well, we're not going to be here."

The subject was taboo, LaPierre said, not only because Flynn was a Communist, but also because her federal prison term and her street protests were simply not ladylike.

"Women in those days just didn't do things like that," said LaPierre, who is proud of Flynn's legacy. "You just stayed home and took care of the kids and did the housework."

By the early 1950s, Flynn had more to worry about than whether her family was talking to her. With the membership of the Communist Party at about 80,000, the Soviet Union in possession of its own atom bomb, and Korea at war, fear of "subversives" led the U.S. Attorney General and the FBI to prosecute Flynn and other radicals under the Smith Act of 1940.

The Communist Party's doctrine of overthrowing the government was by its nature violent, the government argued. By definition, anyone affiliated with the party embraced and advocated violent revolution, authorities said. In 1951, Flynn was arrested in New York City. She was convicted of conspiracy on evidence that stretched back to her early days as a Wobbly.

When Flynn finished serving her twenty-eight-month federal prison term and her probation, it was July 1957. She was sixty-six years old—but she wasn't finished making headlines. Flynn became the first national chairwoman of the American Communist Party in 1961. Mainstream newspapers were intrigued by the idea that the grandmotherly Flynn, with her thick glasses and her gray hair pulled into a neat bun, was now running the dreaded Communist Party of America. "Mrs. Flynn is obviously a nefarious Communist plot," wrote the *San Francisco Chronicle*. "They want us to think that all they've got left to run the insidious Communist conspiracy is a Sweet Old Lady."

Flynn died in Moscow at age seventy-four, while on a trip to work on her autobiography. The Soviet government gave her a state funeral on Red Square, as they had Haywood and several other American Communist leaders. Soviet Premier Nikita Khrushchev stood as part of the honor guard beside her casket toward the end of the eight-hour vigil.

The next day, thousands of Russians holding large photographs of Flynn filled Red Square to say goodbye, as some of her ashes were buried beneath the Kremlin Wall. Herbert Aptheker, a representative of the American Communists, told the crowd, "The mind rebels and the heart bleeds . . . Comrade Elizabeth Gurley Flynn is dead. Out of the marrow of the American working class she came. . . . Tens of thousands who did not altogether share her views respected and loved her."

Toni Matt

A world-class skier, his legend is tied to one daring run down Mount Washington.

BY JIM GRAHAM

Looking down from the windswept shoulder of Mount Washington's Tuckerman Ravine during winter, you see only a deep, forbidding chasm far below. Filled with snow, it is dotted by tiny dark specks that are actually mature spruce trees and granite boulders the size of houses. The illusion is that you are looking over the lip of an icy, death-hungry cliff dropping straight down some 1,000 feet.

The illusion is damn near the truth.

The drop is skiable, in fact, but it is also impossibly steep, absolutely exposed to the raw, unforgiving elements, and so flat-out frightening that the

Matt, second from left, was a world-class skier made famous by a single, daring run.

New England Ski Museum.

Tuckerman Ravine Headwall is famous as the ultimate extreme ski challenge in the East. For experts, surviving it is a legendary rite of passage and courage.

Nobody has skied it better or more courageously than nineteen-year-old Toni Matt did in 1939.

"He's the only one up to this point to ski it that way—and probably the only person who ever will," said Jeff Leich, director of the New England Ski Museum at Cannon Mountain. "A few other people have schussed it, but Toni is the only one who skied straight over the Headwall already carrying a good amount of speed."

Six decades later, mountain people still talk about what Matt did that April day.

The Headwall drops at a 45° angle for at least 600 feet, but it is near vertical in places. You do not so much ski it as control your rate of free fall. For most mortals, that means carving a series of powerful, quick S-turns during the descent, digging razor-sharp steel ski edges deep into the snow and scraping them broadside against the mountain to slow down. It is, practically speaking, the only safe way to ski the Headwall, if there is such a thing.

Matt would have none of that. He skied it straight, or "schussed" it.

An entrant in the 1939 "American Inferno" ski race, which brought together some of the best skiers in the world, Matt started from Mount Washington's 6,288-foot summit. He was already traveling about 45 mph when he reached the lip of the Headwall less than a mile later. Then he pointed his skis straight down the fall line—and let fly.

He did not slow to survey the route or control his speed. Somehow, he reached the bottom without falling, and kept right on skiing.

"Look, I was young. I was strong," Matt said years later. "And I couldn't turn!"

Below, more than 3,000 spectators watched in awe. A black-and-white film of the event shows Matt, first appearing as a grainy black dot, suddenly blasting over the edge and plunging directly into the void. Legs set wide apart, his body coiled far forward, arms gripping bamboo poles, he appears as a rocketing blur trailed by puffs of snowy contrails. Within seconds, his speeding form grows large in the lens and then disappears just as quickly.

"I won every downhill (race) I entered during the 1938–39 season, and I even won a few slaloms, too. I never practiced that event, though. I just wanted to go fast," Matt wrote in 1964.

A careful analysis of the film shows Matt schussed the Headwall at close to 90 mph.

"I was coming into the sudden drop-off at 40 or 45 miles an hour," Matt wrote. "That's not at all like coming in from a dead standstill. It's more like jumping into a 600 foot deep hole from a speeding car."

He reached the Appalachian Mountain Club's Pinkham Notch Camp—covering 3.8 miles and dropping 4,200 vertical feet—in 6 minutes, 29.2 seconds. The next-closest competitor, national champion Dick Durrance, was a full minute behind.

The top-to-bottom race is no longer held because it is deemed too dangerous. Even today's modern ski gear, a marvel of high-tech materials, computer design, and custom fitting, is suspect in such a place, where notoriously fickle weather can turn the mountain from peaceful to perilous in seconds.

Yet Toni Matt is a legend partly because of the rudimentary equipment he used.

His skis were made entirely of wood, and they stood 7 feet, 6 inches—unimaginably long and unwieldy by today's standards. They had metal edges, attached by hand with tiny screws. His bindings consisted of a small metal toe-piece, with a single steel cable wrapped around the heel and a leather strap securing his instep.

His leather boots? Call them ski boots if you must, but today a pair of $40 bargain-basement hiking boots offers more support.

A display of ski equipment from the period, now shown at the ski museum, leaves modern skiers in awe of the terrain tackled by Matt and his contemporaries, like Durrance, Hannes Schneider, Harold Hillman, and Carroll Reed. In the 1930s, their exploits in the White Mountains were fodder for newsreels shown the world over.

Although it receives snow virtually year-round, Mount Washington is an unlikely place for a ski race. Typical winter days find average wind speeds above hurricane force. Snow blown off the summit and into Tuckerman Ravine can pile up more than 100 feet deep. But the day of the 1939 American Inferno, the third and last top-to-bottom race on the mountain, dawned sunny and relatively calm. Snow conditions were ideal, with plenty of firm, packed powder and corn snow covering the mountain. So after weeks of planning, Matt and forty-one other racers hiked to the summit and huddled around a cantankerous wood stove in the tiny observatory, awaiting the start.

Outside, the wind averaged about 65 mph, and the mercury held steady at zero degrees. Strong gusts blew puffs of smoke back down the chimney.

Matt's feat, in 1939, was still remarkable six decades later.

New England Ski Museum.

Racers started individually, and Matt recalled how the wind pushed him from behind as he braced himself for the start signal.

"It was the only race I remember ever standing in the starting gate, using my poles to hold me in the gate instead of trying to pole out of there," Matt told a reporter in 1989. "The wind was at your back, and all you had to do was lift your poles and away you went."

Watching his progress were twenty ski patrollers, two first aid crews, and emergency workers equipped with five toboggans for carrying out injured racers.

"Matt . . . was beautiful to watch as he shot from sight with tremendous vorlage, taking everything in one straight schuss," wrote Oscar Cyr, who finished twenty-eighth overall, in the June 1939 issue of *Appalachia* magazine.

Matt started third overall. And unlike the previous two racers, whose ski tracks carved wide, graceful turns down the slope, Matt left two grooves running straight down the Headwall. The only turn he made was a shallow arc nearer the summit, allowing him to hit the lip head-on.

"When I left the starting gate, I didn't have any idea that I would dare schuss the Headwall," Matt wrote in *Skiing News*. "I had no idea how much speed I would build up or whether I could stand the strain. I had figured on making at least two or three turns while going over the lip, which, even at slow speeds, feels like going down an elevator shaft."

His increasing speed was a problem. Matt was traveling much faster than he planned—too fast to turn safely at the top of the treacherous ravine and too fast to bail out.

"I knew the lip was fast and treacherous and that if I made a false move I would take a terrible fall. I figured it would be safer actually to run straight than to turn. So on the spur of the moment I decided to go all out."

Matt had never skied Tuckerman Ravine before. Ski experts say that is probably why he was able to schuss it. A sane person, a careful person, or even an expert racer would not have attempted it. Matt himself admitted he was lucky to "be nineteen, stupid, and have strong legs."

But was his once-in-a-lifetime schuss really just a happy misfortune? Or was it part of a grand plan? Pictures of Matt, a renowned skier who had just immigrated from Austria to North Conway to teach skiing with Schneider, invariably reveal a mischievous smile. It is a smile that exudes youthful derring-do, completely at home on a rugged, robust face that knew no fear.

He was already one of the world's best downhill skiers. And while he had not skied the ravine before, he certainly had time to study it up close during the long, slow hike up. If anyone was capable of daring the Headwall, it was Matt.

After clearing the wall, Matt continued down the gentler, but still tricky, Sherburne Trail to Pinkham Notch. Exhausted by the upper mountain, he narrowly missed a tree as he approached the finish line. And when he crossed, he—and anyone who witnessed the spectacle—was breathless.

Matt went on to win the national downhill championship at Mount Hood, Oregon, that season. In 1941, he won the combined downhill and slalom nationals in Aspen.

After gaining citizenship and serving in World War II with the famed ski troops of the 10th Mountain Division, Matt returned to captain the U.S. Ski Team for the 1950 world championships in Aspen. He gave up serious competition in 1953, when he broke his leg during a race in Sun Valley, California. Matt later served as president of the Northern Rocky Mountain Ski Association. In 1967, he was elected to the National Ski Hall of Fame. But his other accomplishments would be forever overshadowed by that legendary schuss over the Headwall.

When Matt died of heart trouble in May 1989, Doug "The Rooster" Campbell, an avid North Conway skier and admirer, got fellow skiers to sign their prayer wishes on a photo of Matt. He hiked into Tuckerman Ravine to pay homage, grabbing a rock from the Headwall and stuffing it into his pack. Returning to the valley, he drove eight hours to the funeral and presented the tokens to Matt's widow, who placed the rocky piece of the Headwall in the casket.

Donald Hall

New Hampshire became home to two poetic voices—his and his wife Jane Kenyon's.

BY MIKE PRIDE

Stone walls emerge from leafy ground
and show their bones. In September a leaf
falls singly down, then a thousand leaves whirl
in frosty air. I am wild
with joy of leaves falling, of stone walls
emerging, of return to the countryside
where I lay as a boy
in the valley of noon heat, in the village
of little sounds; where I floated
out of myself, into the world that lives in the air.

In her old age Kate Wells asked her grandson if, when he was away from it, he called New Hampshire home. The grandson, Donald Hall, had grown up in Connecticut, the son of a suburban dairyman. He had gone to Phillips Exeter, Harvard, and Oxford. He was an English professor at the University of Michigan. Although some part of him had always been "a cellar hole poet," as his friend Robert Bly put it, Hall toiled in the modernist tradition. He chose surrealism and fantasy and wrote a short line with sonic bursts.

When he was away from New Hampshire, Hall did not call it home. Yet when his grandmother asked him if he did, he could not say no. Respectful of her feelings, he evaded the question.

Not long afterward, the grandmother, Kate Wells, who had been born on Eagle Pond Farm in 1878 and lived her life there, died at the age of ninety-seven. Her grandson quit his job as a professor and moved to the farm with Jane Kenyon, his second wife. He had decided to make his living as a writer, but coming to the farm was equally bold of Kenyon. Her challenge was to discover whether she was really a poet.

Today Hall speaks in mystical terms of the move and of the change that came over his poetry at around the same time, as though a force outside him compelled it. "Something had begun to speak that could not speak before," he says. He welcomed this voice—he had little choice—and embraced the mission that came with it.

New Hampshire was a lost dream, Eagle Pond Farm a farm in name only. But the poet could rescue the past—if not the fact, then the myth of it. He could reclaim what the progress of the century had turned under. He could give rural New Hampshire, or at least his youthful memories of it, the permanence of the printed word. He had come to a sacred place that needed preserving, and readers near and far would soon see that he had the art to fulfill the task.

> This year the poems came back, when the leaves fell.
> Kicking the leaves, I heard the leaves tell stories,
> remembering, and therefore looking ahead, and building
> the house of dying. I looked up into the maples
> and found them, the vowels of bright desire.
> I thought they had gone forever . . .

On a fall day, if you listen to a tape of Hall reading the poems of *Kicking the Leaves* as you drive Route 4 north toward his farm, his voice will connect you to a rolling landscape broken only by the ribbon of asphalt beneath your wheels. As you follow the road over the hills, and ride the wave of Hall's easy lines, as you drive between stone walls and past grown-over fields, past swamp maples and weathered barns, cemeteries, a stately white church and a roadside brook, the poems rise right up out of the country, inviting you in.

The poet knew this territory before he moved here. He knew what had happened to it since his boyhood summers at his grandparents' place: modern

Donald Hall gave rural New Hampshire the permanence of the printed word.

Ken Williams/Concord Monitor.

life displacing farm life, the countryside rarely relied upon now for what it could produce but universally admired for its beauty, its remnants, and its ghosts.

The old life is richly imagined in the poems. Through the admiring eyes of the grandson, the reader meets the old farmer, carrying a backless chair for milking or hollering "Ke-bosh! Ke-bosh!" in pursuit of wayward Holsteins. The farmer shoots his decrepit horses behind the ear; their monument, a year later, is a dent in the ground. While exploring Eagle Pond Farm, the new owners discover a twenty-five-year-old quart of maple syrup and taste its sweetness—but they are interlopers, and only figuratively will the sap flow again.

The poet wants you to hear the creaking floorboards and smell the burning maple as you linger around the stove at the corner store, which is far from any corner, and listen to the old people talking. You may wonder at times if a story is a whopper, or too pretty, too perfect, even too sentimental, but if you are drawn to this place, you will be taken with these landscapes painted with words.

> Now the railroad draws
> a line of rust through the valley. Birch, pine, and maple
> lean from cellarholes
> and cover the dead pastures of Ragged Mountain
> except where machines make snow
> and cables pull money up hill, to slide back down.

In hindsight, life seems inevitable. We call it destiny. But when Hall and Kenyon came to Eagle Pond Farm in 1975, there was no guarantee things would turn out as they did.

Kenyon, Hall's former student and his wife of three years, had written only one promising poem—"The Needle." Hall could fall back on readings and the royalties of a popular writing textbook, but these would not add up to a living. He had given up tenure, health insurance, and the other perks of a good job. Now he would have to rely on pen and hustle.

The first year there were moments of panic. Hall wrote reviews, read manuscripts, sought out magazine gigs. *The Ford Times* paid him $500 for a piece on Gertrude Stein and her love of Ford cars. He tried, and initially failed, to write for *Yankee*. He did not know where the money would come from six months from now.

Hall scored a financial breakthrough with *Ox-Cart Man,* a children's book about the annual cycle of a New Hampshire farmer. He heard the story from a relative, Paul Fenton. In frugal Yankee fashion, he also turned the story into a poem in *Kicking the Leaves*. The children's book's first payoff was a modern toilet in the old white farmhouse. Hall and Kenyon named the new bathroom "The Caldecott Room" after the prize the book won.

Kenyon, meanwhile, learned what it meant to be married to poetry. She had grown up in a musical family with varied artistic interests. In Hall's view, to succeed at poetry, she needed to focus on it exclusively. His concern was that when they moved to the farm, his famous work ethic would put her off.

"I worried that I would be a living reproach and she would give up poetry because she was living with this fanatic," he says. "But instead of that she threw herself into the one thing. She developed tunnel vision. Earlier, poetry had been what she loved most, but she had loved other things."

Although Kenyon applied her gift to the same landscape and the same farm that Hall was writing about, she drew from an inner life that was all her own. What made poetry possible, for both of them, was the silence. The two poets lived separate lives in the same house—"the double solitude," he calls it now, or, in a poem, "a government of two."

Kenyon came out with her first book of poems in 1978, the same year Hall published *Kicking the Leaves*, his seventh. They never looked back.

> I grow old, in the house I wanted to grow old in.
> When I am sleepy at night, I daydream only
> of waking the next morning—to walk on the earth of the present
> past noons of birch and sugarbush, past cellarholes,
> many miles to the village of nightfall.

As a book, *Kicking the Leaves* is too transitional in both style and subject to hold together. Hall wrote the title poem while living and teaching in Ann Arbor. "I was full of an inward New Hampshire before I came here," he says. But some of the poems in the book came out of his old life.

The hands of sculptor Winslow Eaves create the likeness of Donald Hall in clay.

Ken Williams/Concord Monitor.

What he found most liberating in his new style was the longer line. "The short-line poems had increasingly excluded the world of reality," he says. Now, instead of striving for the fantastic image, he could admit everyday life into his poems.

Hall is careful to say he is not a New Hampshireman, meaning he is not a native and did not grow up here. But it was in Wilmot that the academic poet became the poet of place. From the moment he and Kenyon moved to the farm, they could have satisfied his grandmother had she been alive to ask her question. When they were away from it, did they call New Hampshire home? Yes, they did.

"When I came here, I was writing for my neighbors in the language of my neighbors," Hall says. "These are not poets—these are not people who read it necessarily, but I was writing in the voice of the landscape. There was a bliss of place, and I was writing out of place—out of it and for it."

In Wilmot, instead of cocktail parties and the other social rituals of academia, Hall and Kenyon connected with community life—the church, volunteer work, the Lions Club.

Hall liked the lack of deference. His literary output counted no more or less than the efforts of those around him. Not long after he arrived, a neighbor from Potter Place mentioned to him that he had seen a story about Hall in the paper. "Oh, I'm everywhere," Hall responded airily. "Just like horseshit," the man replied.

The critics were more respectful than his neighbor of the change that came over Hall's poetry in Wilmot. A standard line in the reviews of *Kicking the Leaves* and the books that followed was that Hall had been writing poems for years—some good, some bad—but had not really found himself until he moved with Kenyon to the ancestral farm in New Hampshire.

> Old roses survive
> winter drifts, the melt in April, the August
> parch,
>   and men and women
> who sniffed roses in spring and called them pretty
> as we call them now,
>   strolling beside the barn
> on a day that perishes . . .

Donald Hall had always been a poet of loss. At the farm he harvested sounds from the silence. He wrote poems about barnyard animals, all gone. He restored life to characters who had long since been reduced to names and dates carved on slate and granite. Writing out of the place he now called home, he put the old world beside the new, lost heifers beside Monday night football.

Unfortunately, although loss is universal, and thus a province of poets, it is not merely a general condition. It is personal and particular, and it comes un-invited and unexpected.

In 1995, after a hard fight with leukemia, Kenyon died at the age of forty-seven. Hall still weeps over the trick time played on them. He had been forty-seven when they came to live on the farm, and that is when the critics say he began to produce his best work. By the time her terminal illness struck, Kenyon had mastered the short lyric and won acclaim, but her best years as a poet, and their best years together, might have lain in the future.

Kenyon died in April, the cruelest month. T. S. Eliot called it that because while nature seems to renew itself in April, people do not; their passage from birth to death is linear and irreversible.

Spring's counterpart on the calendar is autumn, when, with one last brilliant stand and a rustle underfoot, nature seems to die. Hall set the title poem of *Kicking the Leaves* in autumn, the season in which it occurred to the happy couple that they might make their life together on Eagle Pond Farm. Grief interrupted their joy, but the poem is all affirming.

> I see the tall bare maple trunks and branches, the oak
> with its few brown weathery remnant leaves,
> and the spruce trees, holding their green.
> Now I leap and fall, exultant, recovering
> from death, on account of death, in accord with the dead,
> the smell and taste of leaves again,
> and the pleasure, the only long pleasure, of taking a place
> in the story of leaves.

(The poems excerpted in this story come from *Kicking the Leaves*. They are quoted in this order: "Stone Walls," "Kicking the Leaves," "The Black-Faced Sheep," "Stone Walls," "Old Roses," and "Kicking the Leaves.")

John Winant

He led New Hampshire through the Depression.

BY ANNMARIE TIMMINS

B y the time the stock market crashed in 1929, New Hampshire had already glimpsed the crisis to come. Half the state's farms had closed, mill owners had cut wages, and nearly every fifth factory worker was out of a job. Never before had New Hampshire needed a governor like John Gilbert Winant.

He was guided by his instincts, not his party's edicts, and embraced valuable Democratic programs when his Republican colleagues wouldn't. The legendary generosity he had for friends extended to strangers: The Concord police were under orders during the Depression to give breakfast to the transients

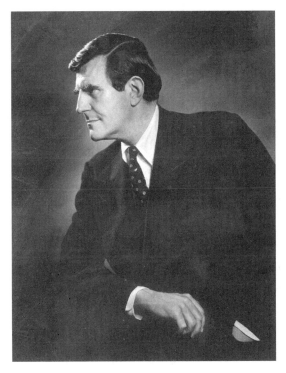

John Winant saw New Hampshire through the Depression.

who wandered in from the cold and to bill Winant personally for the food. He took people's troubles to heart, trying to find them jobs or paying their children's college expenses.

"His administration was marked by a sincere and vigorous effort to serve the interest of the state without respect to who might have been pleased or displeased," Rep. Laurence Whittemore told the legislature in 1951 when Winant's portrait was hung in the State House.

It took Winant many tries to find support for his progressive ideas. Unlike most of his contemporaries, Winant looked on despair and economic decline and saw a responsibility and role for government. He enacted old-age assistance, a minimum wage, emergency relief, and prevention of foreclosures on farms and factory workers' homes. He was less successful in abolishing capital punishment and securing a 48-hour work week for women and children.

His work in New Hampshire caught the attention of Franklin Roosevelt, who made him the nation's first commissioner of Social Security. (It is Winant's doing that got New Hampshire-born residents the first batch of Social Security numbers, 000, 001, or 002.) Roosevelt later named him ambassador to Great Britain, a position he held during World War II.

But it was during the Depression, some say, that Winant showed the most imagination.

He shifted the cost of highway construction, which was necessary to encourage industry to come to New Hampshire, from communities to the state. He relieved municipalities of half of their welfare expenses by looking to Roosevelt's New Deal programs.

As a result, New Hampshire's cities and towns stayed afloat, and people had work longer than they otherwise would have. And taxpayers actually got a small break.

Winant also assumed a greater personal responsibility for the people he served than any governor before or since. For his predecessors, the job had been part-time. Winant typically stayed long after he had sent his staff home. There are stories of Winant arriving at work to find jobless people standing outside the State House, warming themselves in the morning sun. By the time he got to his desk, Winant had emptied his pockets of coins into the hands of the unemployed. Inside, the unfortunate formed a line outside Winant's office. The governor insisted on seeing them all.

Allen Lewis, for instance, graduated from the University of New Hampshire in 1931 with a degree in engineering and little hope of finding work. Lewis, who lived in Contoocook, stood in that line one day and came home with a job—counting cars for the highway department.

"It was the only job he had at the time," said Lewis's widow, Mary Ann. "(My husband) eventually became an engineer with the highway department, and Governor Winant did contact him many times (over the years) to see how he was doing and whether he had any problems. He did that for many employees."

Winant's affection for New Hampshire began at age fourteen, when he came to St. Paul's School in Concord. Twelve years later, he made his first run for elected office. At thirty-five, he became the state's youngest governor.

From his thirty years of public service, Winant left an example some historians say hasn't been matched. In his 1968 biography, *He Walked Alone,* Bernard Bellush called Winant the most indefatigable governor of the twentieth century.

"He was out ahead of the trend," suggesting government had a place in people's lives, said Charles Clark, a retired professor of history at the University of New Hampshire. "It would be pretty hard to come up with people who would be similar today. For one thing very few people have the integrity he had." Winant's earliest campaign flier said he had "no greater ambition in life than to be useful to my fellowman." What he didn't tell voters was that he had believed that long before he hit the campaign trail.

Winant wasn't much of a scholar, at St. Paul's or at Princeton, where he didn't graduate. He loved to read and was influenced by books about Abraham Lincoln, whom he quoted throughout his life, and the bleak lives described by Charles Dickens. (It's thanks to Winant that the State House has a portrait of Lincoln; he paid for it with coins donated by schoolchildren.)

Winant returned to St. Paul's to teach history. As he would later as a legislator, he welcomed students to his office after class to continue discussions. He persuaded students and administrators to abolish secret societies on campus and open the school's government to more people.

Winant won a seat in the House at age twenty-eight and wasted no time proposing sweeping reform. He supported a shorter work week for women and children and better health and educational opportunities for everyone. He lost, initially, but wasn't discouraged. "Neither apathy nor outright hostility on the part of party leaders dissuaded him from pressing for social welfare goals," Bellush wrote.

Winant served his first term as governor in 1924, winning on a platform of reform before it was popular. Especially at first, he struggled through speeches and wasn't talented at explaining himself. Strangely, that difficulty won Winant sympathy.

Frederic Upton, a retired lawyer who lives in Contoocook, remembers how difficult it was for Winant to deliver a speech. "There would be these long, embarrassing pauses where he'd be groping for words, for just the right word, and people would want to shout out to him, but they never did," Upton said. "But he projected great sincerity, and that was what elected him. If we had had television in those times, he wouldn't have been a star."

Winant lost his bid for reelection because he didn't campaign, assuming his work as governor would win him a second term. He returned to office in 1930, aware the state's economy was in decline but determined not to look to the federal government for help. "We are a small state," he said, "but we intend to take care of our own." A year later, he changed his mind. Unemployment had doubled to twenty-six percent. Cities and towns were being asked for thousands more dollars for relief, from both the unemployed and workers who couldn't earn enough to feed their families.

Winant, who had initially opposed programs that created work as a way to dispense relief, used state money to put men to work building highways. He called on industry to stop cutting wages. He arranged for state assistance to keep one factory open so it could pay its local taxes and keep people working. He asked another to delay its closing until April, when the days were "longer and brighter," according to historians Kathryn Grover and Mary Rose Boswell in a book about the period.

Before Roosevelt came out with the New Deal, Winant lobbied for what he called the New Hampshire Plan. On newsreels shown to moviegoers across the country, Winant suggested a nationwide flexible work week. Those with jobs would cut their work week from six to four days and give their two remaining days to the unemployed. The plan wouldn't add to operating expenses, he argued, and would put more people to work.

His proposal wasn't in line with President Herbert Hoover's policies encouraging states to manage their own financial problems and failed. But Winant had begun to see the Depression as a national problem and, as a result, was among the first to sign on to Roosevelt's New Deal programs in 1933. "Relief giving," Winant told a Manchester Rotary group in 1933, "must be divorced from politics."

With federal and state money, Winant saved and even strengthened the state's strongest money-making operations: industry, agriculture, and recreation. He helped farmers better market their milk and used work relief programs to improve rural roads, add ski trails, build parks and bathing houses, and cut new trails in the national forests. "He should be remembered as someone who put principle above politics," said Clark, the history professor. "He left a legacy of political virtue that really ought to be studied."

On a personal note, Winant was feeling the effects of the Depression at home. By the mid-1930s, he did not have the income to justify keeping his personal staff, which included nurses, a maid, cook, butler, chauffeur, finance secretary, groundskeepers, and staff for his wife's dog kennels. At the same time, he refused to lay any of them off because he didn't want to contribute to unemployment. He got rid of his yacht instead.

Any person as public as Winant is survived by stories. But they are seldom recalled with such admiration and awe.

When Winant headed to war in 1917, he left a friend money and instructions to take care of his business affairs. Winant's greatest expense was the milk he'd been buying for the needy people in Concord.

During a campaign stop at a home for delinquent boys, one of the boys, who was very sick, admired the governor's fur coat. Winant sent him one of his own the following Christmas.

On the way to the train station in Concord, Winant ran into a custodian he knew at St. Paul's and learned she was out of a job and caring for sick kids at home. He gave her the cash in his pocket and then had to borrow money for his train fare.

Winant came from a well-to-do family but did not earn much. The scrutiny and care Winant took with the state's money—it was he who first ordered a proper accounting of state revenue—did not extend to his own finances. By 1935, Winant had either lost his money in the stock market or given it away. He was bankrupt the rest of his life.

Winant came back from England in 1946 to rest, finish his memoir, and return to private life. But according to Bellush's biography, Winant was sick and exhausted and had begun drinking. He had completed one volume of his memoirs but was tormented, knowing he owed his publisher two more.

Rob Bass, an attorney whose father, former governor Robert Bass, was close to Winant, recalls a visit the two made to Winant's Pleasant Street home. During the conversation, Winant said he'd begun to doubt his recommendations as ambassador to cooperate with Russia during postwar talks.

"He was downcast and gloomy, and he was beginning to realize, I think, that he had been wrong," Bass said. "He was gloomy about how things would go in Western Europe. He felt beleaguered."

On November 3, 1947, Winant left his supper untouched, took something for a headache, and went into what had been his son's bedroom. He knelt on the floor and shot himself in the head.

His funeral two days later was attended by dignitaries and regular folks. Mary Ann Lewis, whose husband had gone to Winant in 1931 in search of a job, remembers tears coming to her husband's eyes when he got the news. From London, Winston Churchill sent four dozen yellow roses. The king and queen sent their condolences by telegram.

At Winant's funeral, Bishop John Dallas offered a brief eulogy, despite the Episcopal tradition against it.

"Today, we thank Thee for our neighbor and friend, John, for his greatheartedness and for his broken-heartedness," Dallas said. "We praise Thee that one so near to us hast shown us the depths of the needs of the world and for his acts of generosity to men here at home."

Jeanne Shaheen

She was New Hampshire's first woman governor.

Had Jeanne Shaheen been elected in quieter times, her tenure might have been remembered chiefly for its firsts: first woman governor, first Democratic governor in a generation (and only the fourth of the twentieth century), first governor to name a woman to the Supreme Court. She erased the state's anti-abortion laws, encouraged public kindergarten, and signed into law the Martin Luther King Day holiday.

Governors, however, only control so much of the news. And when Shaheen was elected in 1996, she had no idea her term would be dominated by a seemingly endless fight over how to finance public schools.

The governor, like Republican governors before her, took the state's anti-broad-based tax pledge in two elections, thwarting tax reform efforts in the legislature and dividing members of her party. "I still think that was the right thing to do," Shaheen said in 1999. "But education tax reform is obvi-

Jeanne Shaheen was New Hampshire's first female governor.

Dan Habib/Concord Monitor.

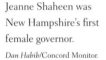

ously a very contentious issue, and it's not something that's going to get solved overnight."

And so, state politics in the twentieth century ended as it began: with concern over the quality of New Hampshire's schools and controversy over how to pay for them.

Jeanne Shaheen

Paul Bofinger and Tad Comstock

They helped forge a compromise to protect Franconia Notch.

otorists driving through Franconia Notch at the end of the twentieth century were universally impressed by the natural beauty: Cannon Mountain, Profile Lake, the Old Man of the Mountain. Taken for granted was the road beneath their wheels, but it was equally impressive: The twelve-mile stretch of Interstate 93 was the result of a dramatic thirty-year fight pitting powerful highway interests against environmentalists. In the end, both sides believed they had won.

At the center of the controversy were old-school engineers like Tad Comstock, head of the Federal Highway Administration for New Hampshire, and

Paul Bofinger, 1996.

Courtesy of Pat Wells.

conservationists like Paul Bofinger, president of the Society for the Protection of New Hampshire Forests.

"This was a boom period, a completely different climate than today, and we thought it was pure foolishness not to build a proper highway," Comstock said in 1999. "I love the Old Man, but the engineers were skilled and it was possible to build the highway the right way."

Bofinger believed blasting a major highway through a narrow, landslide-prone passage threatened the Old Man, who had had major surgeries to hold together the jagged rocks that form his face. "The Old Man was everyone's baby," said Bofinger. "Preserving him inspired a national effort."

The result: plans, studies, a lawsuit, and ultimately a simple solution—the scaled back two-lane parkway that exists today, under the safe gaze of the Old Man.

Laura LeCain

She lived through the Spanish flu of 1918.

Laura LeCain of Concord nearly bled to death at the age of fifteen. As it turns out, she was one of the lucky ones.

To live in New Hampshire in 1918 was to live through the Spanish flu, a fierce, fast-moving epidemic that killed 3,000 people in the state and up to 40 million people across the globe. It lasted from March 1918 to the spring of 1919 and brought with it fever, headaches, and, in the most serious cases, a lethal pneumonia. When it turned, the virus shredded its victims' lungs. Organs hemorrhaged and lungs filled up with bloody fluid. The victims drowned inside; many died within forty-eight hours of the flu's first symptoms appearing.

Laura LeCain, in 1999, at age 96.

Andrea Bruce/Concord Monitor.

In New Hampshire, the flu had most likely arrived from Camp Devens in Massachusetts, with soldiers from the Boston shipyards after months of worldwide travel. In LeCain's hometown, schools and churches shut down. Labor was scarce. Doctors and nurses got sick. The fact that LeCain didn't infect her whole family was unusual. Nonetheless, there wasn't much they could do to ease her affliction.

Her treatment? Chicken soup. "That's all they could do for you then," LeCain said in 1999. "We didn't have any special medicine."

Tomie dePaola

He brought dozens of children's books to life.

To call Tomie dePaola prolific is an understatement. By the end of the century he had written eighty-seven children's stories and illustrated 118 others. And he was still going strong.

DePaola, who lives in New London, has sold more than 5 million kids' books in all, including such classics as *Strega Nona* and *Nana Upstairs & Nana Downstairs*. He's won nearly every major honor in the world of children's literature, and, more important, has legions of loyal fans among the young and nearly young alike.

What's so good about his books? His themes are complicated but his writing is simple. He's funny. He's respectful of his readers. His drawings are easily

DePaola is among the world's most prolific children's authors.

Ken Williams/Concord Monitor.

recognizable. And he remembers details of his childhood so keenly that kids easily identify with him.

"My job is to say to children, 'Look, life is wonderful. Life is funny. Your life is important,'" dePaola said in 1999. "'I'm telling you stories about my life. You have stories about your own life. You're just as important a person as I am.'"

Tomie dePaola

Bob Morrell

The founder of Story Land was a tourism guru.

BY AARON BOWDEN

Winter 1953. Walt Disney was preparing to open a new kind of business in California.

At roughly the same time in Glen, New Hampshire, Bob Morrell was building a village of colorful little houses in his backyard. People in the White Mountains thought he might be going crazy. There wasn't even a word yet to describe what Morrell was proposing.

He was calling it Story Town.

"I remember him telling me that people would pull off the road and say, 'Boy I'd like to buy one of those fancy doghouses,'" longtime friend Jack Mahaney said.

Robert and Ruth Morrell in a 1923 Maxim fire truck, which became part of the first ride at their theme park.
Courtesy of Story Land.

Today those fancy doghouses mark the entranceway to the biggest tourist attraction in northern New Hampshire. Unique as its creator, Story Land—as it's been known since 1955—is a family theme park with rides and attractions based on classic children's stories. And true to Morrell's life philosophy, Story Land remains unfinished, always suggesting new projects and more novel attractions, ever expanding, refusing to stand pat.

In 1959, Morrell went out on a limb and spent almost the entire previous year's profit on a little steam train. Today, it is joined by two other trains as part of "The Huff, Puff, and Whistle Railroad."

"That little train is a great symbol of his refusal to sit still," said his son, Stoney Morrell. "He just took a chance and pushed ahead."

Morrell applied that strategy to everything he did: running a business, raising a family, getting involved in politics, serving the community. "Don't sit still," his gut kept telling him. "Listen to people, work hard, and don't be afraid to fail." Simple, but effective.

When he died in 1998, Bob Morrell might have been the most revered person in North Conway. "I think he's one of the greatest citizens New Hampshire has ever produced," former governor Hugh Gregg said.

Morrell's influence on the White Mountain region is difficult to quantify. Story Land and Heritage New Hampshire—the interactive museum of New Hampshire history he built in 1976—are just his most visible successes. More important, he woke the White Mountains up to their potential as a tourist economy. He championed small businesses and led the effort to unify all the White Mountains attractions. Morrell helped convince well-established businesses they'd do better to sell the whole region, not just its disparate parts.

"Before, there would be a ski resort next to a lodge, and nobody talked with each other," White Mountains Attraction Association President Dick Hamilton said. "Bob would say that whenever a tourism dollar is spent in the White Mountains, all the attractions benefit."

Tents that spray a refreshing mist on visitors are situated throughout Story Land.

Robin Shotola/Concord Monitor.

The other attractions listened up. Story Land had only been around a couple of years, but Bob Morrell's reputation was growing.

Morrell was born in Manchester and moved to North Conway when he was ten. His father was a railroad man, and his mother built and ran the Pine Hill Cabin lodge in North Conway. At his mother's urging, he went to the Bay Path Institute in Springfield, Massachusetts, to study business. His letters home reflected his lack of interest in school. He saved any enthusiasm for the harvesting work he was doing in a local cranberry bog and the skiing he'd do in the winter.

On February 1, 1942, he went to Cannon Mountain with his buddies for one last hurrah. The next day, they all took a train to Boston and enlisted. A lot of them, Morrell included, ended up as ski troops in the 10th Mountain Division. He was stationed in Wisconsin and Canada before coming home in 1944, having avoided the carnage of World War II.

He felt lucky. Losing two years of his life to the war helped him realize he didn't have any time to waste. Morrell quickly proposed to a local girl who had worked at his mother's lodge. Practical-minded and smart, Ruth Morrell would play a major role in the future success of Story Land.

The Morrells moved to Manchester around 1945. Morrell attempted to parlay his business education into a job as an insurance salesman. "I nearly starved," Morrell once said.

Then, in 1947, his daughter Nancy was born. Morrell gave up the insurance business to open the East Slope Ice Cream Company in North Conway. The ice cream stand fared reasonably well, and Morrell got a supplementary job as a salesman at the Carroll Reed ski shop. He watched the way Reed ran his business and learned the customer service skills he would later perfect at Story Land.

In 1950 the Morrell's life took what he called a "serendipitous" detour. He was called back into the service. The Korean War was going strong, and this time he'd be stationed in Baumholder, Germany, with the Quartermaster Corps. The Morrells spent the next three years in military housing, while the Quartermaster Corps helped rebuild Germany.

Then one day, the idea for Story Land came knocking at their door. An old woman named Edith Von Arps was going door-to-door selling hand-made dolls. The couple struck up a friendship and bought more than twenty-five dolls. When Von Arps suggested Americans might enjoy a small village created around her dolls, the Morrells listened.

The dolls wouldn't be enough, they decided, but if they added a few animals, some land, and a fairy-tale theme, it might be a viable business. Morrell had already sold the ice cream stand. When his family returned home, he used the money to buy a piece of land in Glen.

"Glen was not any kind of crossroads," Stoney Morrell said. "And in 1954 no one had a frame of reference for anything like this. Disneyland was being built at the same time, but information wasn't as freely dispersed then and not many people in New Hampshire knew about it."

Morrell's timing was perfect. Anywhere could be a crossroads with the new interstate highway system, and tourism was about to explode. Disney built his park on an orange grove and spent $17 million. Morrell built Story Land on what he referred to as "a wide spot in the road" and wouldn't admit how much money he spent. "It was the most pathetic presentation you can imagine," he once said.

He built it himself, with loaned bulldozers and lumber purchased on credit. He was in his backyard building fancy doghouses in the dead of the New Hampshire winter.

With not much more than three little pigs, a billy goat's gruff, and Little Miss Muffet's spider, Morrell opened for business. He charged eighty-five cents and made $237 the first day.

With Ruth taking care of the books and Bob coming up with new ideas, Story Land was off and running. They reinvested everything they made, working hurriedly through the snowfalls to have new attractions ready by Memorial Day.

Then in 1958, there was a recession. Business fell off by 38 percent from the previous year. It was the first downturn. "Dad would say that 1958 turned him into a fiscal conservative," Stoney Morrell said.

The ski resorts also felt the crunch that year. Morrell took a trip to Disneyland to check out the competition. When he got back to Glen, he knew all the White Mountain attractions needed to get organized if they were going to survive.

He got two of the oldest attractions, the Cog Railway and the Skimobile at Mount Cranmore, to sit down together and talk about tourism. Out of their meeting came the White Mountain Attractions Association, with Bob Morrell—then the little guy on the block—as chairman.

The ten-member association dispatched a guy with a station wagon to disperse 100,000 vacation guides extolling the beauty of the White Mountains. Morrell helped make a promotional film about the region and had it shown in first-run theaters.

Grownups and kids alike ride the teacups at Story Land.

Robin Shotola/Concord Monitor.

"The promotional material never mentioned any single attraction by name," said current White Mountain Attractions Association chairman Dick Hamilton. "That was pretty radical at the time. They sold the region as a whole."

It's not radical anymore. By 1999, the association was printing 1.4 million maps and 650,000 travel guides for the White Mountains.

Cooperating was a boon to all the businesses and helped solidify Story Land's place in the region. By 1960, business had returned to a pattern of steady growth. It was hard to call Story Land a small business anymore, but Morrell never forgot that was where it had started.

When the tourist industry was having trouble financing itself, he became chairman of the White Mountain National Bank in North Conway with a goal of helping seasonal attractions survive.

"He became the entrepreneur you looked up to here in the valley," said Chuck Henderson, head of Malden Polartec Fleece Outerwear. "A word of encouragement from somebody like him could keep you in business an extra year."

Morrell was also fond of giving people their first jobs. Henderson's sister worked at Story Land one year, rotating days of being Cinderella and cleaning toilets.

Jack Mahaney's first stint with Story Land was in the early days. He married the Cinderella they had back then. Years later, a doctor told Mahaney his legs couldn't stand another year as an automobile mechanic. He didn't know what to do. Morrell called him as soon as he heard and offered him a job. Today Mahaney is Story Land's public relations man.

David Dorsett's first job was also at Story Land—at a time when his cerebral palsy made it nearly impossible for him to work anywhere else. He had recently graduated from the Crotched Mountain Rehabilitation Center. Story Land was one of the largest donors to that facility.

"If Bob hadn't given me a job, I don't know if I'd be able to have done what I did in my life," Dorsett said. "He was like a father to me."

In his later years, Morrell reluctantly began to turn the family business over to Stoney. When Ruth died in 1990, the transition was hastened. In 1991 he remarried. Miriam Andrews was a widow, and Morrell had served with her late husband in the 10th Mountain Division. "He traveled a lot," Stoney Morrell said, "but he was always tethered to Story Land, keeping both eyes open for new ideas."

Those who knew him say that was his knack—he listened to people, asked the right questions, and then really listened.

He had always come home angry over something someone said at church, Miriam Morrell said. "I'd ask him, 'Why didn't you say something Bob?'" Miriam said. "He'd say, 'Well I wanted to listen to what they had to say.'"

That's how he kept innovating. He listened. That and he wouldn't get complacent. He wouldn't sit still. He'd rush to get one project done so he could get on to the next bigger one.

Even from beyond the grave he has left specifications for the next big project. In 1991 he bought a 1935 diesel-electric train called the *Flying Yankee*. It was operated by the Boston & Maine Railroad in New Hampshire for twenty-two years. In 1993 he sold the train to the state for $1. His will set aside $1.8 million to create a nonprofit foundation to raise money to restore the train. Morrell wanted it to travel outside the state's borders as an ambassador for New Hampshire.

"He was a great promoter," Hugh Gregg said. "A loving man with more ideas than anyone I've ever known."

Not only that, but he also enjoyed it. "Almost everyone has a latent desire to strike out and do something different, something fun, something creative, something unique," Bob Morrell once said. "Boundless opportunities lie ahead. . . . I told you, it is just having fun while making a living."

Jonathan Daniels

When Southern blacks fought for civil rights, he went to help. It cost him his life.

BY MARY ALLEN

It was hot. The civil rights workers—two young black women, a white Catholic priest, and a white Episcopalian seminarian—had just been released from jail after being held six days for their part in a voter registration drive. The heat of that August day scorched the streets of Hayneville, Alabama, and the foursome walked to Varner's Cash Store to buy Cokes.

Before they made it through the door, an angry white man confronted them. He swore, leveled a twelve-gauge shotgun at one of the women, and ordered them off the store steps. Jonathan Daniels, a twenty-six-year-old from Keene just months shy of his ordination, didn't hesitate. He pushed seventeen-

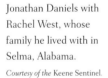

Jonathan Daniels with Rachel West, whose family he lived with in Selma, Alabama.

Courtesy of the Keene Sentinel.

year-old Ruby Sales to the ground, and the shotgun blast meant for her hit him in the stomach. The priest, Richard Morrisroe, grabbed the other girl and turned to run. A second shot hit him in the back.

When it was over, Daniels was dead. Morrisroe lay bleeding on the hot pavement for more than an hour before help arrived. It would take him years to recover and walk without aid.

Thomas Coleman, a part-time deputy sheriff, was charged with manslaughter in Daniels's death. An Alabama jury took just twenty minutes to acquit him. Coleman said he saw a knife, a claim black eyewitnesses disputed and white eyewitnesses supported. Later, a grand jury cleared him of any charges in Morrisroe's shooting.

Daniels died August 20, 1965, just fourteen days after President Lyndon Johnson signed the federal Voting Rights Act into law. It also was Connie Daniels's birthday. The day after her son was killed, a card arrived at her home in Keene. It had been mailed from the Lowndes County jail.

In the years since Daniels's death, much has changed in the way Americans view racial tensions and solutions. In part, Daniels's death brought the social turmoil of the 1960s home to New Hampshire, a state that had been little touched by that debate—until then.

Daniels was the only New Hampshireman killed during the civil rights movement in the South. His death has had a quiet, lasting effect on those who knew him, the Episcopal Church, the city of Keene, and even those who sit in the legislature. The story of Jonathan Daniels has filtered slowly, a drop at a time, into the state's consciousness.

Jonathan Daniels was the only son of Philip and Constance Daniels. His

Ruby Sales, the young woman whose life Daniels saved, followed in his footsteps, completing her divinity degree at the Episcopal Theology Seminary in Cambridge, Massachusetts, in 1998.
Courtesy of the Keene Sentinel.

father was a well-loved family doctor. Connie Daniels spent her time raising the couple's two children, Jonathan and Emily. The family lived in a white clapboard home on the corner of Summer and School streets.

At Keene High School, Daniels is remembered for being smart, not too good at sports, and a lover of life. He was high-spirited and willing to take risks but also intent on pleasing his parents.

"He was a fine fellow—enthusiastic, energetic, concerned for others," said the Rev. Chandler McCarty, former pastor of St. James Episcopal Church in Keene.

In most ways he was a typical kid. He had a girlfriend and loved fast cars. But a couple of things stood out, according to filmmaker Larry Benaquist, who created a documentary about Daniels's life. In the margins of a school notebook given to Benaquist were doodles drawn by Daniels at age nine or ten. The sketches were of tiny crosses, a crucified Christ, and a figure of a priest. And at fifteen, Daniels wrote a short story for the high school literary magazine. In it, two high school sweethearts grow into adult lives that are worlds apart. The boy has become a priest; the girl is a gangster's moll. In a classic film-noir ending, the two are on the same rain-swept street when the cops corner the gangster's mob. The priest hears her familiar voice coming from an alley, pulls his raincoat collar over his white clerical collar, and rushes into the fray shouting "You'll never take me alive." He is mistaken for the gangster and killed in a hail of bullets. She escapes.

"Did he have a predisposition for sacrifice?" Benaquist wonders. "I don't know, but it makes you stop and think."

A love of God and a willingness to serve soon became the focal points of Daniels's life. At seventeen, he left his family's Congregational faith to be baptized at St. James Episcopal. After graduating near the top of his high school class, he surprised friends by choosing Virginia Military Institute.

Some speculated that Daniels craved the discipline to curb his wilder tendencies. It seemed to work. He graduated as class valedictorian in 1961. That fall, Daniels enrolled at Harvard University to study English. But that track would lead to life as an English professor, he realized, and it didn't feel right.

Next stop: the Episcopal Theological School in Cambridge, Massachusetts, where he worked with an inner-city church in Providence. He embraced the experience, especially working with teenagers.

But the world was changing. In the spring of 1965, violence erupted in the South. The Rev. Martin Luther King Jr. called on activists from the North to join the blacks fighting for their rights in the South. Sit-ins, protests, and marches were daily events and the violence grew. Friends remember watching the evening newscasts from Selma and Montgomery with Daniels. When he saw demonstrators attacked by the police with clubs and dogs, he wanted to leave for Alabama immediately.

Some students, including Judith Upham, now a minister in Syracuse, New York, joined the trip to Selma. Their first night in Alabama was spent sleeping on the floor of King's office in Montgomery. Daniels and Upham tried to attend services at a local Episcopal church, but they were rebuffed because they invited several young black children to go with them.

The more Daniels saw injustice, the more he was determined to stay. The students flew back to Cambridge and begged the dean of the seminary to allow them to spend the rest of the semester in Alabama. Daniels, Upham, and the others spent about ten weeks—from March through May 1965—in Selma. They handed out relief supplies, worked with teenagers, and wrote letters telling others of the stark reality of the civil rights struggle.

They were hated by the whites and often feared by the blacks they were trying to help. Their cars were followed or stoned, including the powerful red Plymouth Fury that Daniels bought in Alabama, figuring it could outrun the pickup trucks that chased them at night.

In letters home, it was clear that Daniels knew his work was dangerous, but he was optimistic and driven by a higher calling. In a letter to a friend dated May 1, 1965, Daniels wrote:

> You should have prepared, in advance, both physically and spiritually, for the possibility of tear gas, arrest, and I suppose, even for death, though that's a bit unlikely. It is true abstractly . . . that no white outsider here is entirely safe and I feel very strongly that one should make a realistic estimate of what that means. I see this because I decided a long time ago that the Holy Spirit had brought me here, that I believe very firmly in the gospel and its faith, that my life is not my own but His—which means that before anything else, I am a servant of Christ . . . and that consequently the possibility of death, whether immediate or remote, cannot be a deciding factor for me.

Hundreds filed past the casket that held Daniels's wrecked body as he lay in state in St. James church in Keene. Telegrams poured in. President Johnson

Connie Daniels still lives in Keene, where her son Jonathan's life and death are studied by schoolchildren.
Courtesy of the Keene Sentinel.

wired condolences to Connie Daniels. Episcopal clergy and civil rights leaders from all over the country attended his funeral.

In the weeks that followed, the Southern press reported that many Alabama whites considered the killing justified. This was a Southern struggle, they argued, and outsiders were twentieth-century carpetbaggers. Northern papers defended the civil rights movement and decried the Southern justice that allowed Coleman to walk away free. Branches of the Episcopal Church, meanwhile, were at each other's throats: Northerners were furious at the Alabama diocese, and especially St. Paul's Episcopal Church in Selma, for refusing to hold a memorial service for Daniels.

That could have been the end of it, but Daniels was not easily forgotten.

For starters, Ruby Sales, the young woman whom Daniels pushed out of harm's way, ended up following in his footsteps. The daughter of three generations of Southern Baptist ministers, Sales completed her divinity degree at the Episcopal Theology Seminary in Cambridge in 1998.

In Selma, Sales's brother was elected mayor. And the city recently opened a community development center that bears Jonathan Daniels's name.

Sales came to Keene in August 1997 to honor him during a service at St. James Episcopal Church. "Truth, crushed to the ground, will rise up again," she said in her sermon.

Days later, Sales and Richard Morrisroe were reunited in Hayneville, where 200 blacks and twenty whites had gathered to unveil a monument to Daniels's memory. The crowd included John Hulett, who had just finished serving as Lowndes County's first black sheriff.

At the end of the dedication the crowd walked 400 feet to the spot where Daniels died. Their voices joined in singing "We Shall Overcome."

Benaquist, the filmmaker, was there that day too, trying, as he had been for ten years, to answer this question: How was it that a young white man from Keene had found himself in the midst of the civil rights movement of the 1960s? He thinks he is closer to the answer now.

"His was an absolute certainty that the value of an individual act would make the world a better place," Benaquist says.

Benaquist and his partner William Sullivan labored for ten years on the film. Friends and family members lent the filmmakers Daniels's letters, journals, stories, and drawings. His life was also chronicled in a book, *Outside Agitator: Jon Daniels and the Civil Right Movement in Alabama,* by Charles W. Eagles.

"He left a lot of paper and it became our task to piece the puzzle together," Benaquist said.

Dealing with Daniels's death has also been a healing process for the Episcopal Church, where his name is forever linked to Martin Luther King's in the *Memorial Book of Heroes and Martyrs.* They are the only Americans listed.

In 1991, Daniels's name was added to the church's Calendar of Lesser Feast and Fasts. In 1994, the Episcopal Church of the United States designated August 14, the date he was jailed in Hayneville, as a feast day in his memory.

In Daniels's hometown, city leaders built the Jonathan Daniels Elementary School a few years after his death. As part of an annual memorial celebration, students act out a play about Daniels's life. Elsewhere in the city, events honoring him are coordinated by a committee on diversity that also bears his name.

And while Daniels is best known in Keene, his name was regularly invoked on the floor of the Legislature in Concord during the 1980s and 1990s. As the state struggled with the question of whether to honor Martin Luther King with a holiday, some legislators wondered whether Daniels deserved one too. But those closest to the Danielses believe he would have wanted King's memory honored, not his.

"King was the catalyst," said Benaquist. "Jonathan Daniels was the witness, the social conscience."

George Hause

*He came within hours of being executed, a symbol of the state's ambivalence
over capital punishment.*

BY ANNMARIE TIMMINS

George Hause came so close to the hangman's noose in 1925 that the
men chosen to witness his execution had their engraved invitations
in hand.

"(You) are invited to attend the execution of George Hause at the State
Prison at Concord, N.H," read the cards sent to the police and newspaper-
men. Court appeals had failed. A hangman was hired, the rope stretched, and
a black hood for Hause's head ordered.

Then, just hours before he was to hang for the beating death of Moses

Hause barely escaped the
hangman's noose.

Concord Monitor.

Goldberg, Gov. John Winant spared Hause the noose and gave him life in prison instead. Hause, twenty-five, collapsed at the news, then asked to be baptized.

"After a most careful investigation," Winant told reporters, "the governor and council do not believe it would react to decrease crime or be good public policy to inflict the extreme penalty in this case."

Few besides Goldberg's family disagreed.

People from all over the state—some familiar with the case, others simply on principle—had written to the governor and Executive Council urging them to commute Hause's sentence. The Merrimack County sheriff and the prison warden said they were relieved Winant had listened. So were the other inmates.

"When (Charles) Clarke entered the prison dormitories and announced to the prisoners the fact that there would be no hanging, a mighty cheer went up and the tense stillness which had characterized the prison atmosphere for forty-eight hours was broken," the *Concord Daily Monitor* reported.

New Hampshire has punished its most brutal criminals with death off and on since 1739, when two women were hanged in Portsmouth for the public to see. Twenty-one people have been hanged since, the last one in 1939. Public sentiment toward capital punishment has softened somewhat over the years and tamed the law along with it.

The case of George Hause—a confessed murderer sentenced to death—illustrates New Hampshire's ambivalence toward capital punishment. This is a state that has fought to restore capital punishment laws, battled those who've tried to abolish them, and then chosen not to use them.

Hause was a twenty-four-year-old boxer and baseball player known as Joe Shine at the time of his arrest. He was separated from his wife and kids and had been sleeping in a Concord stable at night and wandering the city during the day. The police knew Hause because he had a felony conviction and had been suspected of breaking into a business just before the murder. They first questioned him two days after the murder because he'd been seen near the scene.

Investigators didn't immediately suspect Hause; they were hoping he would give them leads in one of the most blinding murder mysteries in city history. Goldberg, a Russian immigrant who had befriended the poor by dispensing clothing and advice from his Main Street shop, was found on the floor of his store. Goldberg's attacker had hit him in the head six times before strangling him and robbing him of nearly $300.

It was no secret that Goldberg did his briskest business on Saturday, the day of the murder, and the police suspected robbery was the motive. But for weeks their investigation turned up few clues and no suspects. In an anonymous letter, a Ku Klux Klan member claimed responsibility immediately after Goldberg's body was found: "1 jew is eliminated. We'll get more." But the police didn't buy it. Investigators questioned several people but turned up nothing. Goldberg's friends offered a $500 reward but got no response.

A month after the murder, the police, aware that Hause and his wife had argued, arrested Hause and charged him with carrying a concealed gun without a license. During questioning, Hause could not give a straight story about where he'd been the night of the murder. The police jailed him on $2,000 bail on the weapon charge for more than a month before they charged him with murdering Goldberg.

The evidence cited against Hause in newspaper accounts is sparse: Despite having no real income, Hause had been paying past debts since the murder and robbery. He had been seen near Goldberg's store the night of the murder. The police got an anonymous note suggesting they ask Hause about the crime. And a piece of gun found at the scene matched a gun found in the stable where Hause had been sleeping.

Hause finally confessed after several days of "grilling," according to the newspaper.

In the months before trial, Hause tried to escape three times and went on a twenty-eight-day hunger strike. He threatened suicide. During one escape attempt, Hause asked a police officer to pray for him in his cell and then assaulted the officer when he knelt down and bowed his head.

Hause was convicted and sentenced to hang. His appeals failed to win him a new trial. As a last resort, Hause asked Winant to spare him death in exchange for life in prison. He returned to his cell to await the decision and grew more nervous as his execution hour approached.

It was the warden who first told Hause the news. "Hause broke down completely and it was some time before he recovered from the collapse," the newspaper reported.

The decision to commute Hause's sentence is never fully explained in news accounts. The governor noted that only twice in the past thirty years had anyone been hanged and that both those men had been convicted of premeditated murder against their wives. Winant also reminded reporters that the state prosecutor had said in recent weeks that he'd be happy with a sentence of life in prison.

Hause's near-death experience made the front page.

Concord Monitor.

Nine years later, the state sentenced another man to death. Again Winant spared him the hangman's noose, this time ninety minutes before he was to die. Winant, who decided to speak with the man in his cell before he made his decision, was so worried reporters would catch him visiting the prison and jump to conclusions that he had his chauffeur drop him at a side door after dark.

When he did explain his decision to the press, Winant said: "I am convinced that there was sufficient evidence that could have been used, had he had (better) counsel, to limit the penalty of the crime to life imprisonment."

In the twentieth century only three people were hanged in New Hampshire. But even before the executions tapered off, the state's residents began demanding they be spared seeing the details.

The earliest criminals died a slow death by strangulation because the hangman's knot, which quickly snaps the neck, wasn't in use until much later. After an angry mob protested the hanging of a Haverhill man in 1868, the legislature agreed to move executions inside the prison.

But by the start of the twentieth century, even that was considered too public. Prison officials, concerned for the mental state of both inmates and staff, began taking great pains to keep the time and location of the executions secret. Previously, "the gallows (had) been erected in the corridor of the cell wing," the *Concord Daily Monitor* reported, "and the prisoners in going to and from their work were compelled to pass under the grisly frame to their utter demoralization."

The last three men executed died in the middle of the night in a storage building that sat in what is now the prison's yard. The bookkeeping office used was so small the filing cabinets and desk inside had to be pushed to the walls to clear space. The room was prepared after the office employee went home for the day and reassembled before he returned to work.

"This morning at dawn there was no longer a death chamber," a reporter wrote after witnessing the last hanging, in 1939. "It again was the steward's office, with the trap door boarded over and a desk again covering the spot."

The state's capital punishment laws have changed with demands from the U.S. Supreme Court and with efforts to expand and abolish the existing laws.

In 1998, Gov. Jeanne Shaheen—spurred by a shooting spree in Colebrook, the shooting death of Epsom police officer Jeremy Charron, and the rape and murder of a Contoocook girl—tried to expand the death penalty to include several new crimes. She lost by seventy-eight votes.

Two years later, the tide turned even further. In 2000, the legislature drew national attention by voting to repeal the death penalty altogether; the repeal was promptly vetoed by Shaheen.

The state's death penalty statute may not be put to the test often, but, at least so far, it will remain on the books. Shaheen explains it simply. "There are some murders so heinous that the death penalty is an appropriate punishment," she said in negating the legislature's repeal effort.

Her 2000 veto frustrated death penalty opponents, who vowed to continue their fight.

Rep. Carol Moore, a Concord Democrat, says her research debunks myths used in support of the death penalty: It doesn't deter crime, and it isn't less expensive to kill convicts than to house them in prison.

"The whole thing is a moral issue," she said. "I think it's wrong to kill. If it's wrong to plan a murder and kill someone, then why is it right for the state to plan a murder and kill?"

That same sentiment spared George Hause back in 1925. While scores of people had written to the governor's home urging him to save Hause, they were not the only ones hoping to see Hause live.

"Approval of the decision was apparently not confined to the prison," the *Concord Daily Monitor* wrote after Hause got the news. "Persons who asked the (*Monitor*) for the decision last night eagerly expressed their approval of the commutation while persons who visited downtown stores during the evening were in general pleased with the change in sentence to life imprisonment."

Alexander McKenzie

When the world's fastest wind blew across Mount Washington, he was there to record it.

BY JIM GRAHAM

Two hours before they measured the highest wind speed ever recorded on Earth, Alexander McKenzie and two other weather observers atop Mount Washington saw an ominous sign that a big, big wind was brewing outside.

Behind a dense blanket of ice covering the entire observatory building, behind a heavy-duty wire mesh screen and behind a stout storm window, an interior kitchen window bulged inward more than an inch and a half each time the wind gusted.

McKenzie recorded the big wind—and spent the rest of his life retelling the tale.

New Hampshire Historical Society.

In a place where winds routinely exceed 100 miles per hour, the window had never bulged like that before, because the wind had never penetrated so far, or so powerfully.

They watched in nervous awe, expecting the glass panes to shatter at any moment and the windy fury to reach inside.

"This was disquieting," McKenzie wrote.

Steel chains draped over the roof and anchored into bedrock kept the building from blowing away. Still, it shook from the foundation to its solid timber rafters.

The ferocious roar outside was "like the passage of a continuous freight train," McKenzie wrote.

When frost feathers—long, frozen tentacles of mist created by passing clouds—began forming on the rooftop instruments and interfering with the wind gauge, Wendell Stephenson donned his arctic gear and set out to hack away the offending rime.

Yanking open a double storm door, the robust twenty-six-year-old was instantly knocked flat on his back by a windy body blow. Fighting his way to a ladder nailed flush against the building's wall, Stephenson was plastered against it by the wind, making it nearly impossible to crawl either up or down.

As he inched toward the roofline—a journey that must have seemed interminable in the near-zero visibility and howling wind—he struggled to lift a wooden club to hammer rime ice off the supports of the anemometer, the station's specially designed wind gauge.

Job complete, he wriggled and clawed his way back down to safety.

"Steve (Stephenson's nickname) had done a very dangerous thing," McKenzie wrote, "not just out of bravery, but because it was simply his job. If he had fallen or otherwise injured himself, who could have known?"

Cleared of ice, the anemometer (built to withstand harsh punishment and heated internally to discourage even worse freezing) recorded the highest wind speed ever measured and verified. The two 231-mile-per-hour gusts at 1:21 p.m., April 12, 1934, have yet to be topped. And the observatory remains one of the few fully staffed mountaintop weather stations in the world.

Alexander A. McKenzie II had helped establish the modern Mount Washington Observatory in 1932, soon after graduating from Dartmouth College. Although his illustrious career would include major advances in weather studies and shortwave radio communications, he will forever be known as one of the men who measured the world record wind.

McKenzie knew it, too, and requests to retell the legend persisted throughout his life.

"Life would never again be quite the same for any of us," McKenzie noted in a 1984 memoir. He died on December 13, 1997, at age eighty-nine—the 1934 crew's last survivor.

To set the historic record straight, he wrote a book, *World Record Wind*. Yet, to his chagrin, it did not stop nagging misconceptions about the big wind and failed to quash the popular notion that 231 mph was the point at which the anemometer blew off the roof.

At anniversary events celebrating the big wind, he often posed with the historic anemometer—still in working order and undamaged—and was happy to detail the design of the world's best weather instrument.

Although scientists say winds elsewhere in the world probably top the record from time to time, no one has ever been able to record them. In the few cases where winds have measured 150 mph-plus, the instruments themselves were later damaged by rising gusts or blown off their moorings.

Modern meteorologists still marvel at Mount Washington's enduring record. It is a testimony, they say, to the crew's ingenious and uncommonly rugged instruments, diligent data collection, and round-the-clock commitment.

To put the record in perspective, storms with winds exceeding 74 mph qualify as hurricanes—strong enough to uproot trees. Recalling his heroic trip on the roof, Stephenson himself said, "If I'd known how strong the wind was, I'd never have gone out there."

Later that night, chief observer Sal Pagliuca also climbed outside to de-ice the instruments again. "I hammered with all my strength, but I doubt the strength of Polyphemus could move a sledgehammer in a 200-miles-per-hour breeze," he wrote in an account recorded in the book *Life at the Top: Tales, Truths and Trusted Recipes from the Mount Washington Observatory,* by current weather observer Eric Pinder.

McKenzie, Stephenson, and Pagliuca were the official observatory crew that day and were joined by two guests, Arthur Griffin and George Leslie.

With few breaks off the mountaintop during winter months, the crew kept cabin fever at bay with hard work—maintaining their weather instruments, reporting observations via shortwave radio, conducting research on clouds, wind, and precipitation, and seeing to the unending chores involved in surviving the world's worst weather.

The observers and their two guests huddled around the array of instruments in the observatory. One that drew most of the attention was a device

Alexander McKenzie

View from the top of Mount Washington.

Geoff Forester/Concord Monitor.

linked to the anemometer, which made intermittent, audible "ticks" indicating the volume of wind passing over the summit.

Translated, the rapidly increasing ticks noted that day revealed the almost surreal weather event happening outside. In addition to the two 231-mph gusts, it recorded one five-minute average wind speed of 188 mph and one hour-long average of 173 mph. And in twenty-four hours, it showed 3,075 miles worth of wind passed the station.

"'Will they believe it?' was our first thought," McKenzie wrote of the moment following the record. "I felt then the full responsibility of that startling measurement. Was my timing correct? Was the method okay? Was the calibration curve right?"

Scientists to the core, the observers remained close to the instruments as the gusts dropped.

"Many people have wanted to know what we did after that," he wrote. "Did we cheer or open a bottle of champagne, or what?

"Well, we didn't do anything special for a while, except make more measurements."

As news of the remarkable record spread, reporters inundated the summit observers with interview requests. Newspaper and radio stations around the world carried the story for days. One radio listener, a twelve-year-old girl who lived near Buffalo, New York, wrote the observers a note, proclaiming that they had "felt the wind of God's will."

"We certainly had," McKenzie concluded.

In 1995, a week after McKenzie died, the wind record appeared to be blown out of the books when a South Pacific typhoon slammed into the island of Guam. Initial reports indicated gusts at Guam's Andersen Air Force Base peaked at 236 mph.

"Someone asked me what Alex McKenzie would say if he heard the record had been broken," said Dave Thurlow, host of the observatory's nationally syndicated radio show *The Weather Notebook*.

"And I'd think it'd be, 'Prove it,'" he concluded.

The challenger failed to hold up. In March 1998, an independent panel of weather experts ruled that Guam's claim to the title was erroneous, and that the typhoon's top winds were probably closer to 180 mph.

Gertrude Soule, Bertha Lindsay, and Ethel Hudson

They were New Hampshire's last Shakers.

Gertrude Soule, Bertha Lindsay, and Ethel Hudson died within four years of each other in the late 1980s and early 1990s, taking with them a unique way of life begun 200 years earlier in Canterbury. "I'm the last pebble on the beach," Hudson said in 1992 just weeks before her death. And she was.

The old women were the last Shakers in New Hampshire, the final members of a peculiar sect that prohibited sex, encouraged industry and invention, and brought the world well-known songs and household items galore. The Canterbury Shakers took in orphans and sold medicinal herbs. They dressed in old-fashioned clothing but had electric lights before nearby Concord.

Eldress Gertrude Soule in her garden.
Ken Williams/Concord Monitor.

Eldress Bertha Lindsay with a birthday bouquet from Bill and Camille Cosby, shortly before her death in 1990.
Ken Williams/Concord Monitor.

Eldress Ethel Hudson, Canterbury.
Gary Samson.

As the last of a dying community, the sisters felt a responsibility to let the world know what went on at Canterbury and other villages across New England. Today, thanks partly to their work, their former home is a thriving museum, teaching thousands of visitors each year about the Shakers.

"They were human," said Scott Swank, director of Canterbury Shaker Village. "We're not trying to present them as perfect. But on the other hand they were remarkable, to say the least. You can stand in awe even if you have trouble understanding or agreeing with some of the things that they did."

Theophile Biron

At the turn of the century, he united New Hampshire's young Franco-American community.

When Theophile Biron came to Manchester from Quebec at the turn of the last century, he was part of a giant wave of Canadian immigrants who would change New England's mill cities for good. But he was more than just a face in the crowd: Biron, who drew his first paycheck from the giant Amoskeag Manufacturing Company at age nine, was one of the mill's first Franco-American workers to rise from laborer to overseer. More important, he became a spokesman for his coworkers, creating the Association Canado-Americaine and leading the growing organization from 1896 to 1908.

A portrait of Biron hangs in the office of the Association Canado-Americaine.
Ken Williams/Concord Monitor.

The group's first mission: providing insurance protection and health benefits to blue-collar workers who received neither from Amoskeag. In time, though, the group became a social, cultural, and political force with hundreds of local chapters across New England; a weekly newspaper, *Le Canado-Americain;* dances and dinners galore.

"In the context of New Hampshire and French Americans, he was a visionary," said historian Julien Oliver. "Biron was not alone, but he had enough drive and leadership to make it work."

The Hubbard Brothers

They were chicken breeders extraordinaire.

In the 1920s, it was no big deal for a New England farmer to have a flock of chickens for meat and for eggs. That's how the Hubbard brothers of Walpole—Oliver, Les, Austin, and Donald—started out too. But they sure didn't leave it at that.

The Hubbards started with a few hundred chickens. They then developed a flock free of polluram, a lethal poultry disease that had previously made large-scale chicken production difficult, and their business took off. Their flock grew to 30,000 in 1924 and 200,000 in 1926. And the business became an international player in poultry breeding, selling out to pharmaceutical giant

Ira Hubbard talks chickens with a boy, 1954.

Courtesy of Hubbard Farms.

Merck & Co. in 1974 for more than $70 million. By producing a cheaper, better chicken, the Hubbards helped change the eating habits of people all over the world. And over the course of a century, they forced out all the local competition.

"Hubbard is the only chicken breeder left in the state," Winthrop Skoglund, former head of the Animal Science Department at the University of New Hampshire, said in 1999. "It has a lot of competition all over the nation. The other breeders saw the handwriting on the wall."

John Sloan Dickey

He brought Dartmouth College into the modern era.

John Sloan Dickey's relationship with Dartmouth began in 1925, when he enrolled as a freshman. Decades later, as he retired from a twenty-five-year tenure as college president that spanned the post–World War II period through the civil rights era, he had changed his alma mater inside and out.

Dickey stressed social responsibility among students. He had served on President Harry Truman's civil rights committee and brought the group's ethic back to Dartmouth, challenging fraternities to end their discriminatory practices. "The world's troubles," Dickey told his charges, "are your troubles."

John Sloan Dickey.
Dartmouth College Library.

He stiffened academic standards, established new departments in international relations and public affairs, and improved the stature of the college's graduate programs. He oversaw the founding of the Kiewit Computation Center that led Dartmouth to the forefront of student computing. And to the outside world, Dartmouth's reputation as a home to serious scholars improved.

"He raised our sights and aspirations for the college," said James Wright, president of Dartmouth in the late 1990s. "He obviously made this a stronger place, which has been good for Dartmouth and the state of New Hampshire."

Judge Hugh Bownes

In his court, civil rights flourished.

BY STEVE VARNUM

Hugh Bownes never liked bullies.

Sometimes the bullies were prison guards. Sometimes they were school superintendents.

Sometimes the bullies were small-town officials trying to deny single mothers welfare. Sometimes the bully was the governor, trying to deprive gay students of the right to dance.

Sometimes the bully was the country's military, a military to which Bownes had very nearly given his own life.

The bullies met their match in the courtroom of Bownes, the son of Irish

Bownes proudly wears the title "activist judge."

Courtesy of Hugh Bownes.

immigrants who was mayor of Laconia, rose to a federal judgeship, and became one of the most rigorous civil rights defenders New Hampshire has ever known.

"He is just a giant, in my view," said Claire Ebel, director of the state Civil Liberties Union. "He has written some of the most extraordinary First Amendment opinions from the bench that you are likely to see."

It's hard to name a civil rights issue in the second half of the twentieth century in which Bownes didn't factor.

As a lawyer he helped defend Willard Uphaus, the accused Communist sympathizer who served a year in jail for refusing to name visitors to his World Fellowship Center in Conway.

As the lone trial judge in New Hampshire's U.S. District Court during the tumultuous decade between 1968 and 1977, Bownes balanced Gov. Meldrim Thomson's civil rights rampage. He sided at times with conscientious objectors to the war, hippie protesters, welfare moms, women seeking abortions, unjustly fired teachers, and environmentalists.

In one of his last written decisions before his 1977 appointment to the U.S. First Circuit Court of Appeals, he capped a series of inmate lawsuits by ordering a comprehensive overhaul of the state prison.

"Time at New Hampshire State Prison costs a man much more than part of his life," Bownes wrote. "It robs him of his skills, his ability to cope with society in a civilized manner and, most important, his essential human dignity."

"He's a great judge because he's a human being and he hasn't forgotten that and the robe didn't change that," says Richard Hesse, of the Franklin Pierce Law Center. The school established an annual civil rights forum named for Bownes in 1992.

Bownes willingly wore the title "activist judge" and is proud to have followed the lead of Supreme Court Justice William Brennan, the liberal jurist who was called "the conscience of the court." "There was a determined effort to enlarge the scope of constitutional protections" during his decade in district court, Bownes said.

It was the era of *Roe v. Wade* legalizing abortion and *University of California v. Bakke* opening the door to affirmative action. It was the era of Martin Luther King Jr., Vietnam, and challenges to authority of every stripe.

As the highest judicial authority in New Hampshire, Bownes was determined to let those challenges be aired.

"You felt that you were doing something more than just reading a case to find precedents. You were helping somebody to get an abortion, to get better food, to get better prison conditions, to have more freedom, to wear what you wanted to wear when you went to school, " he said. "It was exciting."

Three speeches shaped Hugh Bownes, the civil libertarian.

One was Jesus' sermon on the mount: "Blessed are the poor in spirit, for theirs is the kingdom of heaven." To his religious mother, he said, those were the greatest words ever uttered.

The second was Franklin Roosevelt's "We have nothing to fear but fear itself" speech, which made a huge impression on a twelve-year-old in the midst of the Depression.

The third came from his father, a member of New York City's then-powerful linotype union. "Don't ever cross a picket line. That's the worst thing you can do," he told his young son.

Bownes wasn't yet in high school when he began working. He received scholarships to the preparatory Horace Mann School for Boys, then to Columbia University. At Horace Mann he learned about class and privilege. He lived in a lower-middle-class neighborhood in the Bronx and had gone to public school with the children of Irish, Italian, and Jewish immigrants. Everyone was poor. That wasn't the case at Horace Mann, where the sons of doctors and professors were the chosen few. He felt intimidated and wondered about his place there.

"They were all going to college. They knew it. And they didn't have to worry about putting food on the table, which was a constant worry as far as I was concerned," he recalled.

For his first day of school he wore a new blue sweater his mother bought. One of the older boys told him, "You know, we don't wear sweaters here. We wear coats."

As a federal judge many years later, he would side with a Pittsfield sixth-grader who lived on a farm and wore dungarees to school. They were all the family could afford. Bownes found the school's dress code unconstitutional because there was no evidence that dungarees "in any way inhibited or tended to inhibit the educational process."

His father could get only part-time work while Bownes attended Columbia, so he lived at home and worked full-time at minimum wage—forty cents an hour at the A&P grocery. He graduated with honors, a history degree, and a budding interest in law.

He received a scholarship to Columbia's law school for fall of 1941. Instead, he enlisted in the Marines, was shipped to the Pacific, and almost didn't come back.

Mortar fire on the beach at Guam severed the artery in his leg and shattered the bone. He was bandaged hurriedly and brought back to a ship, where he received last rites and drifted in and out of consciousness.

His fellow fighters stripped his watch, pocket knife, jungle knife, and revolver as he lay bleeding on the ship's deck. He heard them say, "You're not going to need these anymore. You'll be dead by morning."

He guesses that if he'd been wounded 100 yards inland he'd have bled to death. That was one break. Another was that the military hospital in Hawaii was overloaded, so he was sent to one in the South Pacific. The first shipments of penicillin had recently arrived, and Bownes's gangrenous leg was saved by injections every two hours.

The wound left Bownes with a paralyzed foot and a limp, but he said, "I really was lucky in the war. All my life I've been lucky."

At age twenty-five, when he entered Columbia Law School, Bownes had already had the seminal experience of his lifetime. "It was an obstacle to be overcome," he would say later, and because of his wound he took an extra year to graduate. When he did, he was invited by Arthur Nighswander to join his firm in Laconia.

Bownes had married a Maine woman, a nurse, and they wanted to stay in the East. So he carried Nighswander's bags to court, learned how to search titles, and took whatever cases walked into the office.

He and his first wife, Irja, with whom he would have three children, shared a passion for politics. Both served on the Laconia City Council and he served a term as mayor. He was a member of the Democratic National Committee and ran unsuccessfully for the state Senate.

Willard Uphaus was Bownes's first foray into civil rights. Uphaus, director of the World Fellowship Center in Conway, was at the center of the state's most infamous case of the Red Scare 1950s.

In 1959 Uphaus was jailed for a year for contempt of court. He had refused to divulge the names of people who attended his camp, which was dedicated to the pursuit of social justice. Attorney General Louis Wyman and Gov. Hugh Gregg suspected he was hiding Communists.

Wyman "saw Communists under every bed," said Bownes, and meant to root them out. Some of the state's foremost attorneys volunteered to defend accused subversives, and Nighswander volunteered to join Uphaus's team.

When Nighswander fell ill just before a hearing, the case became Bownes's. They argued it twice before the state Supreme Court and once before the U.S. Supreme Court, losing by a vote each time. Uphaus never turned over the names.

Bownes was appointed a state Superior Court judge in 1966 by a friend and fellow Democrat, Gov. John King. Less than two years later he was nominated to the federal bench by President Lyndon Johnson. The nomination was nearly blocked by Sen. Strom Thurmond, who had a telegram from *Union Leader* publisher William Loeb suggesting Bownes was a Communist and confirming he was a bleeding-heart liberal.

Bownes was backed by another close friend and drinking buddy, Sen. Tom McIntyre, and Thurmond asked the two to come by. He said he'd talked with Sen. Norris Cotton, learned that Bownes was a Marine major with a Silver Star and Purple Heart, and decided to withdraw his opposition.

"I didn't know what the hell to say," said Bownes. So he thanked Thurmond and told him, "You know, Sen. McIntyre has told me on more than one occasion that you are the most popular senator to come out of South Carolina, with the possible exception of John C. Calhoun."

"He really liked that," Bownes said. It was total blarney.

Bownes was happy to get away from the divorce cases in superior court. Plaintiffs in uncontested divorces had to show that cruelty had resulted in physical injury and produce two people from the community to testify to their veracity. The process struck him as hypocritical.

"When I was on the federal bench I said to myself, 'Oh, thank God, no more uncontested divorces!'" he said. "Then the draft cases start coming, and they were even more difficult."

It was 1968, the Vietnam War was escalating, and many young people were doing whatever they could to avoid military service. Draft-dodging was a federal crime, and New Hampshire's only federal judge was Bownes, the decorated Marine veteran.

Yet in the thirteen draft cases in which he wrote decisions, Bownes acquitted ten of the young men who stood before him. Overall, he guesses he let more than half go free. He often found that local draft boards acted arbitrarily.

In the beginning, he observed that while ghetto kids and high school kids went to Vietnam to be maimed or killed, "the cream of the crop . . . were not serving at all. That was a stark contrast to World War II, where everybody went," he said.

Before long, he considered them the most emotionally difficult cases he heard. "As time went on, it was more and more apparent to me and to a lot of other people that this war wasn't going anywhere and that it was just chewing up people's lives right and left. I tried to give as light sentences as possible where it was deserved."

As the draft cases tapered off, other civil rights issues flooded his courtroom. In 1970 he refused to squash a nonunion strike at Simplex Wire and Cable and issued a ruling allowing three "Chicago Seven" defendants to speak at the University of New Hampshire. In 1971 he ruled that a man convicted of a felony and later granted a full pardon was entitled to keep eighteen guns seized from him eight months before the pardon. He reinstated a Langdon teacher, a negotiator for the teachers' union with an excellent record who was fired as a result of "uninvestigated complaints and unverified rumors."

In 1972, he found that New England Telephone and Telegraph's promotion policies discriminated against women. "Ma Bell's voice to the public may be the feminine voice with the smile, but the voice of command and decision is a gruff and masculine one," his order read.

That November, Mel Thomson was elected governor. He and his administration kept Bownes's courtroom busy, and more often than not the judge spoiled their schemes.

Beginning in 1973, Bownes issues a string of decisions siding with individuals against the state or its agents. Some of those rulings:

- That termination of unemployment compensation without a hearing was unconstitutional.
- That the state's flag desecration law was unconstitutionally broad, after a Wilton student was convicted for drawing a peace sign over an American flag patch.
- That public schools could not have blanket prohibitions against the distribution of all non-school-sponsored written materials.
- That construction of Interstate 93 through Franconia Notch must halt until a full environmental study could be made. (Borrowing from Daniel Webster, he said, "In New Hampshire the White Mountains breed men. Highways breed traffic.") Eventually, a two-lane parkway was built.
- That child care must be considered a work expense when calculating Aid to Families with Dependent Children.
- That equal opportunity laws put the burden on employers to show legitimate, nondiscriminatory reasons when rejecting qualified minority applicants.
- That a statutory rape law was unconstitutional because it applied only to males.

- That UNH gay students had the right to sponsor and hold a dance. ("In short, the University may not censor expression because it does not like its message.")

His decisions were not always popular. They provoked howls of indignation from Thomson and Loeb, who called for Bownes's impeachment.

Attorney Steven Gordon, who clerked for Bownes during that time, says the judge provided some much-needed constitutional balance at a time when there was "a tremendous blanket of political conservatism" in the state. "He didn't care about the heat he was going to take . . . and people like Gov. Thomson who were screaming about the federal courts taking over our lives. He was not to be intimidated," said Hesse.

Perhaps Bownes's most ambitious order was one of his last written decisions before stepping up to the appellate court in 1977. In *Laaman v. Helgemoe,* he stopped just short of taking the state prison into receivership. Instead he issued an opinion that ran longer than a hundred pages and ordered sweeping changes at the Concord prison.

It was "a broad assault on the entire prison system," said Concord attorney John MacIntosh, who, as a law student, cut his teeth on the case. Legal Assistance attorney Elliott Berry says the decision was remarkable in its insight into the debilitating effects of prison life.

After laying out a long list of specific wrongs done by the prison system, Bownes wrote: "Deep anger and hatred of the society that relegates prisoners in the name of reform to cages with nothing to do, frustration and hostility engendered by false promises, and the loss of pride and self-esteem inherent in such a degrading experience spawn anti-authoritarian and often violent criminal behavior."

He said he meant to make the order, and the consent decrees that followed, as detailed and specific as possible because he knew Thomson wouldn't like it.

The state never appealed. Instead, the decision was used for leverage for a new prison. Berry, who calls the decision one of the best ever by a federal court in a prisoners' rights case, says without it the prison would not have the vocational and rehabilitative services it now offers.

By the end of the twentieth century, as a senior judge on the appeals court, Bownes was working three or four days most weeks. He still considered himself an activist jurist, but said, "The further you get away from the action, the less activist you become."

During his decade in federal district court, judges like him broke down civil rights barriers. Others, no less activist, jailed peaceful protesters and issued twenty-year prison terms for smoking marijuana.

"You should be an activist when you think that activism is going to promote justice. It's a hard line to draw at times," he said.

Where was his line? "If you're an activist in the pursuit of justice and expanding the constitution, that's good activism," he said. "If you're a negative activist who wants to just throw people in jail willy-nilly for offending your own sense of propriety, that's bad activism."

Do bullies still get under his skin?

"Yes, and sometimes that's not good," he said. "I mean, I think you can carry personal feelings too far. . . . You might react against a bully even though the bully is right, and you have to try to take that into consideration too.

"There are a lot of bullies in the world, unfortunately."

Judge Hugh Bownes

Fritzie Baer

His first motorcycle rally drew 10,000 people. It has grown bigger and more outrageous ever since.

BY ANNMARIE TIMMINS

W ere he alive today, Fritzie Baer might be the one man who wouldn't mind sitting in Motorcycle Week traffic. What a chance to stop and enjoy how well a little race he brought here in 1938 had caught on! "He'd love it—he'd just gloat in it," said Peter Karagianis, a Laconia merchant who helped Baer raise money for the early races. "It was through his early efforts that it has become the race it is today."

By the end of the twentieth century, most of the people who jammed Weirs Beach for its annual summertime motorcycle rally couldn't pick Baer out of an

Baer's rally has grown into a nationally known phenomenon.

Courtesy of Ruth Baer Arnold.

old race program. He died in 1984 at the age of eighty-three and had handed the race over to others long before.

But had Baer not brought his love of motorcycles and advertising flair to the Lakes Region, thousands of visitors would likely spend their annual holiday somewhere else.

"The Lakes Region owes Fritzie a tremendous debt of gratitude," Robert Lawton, editor of the *The Weirs Times,* wrote in 1998.

"His lifetime contribution to the area is monumental."

Baer, born Frank Baer in Clinton, Massachusetts, in 1901, wasn't an educated man or a wealthy one. He wasn't even the first to recognize the Lakes Region as a great summertime motorcycle destination: The Bay State Cycle Club brought about three hundred motorcyclists from Boston to Laconia twenty years before Baer did for an evening cruise, concert, dinner, and an overnight stay in a hotel.

But Baer was smart and a master promoter. After a friend told him of a fine resort in Gilford called the Belknap Mountain Recreation Area, he lobbied the American Motorcycle Association to hold its annual championship here. By then he was a well-known race announcer and a decent rider himself.

Baer's first race drew 10,000 people. Sixty years later, the crowd had grown to 350,000, and the event had become a week-long party.

The crowds have been good news for Weirs Beach property owners, who rely on revenue from the rally to survive the rest of the year. The Weirs Beach Chamber of Commerce, which once shunned bikers for their sleazy, honky-tonk image, now does all it can to welcome the crowds.

Of course, not everyone celebrates the rally's growing popularity. City officials have complained about the crowds' rowdy, crude behavior. In 1998, a fight between the Hells Angels and local police sent two gang members to jail and injured several officers. There have been naked coleslaw wrestling, topless dancing, and porn stars taking baths with anyone interested. By the end of the week, when true motorcycle enthusiasts are outnumbered by thrill seekers, a wet T-shirt can be considered formal attire.

Fritzie Baer's promotion of the Lakes Region began in more innocent times, with promotion of himself. He was rarely seen without a red hat atop his head because he knew it made people recognize him. He adopted his nickname Fritzie, which began as Fuzzie, as his legal name because it was catchier. Some said he was such a good salesman he could make the public clamor for an ice cream cone in the dead of winter.

Baer once flew snow to Puerto Rico to promote skiing. During his ten years as the general manager at the Gunstock ski area, he trucked in ice for summer hill jumps. And after he died, he was credited with saving Gunstock with little more than his personality and flair for attracting public attention.

Baer's talent was a natural one. He quit the eighth grade, not unusual back then, to take a job in a Massachusetts mill. He became an expert at carpet making but already had his mind on motorcycles. With money borrowed from his brother, Baer bought his first motorcycle, a Smith Motorwheel, at age fifteen. From then on, motorcycles brought Baer his greatest joy.

He became a well-known amateur rider. His rapid-fire delivery made him such a popular race announcer he could earn a week's pay at a single race. He worked at the Indian motorcycle company in Massachusetts. He was even riding his motorcycle the day he met the woman he'd marry.

Before Louise Baer died in 1991, she often told the story of Baer slowing down on his 1923 Indian Chief with a Princess sidecar as he passed her and her friend. He circled back, got her name, and began courting her with chocolate and gifts. A year later, they married.

Baer went back to work for Indian in his thirties and eventually took over a Massachusetts dealership for the company. He started his own riding club, Fritzie's Roamers, which was so busy and dedicated to safe riding that it was honored for both in its first year by motorcycle officials.

During his years with the riding club, Baer tested some time-honored rules and held fast to others. For example, his was a club for Indian riders; Harley Davidson owners were not welcome. Women rode on the back of the bike, not the front.

But when the American Motorcycle Association made a stink about Baer's plans to grant a black rider membership with Fritzie's Roamers, Baer fought back. He threatened to cancel his membership with the club and stop refereeing events until the national association backed down.

The end of World War II allowed Baer to revive his riding club, but his prospects with the Indian company were not as promising. The postwar machines didn't sell well. The dealership Baer once managed folded.

But again, motorcycles saved him.

In 1950, the Belknap County commissioners were looking for someone to manage the area ski resort. Baer had done such a good job of making himself and the area known through the annual motorcycle races he got the job.

He moved his family—by then most of the kids were grown—to Weirs Beach. James Baer, who was in eighth grade, remembers being excited about coming to Laconia.

"I thought it was a great adventure," he said.

The young Baer learned it was less thrilling than he imagined. Fritzie Baer worked seven days a week from morning to night and expected the same of his family. James Baer worked as a short-order cook and ticket taker at the county resort. When his father wanted someone to help groom the ski trails at 2:00 in the morning, Jim Baer was hauled out of bed. When it came time to promote the annual motorcycle races, Baer enlisted the help of his son.

"I had to sell ads for the motorcycle program, and we'd drive all around the lake," Jim Baer said. "He'd send me in (to merchants) and say, 'Just tell them you're Fritzie Baer's boy.' I lived in the shadow of a man who cast a very big shadow. I was always his son. I was never just Jim."

During Baer's tenure, the resort replaced its tow ropes with a T-bar. President Dwight Eisenhower stayed one night during a campaign swing through the area. And there is still an expert trail named for Baer, who didn't ski himself: It's called the Red Hat Trail.

A poor ski season combined with politics put an end to Baer's tenure. The county commissioners fired Baer in 1959. His disappointment was made worse by a newspaper column the next year that questioned his management of the resort.

Alfred Rosenblatt, in the *Laconia Evening Citizen,* questioned what Baer had done with the money he earned. Baer sued Rosenblatt for libel and won in a case that was appealed all the way to the U.S. Supreme Court.

The victory won Baer $31,500 but cost him his spirit, James Baer said. "He was never the same after that," he said. "That lawsuit punctured his balloon. Everything after that was anticlimactic."

Baer stayed active in the motorcycle world, although more from the sidelines after his retirement. He was dismayed by the riots at the Laconia rally in the 1960s because he continued to expect decency from the crowds.

In 1973, the Baers celebrated their fiftieth wedding anniversary at the Gilford Country Club. The event was reported with pictures and a story in the *Union Leader* and the August edition of the *Motorcyclist's Post.* The story referred to Baer as Mr. Motorcycling. President Richard Nixon, a U.S. senator, and Gov. Meldrim Thomson sent their wishes to the couple.

Those who knew Baer well didn't deny he loved the attention. But they were also quick to remind that Baer shared that attention, especially with the Lakes Region.

"I remember him sitting down by the ski jumps in the middle of the (race) track," said Loran Percy, a local photographer who worked with Baer. "He was happy as a clam. All the big names were there and everybody knew him. I think he'd be pretty surprised (by the event's success). But pleased."

Willard Uphaus

A victim of the Red Scare, he went to jail to protect his principles.

BY AMY MCCONNELL

T he old Methodist measured the threats of the state and the weight of his conscience and chose the lighter burden. In December 1959, Willard Uphaus said goodbye to his wife and followed the sheriff through a crowd of supporters and toward the Merrimack County jail. He had chosen to protect the names of friends accused of subversion and was sentenced to a year in jail for contempt of court.

In Boscawen, jailers frisked Uphaus, sixty-nine, for dangerous weapons, led him to a six-by-eight-foot cell lit by a single bulb, and locked the steel door behind him.

Willard Uphaus waves to supporters as he is led off to jail.

AP/Wide World Photos.

His first night of imprisonment seemed endless, Uphaus later wrote. "My bones ached fiercely on the hard narrow cot. A car swishing past on the highway tantalized me with the sound of freedom. I had just managed to doze, it seemed, when, with a bang and a clatter, a guard that I had not yet seen came to rouse us."

Uphaus served all but two days of his sentence. During that jail term and the long legal battle preceding it, his struggle brought the nation's hunt for suspected communists home to New Hampshire in a fierce way.

In protecting the identities of his colleagues, supporters said, Uphaus was a symbol of resistance against a dangerous witch-hunt in New Hampshire. In withholding the names of guests at his summer camp in Conway, according to Attorney General Louis Wyman, Gov. Hugh Gregg, and the legislature, Uphaus might be hiding Communists who were plotting to destroy the American way of life.

Uphaus, an Indiana farm boy who graduated from Yale with a doctorate in religious education, had spent much of his life trying to reconcile such apparent paradoxes. After years of teaching in religious schools and Southern colleges for blacks—and seeing many churches ignore the racism and poverty around them—Uphaus tried to bridge the gap between religion and the labor movement. From 1934 to 1953, he ran a small organization called the National Religion and Labor Foundation, which encouraged religious leaders to help labor unions during strikes. He sponsored organizations that advocated civil rights, better working conditions, and world peace. In 1953, he became director of World Fellowship Center, a secluded camp in Conway still used by many liberal and radical workers, intellectuals, and social activists for summer vacations.

The Uphaus controversy began in the summer of 1953 as momentum began to slow behind the national hunt for Communists led by Sen. Joseph McCarthy and the House Un-American Activities Committee. With the memory of World War II fresh in the national mind and with apprehension about the Soviet Union's atomic capabilities rising, fears of a Communist takeover grew virulent in New Hampshire and across the country.

James O'Neil, the Manchester police chief in 1947 and vice-president of the American Legion's Americanism Commission, claimed that year that as many as 1,000 enrolled communists and as many as 10,000 sympathizers might live in the state, based on what O'Neil called his personal information. (The year before, Elba Chase Nelson, the state Communist Party's candidate for governor, won only sixty-seven votes.)

The *New Hampshire Sunday News* reported O'Neil's charge, in the first of what soon became a drumbeat of articles and editorials by it and *The Union Leader* of Manchester about the "red menace."

Two years later, the legislature passed a bill to prohibit "subversive organizations." The State Subversive Activities Act outlawed any organization from committing or advocating any act intended to overthrow or destroy the constitutional form government by force. Conviction was a Class A felony. Anyone remaining a member of an organization advocating violent revolution was guilty of a Class B felony. The law remained on the books until 1994.

Violators were barred from working for state government and running for public office. When the attorney general had information about possible violations, he had to investigate and report the results to the legislature along with recommended actions, according to the statute. He could subpoena correspondence, books, and interviews, and make public any information he possessed, including the identities of people under investigation but not charged with any crime.

In 1953, the first season Uphaus ran World Fellowship, a *Union Leader* reporter appeared at the center, Uphaus later wrote in his memoir, *Commitment*. The reporter said he wanted to write a feature article about the camp, and Uphaus gave him pamphlets and showed him around.

In early September, the newspaper published a front-page story with the headline "Pro-Red at World Fellowship." It claimed Uphaus supported the Communist Party and was harboring members of subversive organizations. In a small box on its front page, the paper published a vow by Wyman to investigate the camp.

Whether or not Communist Party members attended World Fellowship—and some socialists and Marxists undoubtedly did—the goals espoused by Uphaus had nothing to do with violent overthrow of the government. The camp was trying to encourage friendship among people of different countries and to find ways to end war, poverty, hunger, and bigotry.

"Among those who come are philosophical materialists—Marxists and atheists—but they wouldn't be drawn to World Fellowship if they were not humanists with a real concern toward those who suffer from discrimination and exploitation, or dedicated peace workers who believe we should topple the walls that separate people and work together to save all from annihilation," Uphaus wrote. Many religious and civil rights activists and intellectuals—and their children—took three-month summer vacations at the camp, during which they debated issues, swam, hiked, and boated.

But according to Wyman, those religious ideals were a front for the Communist conspiracy. He quoted Benjamin Gitlow, one of five paid witnesses who testified before McCarthy's committee, in asserting that ministers acting as agents of Communism tried to poison the minds of the pious with "a destructive atheistic ideology cloaked in the name of social action."

Gitlow and the other witnesses alleged that 600 ministers had joined with Communists to carry out a pro-Soviet plot. In September 1953 Gitlow claimed Uphaus was one of the "principal individuals involved in the Communist conspiracy to convert the Methodist Church for Communist purposes," prompting another article by *The Union Leader*. Wyman continued to promise an investigation of the center.

Uphaus hadn't heard from Wyman by the next spring, so he sought him out in Concord before opening the camp for the summer. He hoped to put the issue to rest. Perhaps Wyman would come speak at World Fellowship and could reassure himself about the camp. Instead, Wyman subpoenaed Uphaus.

During a meeting in June, Uphaus answered Wyman's questions about the organizations he had supported or worked with during a lifetime of political activism.

That fall, another subpoena arrived just as Uphaus and his wife were closing World Fellowship for the winter. Uphaus was ordered to bring a 1954 guest list, information about the camp's employees, a list of speakers and any correspondence Uphaus had with them, and any letters or documents that showed a relationship with organizations the federal authorities had labeled as subversive.

Uphaus refused. "I had been harried, pilloried, and branded," he wrote. "My actions, and my motives, had been publicly misconstrued. . . . To expose the good, law-abiding people who had been with us at World Fellowship would be a degrading thing to do."

Uphaus refused again in January 1956, when he appeared in Merrimack County Superior Court in response to yet another subpoena from Wyman. Satisfying the demands of his conscience, Uphaus said, took precedence over obeying the orders of the attorney general, the courts, and the legislature.

"It is wrong to bear false witness against my brother," Uphaus told the court. "And inasmuch as I have no reason to believe that any of these persons whose names have been called for have in any sense hurt this state or our country, I have reason to believe that they should not be in possession of the attorney general."

Judge George Grant Jr. declared Uphaus in contempt of court and sentenced him to jail until he surrendered the guest list and other information. Released on bail, Uphaus appealed to the state Supreme Court, which upheld Wyman's right to investigate possible subversive activities based on hearsay evidence and to demand the guest list.

In 1958 Uphaus's case was heard by the U.S. Supreme Court—a development he believed would vindicate him. Instead, the justices ruled that public interest outweighed Uphaus's private rights; given the power granted Wyman by the legislature, the attorney general could force Uphaus to produce the guest list or prosecute him.

In his dissenting opinion, Justice William Brennan wrote that he disagreed not only with allowing the rights of the state to take precedence over the rights of the individual, but also with the purpose of the investigation. "This record, I think, not only fails to reveal any interest of the State sufficient to subordinate appellant's constitutionally protected rights, but affirmatively shows that the investigatory objective was the impermissible one of exposure for exposure's sake," Brennan wrote.

Although Wyman eventually questioned 131 people he suspected of subversion—most of whom he identified in a public report to the legislature in 1955—none, including Uphaus, were ever indicted on criminal charges.

Having exhausted his appeals, Uphaus returned for a final hearing in Merrimack County Superior Court—his last chance to turn over World Fellowship's guest list to spare himself a jail sentence. He refused. On December 14, 1959, he began serving a one-year sentence for contempt of court.

Letters of support and criticism poured into the jail. Allies gathered outside the jail on Sundays to sing hymns and old labor songs. Over time, Uphaus's fellow inmates learned the songs and sang along.

"It was a center for discussions—definitely left of center but certainly not revolutionary," said Annette Rubinstein, an Uphaus supporter who was black-listed in 1952 for her participation in the American Labor Party.

The so-called "red menace" used to justify Wyman's investigations of World Fellowship had never posed a threat to the country's security, Rubinstein said. "Anybody who said black people had a right to live where they wanted or who asked for higher wages was called a Communist," she said.

Audrey Rogers, who grew up in Conway and now lives near World Fellowship, said she saw firsthand how fear of the unknown—of "foreigners" and Communists—created prejudice against people at the camp. When she was a girl in the 1950s, Rogers said, people in town hated the center and were "petrified" that a Communist takeover might begin there. "You've got to remember that we live out in the country," Rogers said. "If you're from a small town and you're hearing people speaking a foreign language, you don't know if they're talking about having a cup of tea or taking your life."

But if fear helped drive the search for subversives during the 1950s, it wasn't necessarily misplaced, according to Stuart Conner, who helped in Wyman's investigation and who wrote most of the attorney general's 1955 report to the legislature. Communists had taken over Eastern Europe and much of Asia after the end of World War II, and they made no secret of their plans to extend that influence, Conner said. There was "absolutely no question" that Communism threatened the United States, Conner said in an interview a half-century later.

"They were able to sugarcoat the public line, but when you go back and read Marx and Engels and Lenin there isn't any question about what their plans were. . . . There's no prohibition against violence there."

The investigation of World Fellowship never penetrated far enough for Conner and Wyman to understand what activities were going on there or to discover whether the camp harbored Communists. But, Conner said, he and Wyman had the right and the duty to perform the job the legislature had ordered, which included questioning people. Sometimes that duty also included threatening public exposure to force witnesses' cooperation.

After all, he said: "How can you ever prove a conspiracy if you don't ask the question of who was involved?"

Andru Volinsky

He forced the state to reform education—and adopt a broad-based tax.

In 1997, the New Hampshire Supreme Court issued its biggest decision of the twentieth century, forcing the state to find a better way to finance public schools and ultimately leading to the enactment of a broad-based tax.

In the Claremont case, the justices ruled that the state's long reliance on local property taxes to pay for education gave the children of wealthy towns advantages over those in poor towns. All children, the court said, deserved an adequate education.

At the center of it all: Andru Volinsky, a crusading lawyer who led the team representing the children of Claremont, Allenstown, Pittsfield, Franklin, and Lisbon. The lawsuit, he said, was a last resort. "Many legislatures and many governors ignored the problems because they were happening only to a small

Volinsky argues on behalf of Claremont and other poor school districts at the state Supreme Court.

Dan Habib/Concord Monitor.

At the State House, reporters get Volinsky's reaction to lawmakers' latest school-funding scheme, November 1998.

Ken Williams/Concord Monitor.

and relatively powerless minority. That's what the constitution is in place to protect against."

His victory shocked the political establishment. "I don't think anybody thought he had a chance of winning," said attorney Charles DeGrandpre. "Most people thought he was going up the creek without a paddle."

The initial results: More money for poor communities, a lawsuit by rich communities, an alarming state budget deficit, and a political campaign issue for years to come. While Volinsky wasn't wholly satisfied with the state's immediate reaction, he said, it was a start. "We're all talking about edging towards tax fairness, which wouldn't have happened without Claremont," he said.

Dennis Theriault

Like those before him, he makes paper.

Dennis Theriault works three twelve-hour days one week, four the next; two weeks on days followed by two on nights. The work is not easy but the pay—especially with overtime—is decent.

Theriault's father, grandparents, and great-grandparents did the same work he does. Unheard of in most of the state, it's not unusual up north, where the paper mills in Berlin and Gorham have kept thousands of residents employed for more than a hundred years.

Their time as an industrial power may have faded, but the mills still act as the financial engine for the region. "Paper is one of the two big industries that set the modern identity of the state," said Stuart Arnett, director of the state office of economic development. In 1997, the forest industry had a $300 million payroll and $1.7 billion in sales.

Even now, the paper mills dominate Berlin.

Ben Garvin/Concord Monitor.

At the end of the century, the mills had been sold, down-sized, and modernized. But to Theriault, some things would never change: "The northern worker is known to be a hard worker," he said. "He doesn't complain too much, works for lower wages, is known as a workaholic type. The northern paper worker is a very regular guy in a lot of ways."

Charles Holmes Pettee

He moved the University of New Hampshire from Hanover to Durham and shaped the early years of the institution.

If you think "the University of New Hampshire" is a mouthful, consider that the school's original name was the "New Hampshire College of Agriculture and the Mechanical Arts." Charles Holmes Pettee, a meteorology professor, recruiter, and dean, advocated the change—as well as untold others that shaped and modernized the state university.

Most notably, Pettee oversaw the school's move from Hanover, where there was friction with the pooh-bahs at Dartmouth College, to Durham, where a farmer had willed his farm to the state in 1890 for the purpose of creating an agricultural school. Pettee's responsibilities were broad: He lured new teachers and students. He negotiated for more land. He haggled with architects. He consulted with the U.S. Secretary of Agriculture and librarians around the country over what UNH should teach—and what it should stock in its library.

Pettee touched the lives of thousands of students at the University of New Hampshire.

Courtesy of Instructional Services, Dimond Library, UNH.

UNH in 1895, as seen
from Nesmith and
Conant Hall.

Courtesy of Instructional Services,

Dimond Library, UNH.

The first classes in Durham were held in 1893 for fifty-one students. The school grew quickly, and Pettee touched the lives of thousands of UNH students, from the turn of the century through the 1930s.

His approach to education was the same as his approach to living: "Service, not a life of pleasure, satisfies," he told the UNH faculty in 1935. "Let us therefore teach an approach to ideals by setting high and higher standards instead of setting up impossible ideals as standards."

Milton and Arnold Graton

They preserved the art of covered-bridge building.

At the end of the twentieth century there were still nearly seventy covered bridges in New Hampshire, reminders of an earlier era that charmed tourists and residents alike. Responsible for the safety and beauty of many of them were Milton and Arnold Graton, father and son builders who did things the old-fashioned way.

Milton Graton built ten new covered bridges and restored more than twenty-five in New England and around the country. Arnold Graton learned what he knew from his father. And with the exception of what his family learned from him, he was possibly the last person alive who knew how to re-store bridges without concessions to modernity. He used no steel girders or boiler plates or glue laminate or any other new-fashioned material. When his bridges were complete, he used oxen to pull them across hand-built tracks.

The work of father and son eventually caught the attention of history buffs,

From left, Arnold, Arnold Jr., and Austin Graton put together a covered bridge at a celebration of New Hampshire folklife in Washington, D.C., 1999.

Robin Shotola/Concord Monitor.

An afternoon jogger
crosses the Henniker
bridge built by the
Gratons in 1972.
*Ken Williams/*Concord Monitor.

writers, and big-name journalists. "In an age in which we do so many things fast, and wrong, Milton Graton still does things slowly, and right," wrote Charles Kuralt, the CBS News personality. "There is an ancient injunction which Milton Graton lives by, whether he knows it or not: 'Remove not the ancient landmark which thy fathers have set.'"

Grace Metalious

Her racy novel scandalized the nation.

BY GWEN FILOSA

There were no calling hours. After a simple funeral in Laconia her body was stored in a graveyard tomb until spring thawed the ground of the Smith Meeting House Cemetery. Death did not give way to quiet. People called her family, saying they did not want that woman buried in Gilmanton.

In the town where she wrote a book that riveted a nation, Grace Metalious was dead but not forgiven.

In 1956 *Peyton Place* made Metalious a star and carried an unwilling Gilmanton along for the ride. Filled with characters immersed in corruption, love

Metalious's *Peyton Place* scandalized the state— and the nation.

New Hampshire Historical Society.

affairs, and violence, the book was labeled indecent and, in some places, banned. Its cover was kept hidden by readers everywhere.

For small-town New England, *Peyton Place* was the literary equivalent of kicking over a rock. Metalious said in 1956: "All kinds of strange things crawl out. Everybody who lives in town knows what's going on—there are no secrets—but they don't want outsiders to know." Her analogy did not please Gilmanton residents, who considered the book an affront.

Millions read it. People who had never bought books bought *Peyton Place,* where they learned of a single mother's romance with the town principal and teenagers' first fumbles with sex. They also saw fourteen-year-old Selena Cross end the sexual abuse from her stepfather by smashing the fireplace tongs into his skull.

"She wrote what I call the second version of the Bible: the filthy version," said her father, Alfred DeRepentigny.

Ten days after its release, 60,000 copies of *Peyton Place* had sold. A film, a sequel, and a long-running TV series followed. Today, sales are estimated at nearly 20 million.

In 1956, however, the attention was on the author, who appeared in magazine photo spreads, newspaper headlines, and public events. Eight years later she had drunk herself to death at age thirty-nine.

"The publicity thing took over and ran her life," said her daughter, Marsha Duprey. "If *[Peyton Place]* had not been such a huge success, she'd probably be fine now and still writing."

Grace Metalious's short life turned rapidly. Her first marriage fell apart during *Peyton Place's* popularity. Other loves followed, as did parties, trips, and constant media attention.

"Everything about Grace turned into a scandal," said her friend Laurose Wilkens MacFadyen. "She had a knack for making people pay attention."

Grace DeRepentigny was born in 1924 to working-class Franco-American parents in Manchester. As a child, she was absorbed by books.

"When she wasn't out playing football with the boys, she was in the library," said George Metalious, who was her first real date. They married right after high school.

The young couple struggled through a succession of jobs and soon started a family. While George attended the University of New Hampshire, Grace started writing short stories, which she later incorporated into her novels.

The inspiration for *Peyton Place* came to her suddenly one August night, George Metalious recalls. "At 3 a.m. she woke me up, and she had the whole plot in her mind," he said. "She hadn't slept. She got up and she outlined what she thought was a good story."

In the fall of 1954 the Metaliouses moved to Gilmanton, into a simple house called "It'll Do." Grace wrote feverishly. "I thought twenty-four hours a day for a year," she said later. "I wrote ten hours a day for two and a half months."

In Gilmanton during the spring of 1955, she finished *The Tree and the Blossom,* which was later given a catchier name: *Peyton Place.* It was a fictitious New Hampshire town on the Connecticut River. Metalious picked an agent with a French name from a directory and sent him her manuscript.

Then, on a dry summer day, Metalious opened her mailbox to find news that her book had been sold. By the next fall a publicity campaign launched *Peyton Place*.

The press descended on Gilmanton. "They surrounded the Corner Store in a crowd, snapping pictures like crazy and quizzing startled townspeople into giving all sorts of strange answers to startling questions," MacFayden wrote in the local newspaper. Readers were glued to the fast-paced book; across the country, its pages were dog-eared to mark the good parts. "The reason it struck people was that it was so real," said John Michael Hayes, who wrote the screenplay. "They felt it. It didn't read like fiction."

Peyton Place is the story of Allison MacKenzie, a fatherless girl who wants to become a writer and does, after discovering she can write about her neighbors in thinly veiled characterizations. Yet the novel's most compelling character is Selena Cross, an impoverished and abused girl determined to escape the "shacks." Grace Metalious, writer Merle Miller concluded in 1965, was "the master of the hopeless situation."

Eventually, Metalious's name was almost as well known as her book. *Life* magazine chronicled her life at home, and she wrote personal essays in *The American Weekly*. One installment detailed her romance and second marriage to Laconia disc jockey T. J. Martin, accompanied by a wedding cake snapshot.

Yet when her daughter sees pictures from that era—her mother posing with her producers or arriving at book signings—she sees a woman terrified.

"My mother had the biggest heart of anyone in the world," said Duprey. "But she was not emotionally stable. She was basically a shy person. She came across as a tough broad because she was scared."

Attacks on the book hit close to home. People appeared at the edge of the family's driveway to holler obscenities and throw rocks. In January 1957 a front-page editorial in the *Union Leader* castigated the *Peyton Place* craze. Without mentioning the book's title or author, publisher William Loeb dismissed it as "literary sewage" that revealed "a complete debasement of taste and a fascination with the filthy, rotten side of life that are the earmarks of the collapse of civilization."

Metalious knew what it was like to go without. At "It'll Do" water had to be bottled from a spring two miles away. Money was rationed for groceries and gasoline.

"I don't go along with all the claptrap about poverty being good for the soul, and trouble and struggle being great strengtheners of character," Metalious wrote. Poverty courses through *Peyton Place*, stripping people of dignity and imploring others to do whatever it takes to get money. In one scene, for instance, a young man convinces his fiancée to marry a rich old doctor, so they can have his house and savings when he dies.

When a $75,000 advance came from the movie sale of *Peyton Place,* Metalious made the rounds to creditors to see the looks on their faces when she held up the check.

"She was instant celebrity and instant fortune," said Lynn Snierson, whose father was Metalious's lawyer. "And an awful lot of people resented the hell out of her for that."

Convinced their lives had been distorted into a lurid novel, locals blamed Metalious for writing a "dirty book" and dragging Gilmanton's name into it.

Money came in, but it went out just as quickly. Relatives, friends, and strangers asked for help. After a car accident in which Metalious was driving, her own mother sued her and won $11,000.

George Metalious, who now lives in Rye, still believes the book played a role in his dismissal as principal of Gilmanton's grammar school. "Everybody thought it was about Gilmanton, and none of the characters are about Gilmanton," he insisted. Grace Metalious, like any novelist, took cues from what she saw in daily life, her ex-husband said, but her characters were inventions. Still, there was no denying that the story line of Selena Cross was lifted from a real-life scandal: Eight years before Metalious finished *Peyton Place*, a twenty-year-old Gilmanton woman confessed to shooting her father to death after years of rapes and beatings. Her younger brother helped her kill him and bury the body beneath the family's sheep pen.

Selena and Joey Cross did the same with the remains of their stepfather. "An old sore had been opened," said attorney John Chandler, who helped represent Metalious. "That was very upsetting to that family."

The "sheep pen murder" settled it for many in New Hampshire: *Peyton Place* must be based on Gilmanton. Metalious denied it, but the belief became imbedded in New England folklore.

Peyton Place and Gilmanton could only agree on one thing: They were stuck with each other.

When Selectman Dave Russell and his wife ran the Gilmanton Village Store, travelers regularly stopped by to ask about Metalious. "We had a time when Barbara Walters came to town and went into the library and there wasn't a copy of *Peyton Place*," Russell said. "So she donated one."

Peyton Place did not break artistic ground but was remarkable for its time, said John Unsworth, a University of Virginia professor who includes the book in his course on twentieth-century American bestsellers.

"It wouldn't be an exaggeration to say America wasn't the same after *Peyton Place*," he said. "It's sort of a watershed moment in American mores." But its place in history rests on its sensationalism, Unsworth said. "Literary merit is not its strong suit."

Metalious, who had no college degree, whose parents had worked in mills, let her sales record answer her critics. "If I'm a lousy writer," Metalious mused, "then a hell of a lot of people have got lousy taste."

Forty years later the argument over *Peyton Place*'s significance continued. In 1999, publishing houses released two new versions of *Peyton Place*—and a new edition of its sequel, *Return to Peyton Place*. Critics weren't impressed.

"*Peyton Place* is, on its own terms, both a perfectly decent popular novel and an honest one," *Kirkus Reviews* declared. "But it never was an important one, and no amount of retroactive puffery can make it so."

But beneath the scandal, *Peyton Place* was a milestone, said Emily Toth, who wrote a 1981 biography of Metalious.

"[She] had a kind of intuition," Toth said, "a gut-level, emotional grasp of all the issues feminists from the early '70s seized."

Metalious's drinking escalated with her fame. At one point she told Bernard Snierson: "I looked into that empty bottle and I saw myself." In her last years Metalious regretted spilling intimate details to the press, but it was too late. *Newsweek* ran an interview in which she lamented her second breakup with George, which was preceded by her divorce from T. J. Martin. Tabloids carried stories with Grace saying George didn't love her anymore. Journalists compared her life to *Peyton Place*. "If I had to do it over again," she was quoted, "it would be easier to be poor . . ."

On the morning of February 25, 1964, Grace Metalious died from cirrhosis in a Boston hospital, the result of alcohol abuse. A deathbed rewrite of her will left everything to Metalious's companion, journalist John Rees, and demanded no funeral so that her body could be donated to science. The fact that her estate was hollowed out by debt—more than $200,000 in liabilities—made the papers.

The Metalious children contested the will, and a state Supreme Court decision allowed the family to hold a simple funeral. Dartmouth's and Harvard's medical schools declined the body because of the legal fight, denying the will's central wish.

A year later, Metalious's home and possessions were auctioned to pay back taxes. The old typewriter, kitchen table, and chair she used in writing *Peyton Place* went for $75.

Christopher Metalious turned seventeen four days before his mother died.

Now a veteran Hopkinton police officer, he has never read his mother's book. If he sees the movie version on TV, he turns it off. Someday he will read *Peyton Place* and research her life, he said—maybe when he retires.

"She was smart but she was stupid," he said. "Stupid in the sense she drank herself to death. What a waste of a brilliant mind."

People often recognize Christopher Metalious's last name, and he has taken jabs directed at his mother's memory. When he was a correctional officer at the state prison, inmates called him "incest baby," a reference to *Peyton Place*'s most notorious story. He purposely avoids Laconia and Gilmanton, he said.

Good memories surface when he talks about his mother. There was the cross-country drive to Hollywood where *Peyton Place* was being filmed. He met Marilyn Monroe and still has a snapshot of his mother with Cary Grant.

The harsh times resonate as well: the brutal arguments and the alcohol that obliterated everything.

To her son, it is clear what killed Grace Metalious.

"Had she not been famous, had she not started drinking, she'd be alive today," he said. "You get all that power and money and prestige. And things aren't what you thought they would be."

Mel Thomson

In the 1970s, he embodied New Hampshire conservatism.

BY CARRIE STURROCK

Plowing a cornfield in the spring of 1968, a Georgia transplant whose heftiest political experience had been chairing the Orford school board made a decision that would eventually change New Hampshire's political landscape.

Meldrim Thomson Jr. shut down his tractor, turned to his son Peter and said, "I've decided I'm going to run for governor." His eldest replied, "Dad, did you have too much sun?"

The decision came out of nowhere, much like the man who made it. Nevertheless, the staunchly conservative Thomson soon attracted the support of

Mel Thomson. In the 1970s, Thomson embodied New Hampshire conservatism.

New Hampshire Historical Society.

the powerful Manchester *Union Leader,* catapulting him into office in 1973 and New Hampshire into some of its more tumultuous years of the century.

A cordial man who made "Live Free or Die" part of the state's vernacular, Thomson, a Republican, never doubted his own wisdom. While his most lasting legacies may be the state's anti-tax fervor and the construction of the Seabrook nuclear power plant, he is remembered for smaller controversies too.

He called for arming the National Guard with nuclear weapons. He raised and lowered the state flag to show displeasure with national policy and mourn Christ's death on Good Friday. A Thomson aide illegally perused confidential tax records, and the governor himself tried to dig up criminal information on political foes. He sought to remove state employees who criticized his policy. When he discovered the University of New Hampshire had a gay student organization, he threatened to veto money for the school and called homosexuality "a socially abhorrent activity." He supported Aristotle Onassis's failed attempt to locate one of the world's largest oil refineries in Durham and make the Isles of Shoals a port for supertankers.

The *Union Leader* regularly lauded Thomson's actions on the front page, giving the governor a bully pulpit for his great crusade: convincing New Hampshire that an income or sales tax would ruin it.

"He changed the mood of the state and got that message across," said Marshall Cobleigh, Thomson's deputy chief of staff. "He got it inculcated in people's minds that spending was wrong. He conveyed the difference between needs and wants."

Thomson attended University of Georgia Law School and started a legal textbook publishing firm on Long Island, New York. In search of quiet, he moved his family of five children to Orford, where he founded Equity Publishing Corp. and bought a nineteenth-century home near the foot of Mount Cube. The year was 1954.

To understand how a man with a southern drawl rose to power in the Granite State, it helps to read the *Union Leader* of the mid-1970s. Published and dominated by William Loeb, the paper became Thomson's biggest cheerleader, first for his gubernatorial campaign and then during his three terms in office.

After unsuccessful attempts to place others in the governor's seat, Loeb set his sights on Mel "Ax the Tax" Thomson, who disparaged welfare, opposed gun control, and supported prayer in schools.

In a front-page editorial on November 2, 1972, Loeb wrote, "Candidate Thomson has not weaseled or wiggled on any of his promises. This newspaper therefore urges all who are interested in protecting their pocketbooks and the state's financial position to vote for Mel Thomson, who will surely give the state a progressive administration."

Thomson took the "Pledge" against an income or sales tax, and for the rest of the century no governor was elected without doing the same. With the backlash against the counterculture movement in full swing, the time was ripe for an arch-conservative. And Thomson had a genial manner. Many liked his candor.

Mary Chambers, the former House Democratic leader, can remember sitting next to an ecstatic young man at Thomson's first inauguration. "He felt he had voted for somebody he believed was committed to making his life better," she said. "Many people felt cut off from their government, and (Thomson) answered a real need."

Soon after his election, the controversy began. He directed an aide to review the business tax files of five taxpayers, three of whom were close allies of a political foe. When the state Supreme Court ruled the search illegal, Thomson called the opinion "bad policy and bad law" and said he would interpret the constitution as he understood it.

Thomson himself sped in a state limousine to the New England Organized Crime Intelligence System in Wellesley, Massachusetts, where he asked for files on political enemies. When questioned about it, he explained he was "testing the security measures."

From the beginning, Loeb and Thomson talked frequently. A reporter who obtained phone records discovered that from January 1973 to the fall of 1974 Thomson had called Loeb at his Massachusetts and Nevada homes hundreds of times at state expense. On days following heavy exchanges between the two, Thomson would invariably make a policy statement or take other significant action.

Some assumed Thomson took orders from Loeb, but supporters say he was too willful and opinionated for that. Thomson just happened to personify Loeb's written word. "It wasn't true that Bill Loeb controlled him," said Thomson's wife, Gale. "No one controlled Mel Thomson."

Cobleigh agrees. "I sat in the room for two-thirds of the phone calls, and (Thomson) would say, 'Here, listen to what I'm going to do to the liberals today,'" he said. "He was gloating about how he was going to get them."

Thomson could always count on liberals getting excited if he blurred the line separating church and state. One year, with the approval of the Executive Council, he placed a crèche on the State House lawn.

"I remember him calling Bill Loeb and saying, 'I'm going to suck them into banning a crèche on the State House lawn. Joe Six-Pack tends to believe in Christmas," said Cobleigh. "He understood the mood of the people. He was constantly doing things the people liked that the do-gooder gang didn't like."

Thomson lowered the state flag to protest passage of the Panama Canal Treaty and President Jimmy Carter's declaration of amnesty for draft dodgers. When he lowered it to mourn the death of Christ on Good Friday, the American Civil Liberties Union contested it all the way to the U.S. Supreme Court, which made him hoist the flag.

Thomson also got his point across through official proclamations and holidays: "New Hampshire Right to Life Day," "Communist Martyr Month," and, because he considered the U.S. ambassador to the United Nations a Communist sympathizer, "Removal of Andrew Young Day." (Less political, he also called for "National CB Day" to honor the assistance of CB radio users to beleaguered motorists.)

Thomson waged a "lobster war" with Maine over a disputed maritime boundary between the states. He proposed legislation that would have run New Hampshire's boundary through Kittery, Maine, and into Canadian waters 200 miles out to sea.

And when Maine arrested a New Hampshire lobsterman in disputed waters, Thomson interrupted an Executive Council meeting to announce: "Maine has declared war on us." The two states finally agreed to a compromise boundary.

"I don't think as he grew up he ever set out to be governor, so when he became governor I don't think he measured his actions against what the immediate political consequences would be," said Concord lawyer Tom Rath, attorney general during part of Thomson's tenure. "He said, 'I'm governor and I'm going to do what I think is right.'"

When, in 1977, sportscaster Howard Cosell suggested New Hampshire was "nowhere" during *Monday Night Football,* Thomson fired off a telegram defending the state and chastising Cosell. Two days later, on *Good Morning America,* Cosell told the nation, "the governor forsook his dignity . . . and he needs a sense of humor."

Thomson didn't think so. He asked University of New Hampshire officials to fire a part-time journalism instructor and *Boston Globe* columnist for describing New Hampshire as an unfriendly, unneighborly, and stingy state. The columnist characterized Thomson as a "bumbling busybody who is best known for butting into situations he doesn't know anything about."

Thomson championed putting the until-then obscure state motto "Live Free or Die" on license plates. He considered the words a call to arms against an oppressive Washington.

When a federal judge ruled that a New Hampshire man had a First Amendment right to excise the motto from his plates, Thomson had this to say: "If the un-American decisions of misguided judges are allowed to continue unchallenged and unchecked, the judiciary will succeed in doing what no enemy has been able to do—namely destroy America."

The state appealed to the U.S. Supreme Court and lost.

Thomson had little patience for state prisoners. When 100 inmates launched a hunger strike in 1975 to protest rotten meat and sour milk, a federal judge ordered the state to answer the charges. Thomson promptly ate a meal there and declared it surpassed his wife's cooking.

"Mel Thomson had the courage of his convictions," Cobleigh said. "If the world thought it was right, and he thought it was wrong, he wouldn't do it. If he thought it was right and the world thought it was wrong, he would do it."

The world had plenty of opportunities to think something of Thomson, whose extensive travel fostered criticism. He traveled to Panama and denounced the treaty giving up U.S. control of the Panama Canal as a "a brazen attempt to rip out the vital organ of our body politic." He journeyed to the Caribbean to study oil refineries.

Once he left office, he traveled to apartheid South Africa. Upon his return, he opposed sanctions against it in his *Union Leader* column, "Mel Thomson's Perspective." The country had reduced apartheid "tremendously," he said, and sanctions would just drive it into the Soviet camp.

That and calling Martin Luther King Jr. a man "of immoral character" who associated with "the leading agents of Communism" prompted some to call him racist.

Gale Thomson defends her husband as anything but. After all, she points out, he appointed New Hampshire's first black judge, Ivory Cobb, and he once personally delivered special farming license plates to a black man who couldn't get them.

Thomson's most sustained campaign was for a new, reliable energy source for New Hampshire. In 1973, the OPEC cartel embargoed crude oil, creating a sense of vulnerability in this state of long cold winters. Thomson already acutely feared dependence on foreign nations.

When Aristotle Onassis quietly purchased 3,000 acres on Durham Point to build an oil refinery, Thomson supported it. That project collapsed under intense opposition, but Thomson's fight for energy didn't. He led the crusade for Public Service Company of New Hampshire to build a nuclear power plant in Seabrook.

"Seabrook was built not because it made economic sense, not because it made environmental sense, but because it was embraced by those who held economic and political power in the state," said Renny Cushing of Hampton, who protested the plant's construction. "Seabrook damaged our economy, our constitutional form of government, and that damage to New Hampshire is the legacy of Mel Thomson."

When Seabrook residents voted at the March 1976 town meeting, 768–637, to oppose the nuclear reactor, Thomson brushed it off. He urged the Executive Council to adopt a policy favoring a nuclear power plant. He removed state employees who questioned the project. "If someone wants to oppose the nuclear power plant, he has an easy way out," he said of state employees. "He can resign and then speak out against it." After a conditional construction permit was granted in July 1976, nonviolent protests began. The following spring, 1,414 people were arrested and jailed. It was the largest mass arrest in New Hampshire history and a watershed moment for the anti-nuclear movement.

Thomson's downfall soon followed, as PSNH struggled to pay for the project. The company wanted to charge ratepayers during construction to help complete the Seabrook plant, and Thomson vetoed legislation that would have prevented that. Democrat Hugh Gallen hammered away at the governor over rising electric rates, unseating him in 1978.

By the late 1990s, withdrawn from public life, Thomson spent most of his time at his Orford home. Parkinson's disease had made walking, communicating, and remembering difficult. Evidence of the once-powerful man sat in a dark basement. On the wall above the stairs there gleamed eight shiny ground-breaking shovels, including one used at Seabrook on August 5, 1976.

His gubernatorial desk was down there, his gubernatorial chair, his wife's "AXTAX" license plate, and the framed words that hung in his office: "Low taxes are the result of low spending."

In Concord, however, much was changed since Thomson's reign. In 1999, for instance, legislators did the unthinkable and passed an income tax (though a threatened gubernatorial veto derailed the effort). The state now recognizes Martin Luther King Jr. Day. A law banning gay people from adopting kids was wiped off the books.

Thomson's family didn't discuss with him New Hampshire's changing face.

"Why not let him live in the past?" Peter Thomson asked.

Augustus Saint-Gaudens

His sculptures memorialized American heroes.

Toward the close of the nineteenth century, the United States longed for heroes. The death, discouragement, and financial doldrums of the Civil War had passed. The country was rebounding, producing the wealth that pays for monuments to its famous.

One American sculptor, more than any other, created the images that matched the nation's sense of strength and confidence. Augustus Saint-Gaudens, who spent much of his life in Cornish, memorialized the leaders of his era—from Abraham Lincoln to Robert Louis Stevenson to Robert Gould Shaw, the Bostonian who led the Civil War's first black regiment—

Saint-Gaudens in 1905.

U.S. Department of the Interior, National Park Service, Saint-Gaudens National Historic Site, Cornish, NH.

Saint-Gaudens's sculpture of Lincoln is
on display in Cornish.

Ken Williams/Concord Monitor.

Close-up of Saint-Gaudens's Adams Memorial.

Ken Williams/Concord Monitor.

capturing the individual while conveying the timeless, mythical quality of
the hero.

Saint-Gaudens lived only seven years into the twentieth century, and his
fame faded in mid-century. But by the 1980s, appreciation of his work rekin-
dled as tastes shifted again toward figurative sculpture and public monuments
returned to the realistic style of an earlier era. "There is a big resurgence," said
Gregory Schwarz, chief of interpretation at the artist's home, now a national
historic site. "And Saint-Gaudens was one of the masters of that style."

Maxfield Parrish

He was the most famous illustrator of the early twentieth century.

In subjects ranging from fairy tales to historical events, Maxfield Parrish's use of bold, luminous color helped capture a vision of ideal beauty for the masses. His paintings—widely reproduced in ads for mundane products like light bulbs and soap—carried fine art into the lives of farmers, merchants, and housewives, who framed his promotional calendars and hung them proudly at year's end. For Parrish, even a box of chocolates could convey images of the sublime. "Do you know what I mean by the spirit of things?" Parrish asked one client, who had commissioned a painting to decorate his company's Christmas candy boxes. "I mean the spirit of the things in which

Parrish's work once hung in one of every four American homes.

we take most joy and happiness in life. The spirit of out-of-doors, the spirit of light and distance . . . that is a quality not lost on the public, I feel sure."

Parrish was so popular that by 1925 one in every four American families owned a copy of his most famous painting, "Daybreak." Children around the world read fairy tales and nursery rhymes illustrated with his drawings. At home in Plainfield, New Hampshire, residents knew Parrish as a gracious, approachable neighbor. He had a sense of whimsy—and he could help them pay their bills by hiring them as models. "He was different—he was a peach," recalled Kathleen Philbrick Reed, who used her modeling money to buy a .22-caliber rifle from Sears. "We talked about all sorts of things, things like catching frogs."

Robert Frost

In Derry, he discovered American speech.

BY MIKE PRIDE

W hile living on a farm in Derry during the first decade of the twentieth century, Robert Frost discovered his poetic voice. He was an
outsider—a Californian by birth—and fame, fortune, and a restless spirit later lured him elsewhere. But no matter where he wandered, his
voice, like his name, fixed the character of New Hampshire in American lore.

His years in Derry tested Frost's own character. Because he suffered chronic
fevers, chest pains, and breathing difficulties, a physician had warned him
against the sedentary life of writing and teaching for which he had prepared.
In 1900, the year he moved to Derry, his firstborn son died of cholera and his

Frost in Littleton, 1915.
Dartmouth College Library.

mother died of cancer. Frost was just twenty-six years old, but life seemed to mock his desire to be a poet.

To make a living in Derry, Frost first farmed, then taught. He was a moderate success as a farmer, yet he bore the whispered stigma of "failed henman" into the classroom at Pinkerton Academy. As a teacher he excelled, urging on his students an approach to writing that had already become central to his poetry: Write about common experience in an uncommon way. But a career in education was not for him. "Why have only your labor for your pains?" he wrote, lamenting that teaching stole from his poetry.

What Frost discovered in Derry was genuine speech—American speech—and a method of posing that speech against the formal meter of poetry. "He wants two things at once: the sound of speech and absolute metrical regularity," said Donald Hall, the Wilmot poet who himself moved to a New Hampshire farm seventy-five years after Frost. Another rural New England poet, Wesley McNair, said that in rebelling against the singsong of nineteenth-century verse, Frost "turned to the life and energy of spoken English to renew poetry."

To renew poetry: Frost's ambition was no less than that. In 1916, five years after selling the farm, he summed up his time in Derry to a Boston reporter: "I kept farm, so to speak, for nearly ten years, but less as a farmer than as a fugitive from the world that seemed to disallow me. . . . I can see now that I went away to save myself and fix myself before I measured my strength against all creation."

Word that Frost had moved to New Hampshire reached readers of the weekly *Derry News* in October 1900. "R. Frost has moved upon the Magoon place which he recently bought," the newspaper reported. "He has a flock of nearly three hundred Wyandotte fowls."

In fact, it was Frost's grandfather who had bought the farm, for $1,700. The Frost family—Robert, his wife Elinor, and their one-year-old daughter Lesley—had been evicted from a farm they rented in Methuen, Massachusetts. The poultry farming had begun well enough in Methuen, but the death of three-year-old Elliott Frost brought despair upon the young couple, and Frost fell behind in the rent.

The new farm, a white clapboard house, a barn, and an apple orchard on thirty acres, promised a new beginning. If Frost managed to hang on to it for ten years, his grandfather said, it would be his. The grandfather also gave Frost an annuity of $500, which would grow to $800 after ten years. A live-in hired man tended the cow, the horse, the apple and pear trees, and the vegetable garden and helped Frost make hen coops, but the poultry farming was Frost's work. Although he would later discount his efforts, he managed to keep his growing family fed.

Elinor gave birth to a son and two daughters during the first five years at Derry. Both parents were teachers, and they taught their children at home. Most of this duty fell on Elinor, but Robert was an attentive father who read to his children, taught them botany and astronomy, and went over their writing with them.

Frost's life in Derry was full of contradictions. He rose late by a farmer's standards, but he also sat up into the night writing poetry at the kitchen table.

He felt alienated from the literary world, yet he developed fast friendships with his fellow poultrymen. "I was never really out of the world for good and all," he later wrote. "I liked people even when I believed I detested them."

As a young girl, Frost's daughter Lesley went on long walks and errands with her father. His love of conversation meant they never got home on time. An acquaintance once said of Frost: "He talks all day and every day." But he was a listener, too, and his keen ear gleaned both the manner of speech and the mastery of subject that transformed his poetry.

Frost's closest friend was a poultryman named John Hall, thirty years his elder, from neighboring Atkinson. Hall was a salty, down-to-earth man who raised prize fowl. Frost admired and learned from Hall's farming expertise, but Hall had a more vital lesson to teach. Frost recognized Hall's speech as "homely, shrewd, and living," and he paid close attention to it. Before long, he had concluded that "real artistic speech was only to be copied from real life."

In 1903, to supplement his income, Frost began writing fictional sketches for $10 apiece for two poultry trade magazines. A recurring character was modeled on Hall, and the speech patterns in the dialogue closely resembled the ones Frost had begun to shape into poems. Sometimes in the sketches, the characters spoke directly to one another with little commentary or context from the narrator—the same technique Frost later used in such talking poems as "The Death of the Hired Man."

In that poem, a farmer's wife tells him that a poor old bum has just returned in search of work, though it is wintertime and there is little extra to do. She beseeches her husband to be kind to the man. The husband replies:

> "When was I ever anything but kind to him?
> But I'll not have the fellow back," he said.
> "I told him so last haying, didn't I?
> If he left then, I said, that ended it.
> What good is he? Who else will harbor him
> At his age for the little he can do?
> What help he is there's no depending on.
> Off he goes always when I need him most.
> He thinks he ought to earn a little pay,
> Enough at least to buy tobacco with,
> So he won't have to beg and be beholden.
> 'All right,' I say, 'I can't afford to pay
> Any fixed wages, though I wish I could.'
> 'Someone else can.' 'Then someone else will have to.'

Frost absorbed more than the language in and around Derry; rural New Hampshire gave him settings and subjects that lasted him a lifetime. "I was interested in neighbors for more than merely their tones of speech," he wrote. He also enjoyed "gossip for its own sake." Poetry was all around him—in conversation, in the woods, in the everyday lives of Yankee farmers.

In 1906, to improve his income, Frost took a job teaching English at Pinkerton Academy. Teaching enforced a new regimen on him. No longer could he write into the night after the children were in bed, then sleep late. He had to grade papers and prepare for class, and he had to rise early and walk the two miles to school each day.

In an era in which Victorian primness governed the dress and demeanor of teachers, Frost behaved otherwise. He always entered the classroom "at a gallop," a student recalled. "His hair, cut at home, was blown in all directions by the wind. . . . His clothes were rumpled and ill-fitting." Before the class, he "would slump down in his chair behind his desk, almost disappearing from sight except for his heavy-lidded eyes and bushy brows."

Whatever his posture, Frost was an engaging, vigorous, and demanding teacher. In addition to a heavy reading load, his freshmen and sophomores had to write or present fifty themes per academic year. He expected correct grammar and spelling. He taught the usual books, but his purpose and his method were singular. Above all, he pushed his students to have ideas of their own. In the classroom he "was seeking kindred spirits—to comfort them and to comfort me," he said. For him, the joy in literature occurred between the reader and the book—and the joy was the point. The pleasure of words, read aloud or recited, had a value all its own.

Frost's superiors noticed his talents. He was soon writing Pinkerton's English curriculum, stating its twofold purpose in the very first sentence: "to bring our students under the influence of the great books, and to teach them the satisfaction of superior speech." New Hampshire's superintendent of public instruction observed Frost's classes and admired his innovation so much that he invited him to speak on his methods at a state teachers' convention.

Over time, teaching displaced farming as Frost's livelihood. He and his family sold the Derry farm in 1911 and headed north so that he could take a job at Plymouth Normal School. Yet what was true of his farming was true of his days in the classroom: He was a teacher out of necessity.

For Frost's calling—poetry—the Derry years were a period of incubation. From age twenty-seven to age thirty-two, he sent no poems to any editor. He

Frost's home in Derry is now a historic site.
Ken Williams/Concord Monitor.

wrote poems, and good ones, but his real achievement was to make his way as a poet. He found plain speech and real life to put in his poems, and he developed a theory about how to do it.

This breakthrough he himself described a few years later in letters to John Bartlett, the valedictorian of the class of 1910 at Pinkerton Academy and a favorite student of Frost's. The idea, Frost wrote, was that the sounds—not just the words—of spoken sentences conveyed meaning to the ear. If a person began a sentence, "My father used to say—" or said, "Put it there, old man," the ear was practiced in receiving the natural rhythms of the sentence. It could take the meaning without hearing the words.

"A sentence is a sound in itself on which other sounds called words may be strung," Frost wrote Bartlett. "A man is all a writer if all his words are strung on definite recognizable sentence-sounds. The voice of the imagination, the speaking voice must know certainly how to behave . . . in every sentence he offers."

Literature, to Frost, was not a matter of presenting readers with some new truth or discovery. "It is never to tell them something they don't know, but something they know and haven't thought of saying," he wrote. "It must be something they recognize." In a journal he kept a few years after the Derry period, he wrote: "A poem would be no good that hadn't doors. I wouldn't leave them open though."

Placing himself as a poet gave Frost a direction for his work. Like his traveler who comes to two roads in a yellow wood, he embraced this direction as his fate. Nearly all of Frost's best poems, even many written years later, flowed from the Derry period.

In "Mending Wall," written shortly after he left New Hampshire, almost any short passage serves to illustrate how he set down in iambic pentameter the sentence sounds of the speech he had so carefully absorbed as a chicken farmer in Derry. Or, as Donald Hall put it, how Frost went about "breaking the American sentence against the English line." Here the farmer narrating the poem is talking about setting stray boulders back in place in a stone wall:

> We have to use a spell to make them balance:
> "Stay where you are until our backs are turned."
> We wear our fingers rough with handling them.
> Oh, just another kind of outdoor game,
> One on a side. It comes to little more:
> There where it is we do not need the wall:
> He is all pine and I am apple orchard.
> My apples will never get across
> And eat the cones under his pines, I tell him.
> He only says, "Good fences make good neighbors."

Although the subject matter is rustic, the sentences in this poem sound as fresh as they did when Frost wrote them. The reader knows from the form and cadences that this is poetry, but it is also plain speech.

Through context and through writing for the American ear, Frost made the last line quoted mean something different from what the speaker intended to say. This is Yankee irony boiled down to the bone: The stone wall has outlived its use, yet the narrator's stubborn neighbor clings to the old saw about good fences making good neighbors.

Frost's poetry has universal appeal, but all New Hampshirites who read him closely recognize in his poems people they know, if not some part of themselves. Frost's imagery—the birches and brooks, the stone walls, leaf-covered trails and snowy woods—are real and familiar. And so is the voice in which Robert Frost wrote, the voice he found as a poultryman in Derry.

Joe Dodge

He turned the wilderness into a public playground.

BY JIM GRAHAM

Joe Dodge would get a kick out of the conclusion made by his biographer and longtime friend William Lowell Putnam: "If you didn't know Joe Dodge, you damn well should have."

The words were Putnam's, but the sentiment was pure Joe. Blunt. Profane. Honest. Humorous.

Volumes have been written and spoken about Joseph Brooks Dodge, huts manager of the Appalachian Mountain Club, founder of the Mount Washington Observatory, community leader, and colorful contemporary of both logger Jigger Johnson and poet Robert Frost. But ask what the White Mountains

Joe Dodge managed the Appalachian Mountain Club huts in the White Mountains.

Appalachian Mountain Club Collection.

would look like today had Dodge never come along, and North Country historians fall into silence. It is as impossible to imagine New Hampshire without Joe Dodge as it is to imagine Franconia Notch without the Old Man of the Mountain.

So try, if you can, to picture the mountains without the AMC's eight huts, each perched a day's hike apart in the high country wilderness. Reachable only by footpath and staffed by resourceful, robust young crews, they provide shelter, food, information, and emergency help to more than 200,000 hikers a year. The club's Pinkham Notch Camp Visitors Center, at the foot of Mount Washington, draws an additional 225,000.

Dodge helped build, rebuild, or expand seven of the huts and Pinkham. Or picture Mount Washington without its weather observatory. Operated year-round, the summit outpost conducts landmark research on everything from the effects of ice and snow on aircraft to changes in global climate patterns.

Dodge founded the observatory in 1932 with Bob Monahan, starting with just $400 for equipment and staff.

Or simply imagine the North Country without its legacy of rugged, independent-minded characters who, with their own creativity and wherewithal, did the work that had to be done.

Dodge personified them all.

In 1955, when Dodge received an honorary master's degree from Dartmouth and shared the stage with Frost, the school's president, John Sloan Dickey, summed it up like this:

> Onetime wireless operator at sea, longtime mountaineer, student of Mount Washington's ways and weather, you have been more than a match for storms, slides, fools, skiers, and porcupines. You have rescued so many of us from both the harshness of the mountain and the soft way leading down to boredom that you, yourself, are now beyond rescue as a legend of all that is unafraid, friendly, rigorously good, and ruggedly expressed in the out-of-doors.

Born the day after Christmas 1898, Dodge did not come from the mountains but from Manchester-by-the-Sea, a bustling Massachusetts fishing town. While he loved the ocean, his passions shifted at age eleven when he made his first trip to the White Mountains. With his father, he traveled by the most convenient means available: by passenger ferry from Boston to Portland, by train to Glen, and, finally, by horse-drawn buckboard to the base of Mount Washington. Hiking from Madison over the Presidential Range to Crawford Notch, he returned home fascinated by the windswept mountains.

In an old gazetteer, he read about the town of Gorham. "I'll always remember those words: 'It is a rough, cold, and unproductive township. Several streams, swarming with trout, descend from the mountains into the Androscoggin River in this town,'" Dodge said, as recorded in Putnam's book *Joe Dodge, One New Hampshire Institution*.

" 'Swarming with trout,' those were the words I kept thinking about," said Dodge.

But it was years before his rambunctious soul finally found its home there. In 1914, he landed his first job as a wireless operator aboard *The Bay State*, a Boston-to-Portland steamship. During World War I, he put his radio skills to work in the U.S. Navy submarine service. After the war, Dodge also worked as a radioman on an oceangoing freighter. He returned home to his family's furniture mill in Massachusetts, staying just long enough to realize "there wasn't enough room" for him to work under his older brother.

So Dodge headed north to find a job near the place where the wild brook trout swarmed.

He hired out to the AMC in the summer of 1922 as hutmaster at Pinkham Notch Camp, then a crude log cabin that served as the club's North Country headquarters and the center of hiking activity in the Presidential Range. At first, the job was just a summer position; during winters Dodge worked at a lumber camp just over the Maine border. Later, as AMC hut manager, Dodge adopted the best attributes of a logging camp boss when he oversaw the crews of college-aged men who staffed the huts and carried up food and supplies each day on their backs. While never rough with his young charges, he assigned them staggering amounts of work and gave them free rein to get the job done—then reeled them in with a vengeance if they strayed too far.

Edwin "Moose" Damp, a longtime hutman, remembered how he became a cook at Madison Hut. "Joe came up to me one day at Pinkham and he said, 'Moose, get your goddamned gear together. Get on the truck and go up to Madison. You're the cook.' I said, '@*!#, I don't know how to cook.'"

Damp didn't forget Dodge's reply.

"Don't give me any backtalk. . . . Goddammit, you're the cook! There's nobody else. Get up there!" Damp recalled in *A Century of Hospitality in High Places,* a book celebrating the 100th anniversary of the AMC huts.

Dodge and his buddies tooled around the mountains in an open-air car.

Appalachian Mountain Club Collection.

"That was it. You didn't argue much with Joe," said Damp, who soon cooked his first meal. "What happened? Everybody got sick."

Today's hut system looks nothing like it did when AMC leaders invited Dodge to open Pinkham year-round in 1926.

In the 1920s, there were just four huts: Pinkham, Lakes of the Clouds, Madison, and Carter Notch. All were small, open sporadically, and unable to accommodate more than a handful of hikers at one time.

Under Dodge's direction, the club developed Lonesome Lake, Greenleaf, Galehead, and Zealand Falls, each capable of handling dozens of overnight guests. It also undertook ambitious renovations at the existing huts.

Decades before red tape and distant bureaucrats governed every move allowed in the federally owned White Mountain National Forest, Dodge worked under his own promise to do things right. He never failed to deliver.

"I'm sure his word was his credit with anybody," said Fred "Mac" Stott, who worked with Dodge in the 1930s. "It was an era when you could get things done simply."

Without that freedom, it's doubtful the hut system would have been developed the way it is today. But from 1927, when he expanded Pinkham and Lakes, through 1952, when he oversaw construction of a shelter at Tuckerman Ravine, Dodge directed projects with the informal blessing of the AMC huts committee, a shoestring budget, and the brawny sweat of low-paid crews.

He conceived of the notion of linking the huts together along a ridge-hugging, fifty-six-mile course laid out from Lonesome Lake in Franconia Notch to Carter Notch, spanning the entire breadth of northern New Hampshire. The route is now part of the Appalachian Trail from Maine to Georgia.

"That's where he had the vision. To make it all a chain, to connect them like that," said Rob Burbank, an AMC spokesman at Pinkham. "And he accomplished it with the kind of public-private partnership that still benefits everyone to this day."

Beyond what he built, it was Dodge's style that makes his legacy as enduring as it is entertaining.

Dodge was a prankster and storyteller who enjoyed a hearty belly laugh—and who often turned a blind eye when the hutmen blew off steam with good-natured high jinks.

Everyone had a funny Joe Dodge story. Like the time an alert hiker discovered a dead black bear floating below Crystal Cascade just above Pinkham.

"Well, we went up there and fished the brute out," Dodge said, as recorded in Putnam's book. "He'd been in there quite awhile, and was kind of bloated. So, I thought maybe we ought to collect the bounty; after all, we had a dead bear. Five bucks was good money in those days when gasoline was only a quarter a gallon."

So Dodge and some buddies loaded the bear into an open-air car and drove into Gorham to collect the bounty from the town clerk. Baking and rotting in the hot summer sun, the bear stank to high heaven.

Paid the $5 bounty, Dodge asked the clerk whether he wanted to keep the bear.

"Get it the hell outta here!" the man said.

"Well, we still had the bear and figured we might be able to get another bounty, so we drove over to Littleton, where we found another town clerk," Dodge remembered.

By the end of the day, Dodge had collected bear bounties in Bartlett and Jackson too. Twenty bucks for a day's work.

Then there was the time Dodge demonstrated his unusual "bedside manner."

When Raymond Davis of Sharon, Massachusetts, died of a heart attack while hiking in Tuckerman Ravine in 1952, Dodge oversaw the recovery operation. After his crew carried Davis's body over nearly three miles of steep, rocky terrain to Pinkham, Dodge searched the man's pockets and found a home phone number.

He called the man's wife and gave a blunt but polite introduction.

"This is Joe Dodge, manager of the Appalachian Mountain Club, calling from Mount Washington, and I'm afraid I've got some bad news for you about your husband," Dodge bellowed into the phone.

The woman started rambling, assuming it was not serious, so Dodge cut to the chase.

"Jesus Christ, no lady! It's worse than that; the sonofabitch is dead!"

It wasn't in Dodge's nature to procrastinate; even his marriage proposal was direct.

After a few months alone during his first winter at Pinkham, Dodge got on the ham radio and relayed a message to another radio operator about his old high school sweetheart.

"Call up Cherstine Peterson over in Cambridge and tell her I'm getting kind of lonesome up here," Dodge said. "See if she'd like to come up and join me."

She accepted, and he sent another radio message asking her to choose a ring.

"Teen" and Joe had two children, Ann and Joseph Jr. Both became expert skiers, tackling the perilous Tuckerman Ravine headwall on wooden skis before they were teenagers. His son competed in the 1952 Olympics.

The Dodges lived at Pinkham through his tenure, which ended in 1959, when he retired as huts manager. His dedication built the hut system but also helped make hiking so popular that the AMC struggled to handle the growing crowds. The increasingly tight rein of the U.S. Forest Service added to the pressures.

"Joe became, in a way, the victim of his own success," Putnam wrote. "Around Gorham and elsewhere, the AMC's Pinkham Notch Camp had become 'Joe Dodge's Place'—to the chagrin of some club officialdom."

Dodge did not slow down a beat when he and Teen moved to a house they dubbed "Our Hut" on West Side Road in Conway.

"You guys figured all I knew how to do was run those goddamn huts," he told Putnam. "Hell, I've got a morning radio show every day of the week, I'm a selectman here in Conway, I'm chairman of Doc Shedd's hospital, and I still manage all the business affairs for the good old observatory. I've got more to do retired than most of you city folk who claim to be working."

When Putnam asked him whether he ever regretted leaving his family's furniture business for the hard life of the mountains, Dodge didn't hesitate.

"Holy goddamn crow, Willie, you gotta take it easy on my sippin' whiskey!" Dodge said. "Any more dumb ones like that and you're turned off.

"Have you ever heard of Charles C. Dodge Furniture Company? Hell, no, of course you haven't, but by the pink elephant's ear, you've damned well heard of me. Sure, I haven't made any fortune up here working for the AMC, but I've had more fun in my life than any city slicker you've ever met, and it gets better all the time."

George Maynard

He won the right to live free of "Live Free Or Die."

New Hampshire adopted the "Live Free Or Die" state motto in 1945, and by the end of the century it was arguably the most well known in the country. That didn't mean everyone liked it.

In the spring of 1974, George Maynard, a Jehovah's Witness from Claremont, blotted out the motto on his license plates. The "Live Free" was covered with tape. The "Or Die" was removed with tin snips. According to Maynard's religion, it *wasn't,* in fact, better to die than to live without freedom.

The upshot: He got pulled over—again and again. He even spent time in jail. Maynard's case made it all the way to the U.S. Supreme Court, where, to the horror of the motto-loving Gov. Meldrim Thomson, he won. "New Hampshire's

George Maynard's religion forbade him from keeping the "Live Free or Die" logo on his license plates.

Patrick Raycraft/Concord Monitor.

statute in effect requires that appellees use their private property as a 'mobile billboard' for the state's ideological message or suffer penalty," wrote Chief Justice Warren Burger. "The First Amendment protects the rights of individuals to hold a point of view different from the majority and to refuse to foster, in the way New Hampshire commands, an idea they find morally objectionable."

Lilian Streeter

She started the state's first visiting nurse association.

Lilian Carpenter Streeter was daughter of a state Supreme Court justice and the wife of a prominent lawyer. In other words, she could have led a life of leisure. Instead, she worked ceaselessly to convince Concord leaders to help her establish a visiting nurse association, a charitable group that would send medical workers into needy residents' homes.

The nurse—at first, just one—started work in December 1899. Ten months later, she had made 1,652 visits to 145 cases for twenty doctors. "Conclusive proof," Streeter wrote, "that the great need of a district nurse in Concord had not been overestimated."

Streeter's vision was replicated across the state.

Courtesy of the Concord Visiting Nurse Association.

Communities all over New Hampshire soon followed Concord's lead. Decades before Medicaid or Medicare, many poor residents had previously gone without care during childbirth or illness. The need was great. "The District Nursing Association is a charity which benefits the whole town, and the whole town should feel it a privilege to help in its support," Streeter said.

One hundred years later, the VNA was still going strong, its role changing always to accommodate new challenges. In the 1990s alone, the Concord group opened a hospice house for terminally ill patients, expanded its team of nurses to provide follow-up home care for heart surgery patients, and helped create a clinic for the city's poor and homeless.

Streeter, no doubt, would have approved.

Lewis Feldstein

In a flinty state, he encouraged charity.

At the end of the twentieth century, New Hampshire consistently ranked at or near the bottom in terms of philanthropic giving. What that statistic conceals is the success of Lewis Feldstein and the New Hampshire Charitable Foundation.

Feldstein has run the organization since 1986 and supported the creation of everything from New Hampshire Public Radio to the Alliance for the Mentally Ill to the Matthew Thornton Heath Plan to the New Hampshire Center for Dispute Resolution. The group's money—its assets topped $200 million by the century's end—helped launch dozens of nonprofit organizations and backed initiatives in others. It thrust itself into the public debate, providing

Lew Feldstein and the New Hampshire Charitable Foundation have encouraged generosity in a flinty state.

Ken Williams/Concord Monitor.

the private component of numerous public/private initiatives, including a giant state land conservation effort in the late 1980s. And it grew to one of the largest community foundations in the country, among the top thirty of more than 500.

"This role of trying to nurture and support a lot of original ideas—almost always we are most influential at the beginning when the risk is highest," Feldstein said. "It's risk capital in the nonprofit side."

Mary Hill Coolidge and
A. Cooper Ballentine

They created the League of New Hampshire Craftsmen, protecting and promoting the state's traditional arts.

Mary Hill Coolidge and A. Cooper Ballentine both came to New Hampshire as summer visitors to the Lakes Region. And in the 1920s, they both had a similar vision: the revival of traditional handicrafts as a way to help their struggling neighbors make some extra money. They met, strategized, and sought the help of Gov. John Winant. Eventually, the League of New Hampshire Craftsmen was born.

The idea: a statewide program of craft instruction and marketing.

The outcome: It worked.

Mary Hill Coolidge's efforts led to the creation of the League of New Hampshire Craftsmen.

New Hampshire Historical Society.

By 1936, the League had 2,000 members and forty-seven local councils, which managed the home industry shops in their areas. As Coolidge and Ballentine envisioned, the money made a significant difference for many rural residents. One widow paid taxes with rug money. Another shingled her roof with savings from her weaving.

The League continued throughout the twentieth century, sponsoring education courses and selling crafts from popular shops around the state. From the beginning, League officials were as concerned about quality as they were about sales. "The League is aiming at something far more permanent than an emergency occupation," wrote Martha Stearns, the League vice president, in 1939. "If and when prosperity comes back and our bank accounts begin to put on weight once more, we hope the League will still go on."

Bob Bahre

His racetrack put Loudon on the map.

BY AMY MCCONNELL

Bob Bahre, a self-made multimillionaire who never takes vacations, built an auto racing empire in a tiny town and transformed the leisure time of people throughout New England.

When New Hampshire International Speedway opened in the 1980s, auto racing had barely begun its rise in popularity in the region. Few people knew what to expect.

Then, thousands of race fans from Maine to Rhode Island and beyond began heading toward Loudon for summer stock car races. Bahre and his son Gary expanded the track into a professional-class facility, adding one Winston Cup race in July and another in September. Television crews beamed the name of Loudon, New Hampshire, onto TV screens across the country. Crowds, advertising dollars, and state revenue spiraled upward. The speedway has won the state the sort of recognition money can't buy—at least on

Bob Bahre at the New Hampshire International Speedway in Loudon, 1999.

Ken Williams/Concord Monitor.

245

New Hampshire's budget—according to Lauri Ostrander Klefos, director of the state tourism office.

Bahre, a gruff and rumpled farmer's son whose scuffed brown wing-tips defy the track's shiny corporate image, seems at first an unlikely tycoon. Auto racing may have turned corporate amid a swirl of money and publicity, but Bahre remains a child of the Great Depression—a tough-talking businessman who seals deals with a handshake and never breaks a promise.

Bahre still works farmers' hours—pre-dawn to past dark. His work habits began on his family's dairy and tobacco farm outside Hartford, Connecticut. Neither he nor his parents had much spare time as they tried to keep their farm going during the Depression. Although the family butchered its own animals and always had enough to eat, his parents worried about making mortgage payments and had little cash. So everyone who could work, did. Bahre and his father did most of the planting, milking, and hoeing, but his mother, a nurse, helped plant and cut tobacco. His two younger brothers pitched in when they were old enough.

Bahre's father began taking him to auto races when he was eight or nine years old. A few times each summer his father would buy him a fifty-cent ticket to watch sprint cars race around dirt tracks.

"There were only these boards for a guard rail around the edge," Bahre said. "When a driver hit it, the timber would fly up in the air."

Auto racing still was an amateur sport held on dusty—or muddy—tracks at ramshackle fairgrounds or in farmers' fields. Down South, stock car racing was developing as a by-product of illegal bootlegging; the first stock cars were souped up to outrun revenuers and ferry moonshine from mountain stills to Charlotte, North Carolina, and Knoxville, Tennessee.

Within a few years of watching his first sprint race, Bahre had become a fan. He never saw a major race as a child, but he tuned the radio to listen to the Indianapolis 500 every Memorial Day. He used the announcer's descriptions to visualize the race. Meanwhile, he started making money. When he was fourteen or fifteen years old, his mother agreed to put down $5 on a $64 welder he wanted. Bahre did welding jobs around their farm but also began welding for neighbors. He soon dropped out of school to work.

After years of using horses to plow the fields, Bahre's father bought a tractor. Bahre borrowed it to plow and harrow other farmers' fields with several neighbor boys—often at night after he had finished the chores on his family's farm.

With the money Bahre saved from those odd jobs, he bought old cars at the junkyard for $5 and salvaged their axles and wheels, which he used to make sixteen-foot trailers for farmers to haul hay. Each trailer sold for about $300.

His business began to pick up speed. Bahre bought a corn chopper and some trucks to cut and haul silage—cornstalks used for cattle feed—for neighbors at $40 per acre. With the profits, he bought a backhoe to dig septic systems in the area. Several neighbor boys Bahre hired sometimes drank so much they missed work; Bahre had to roust them out of bed with hangovers. After watching their misery, Bahre said, he has never tasted alcohol or smoked a cigarette.

"I said to hell with it, why be like these guys?" Bahre said. "I needed every penny I had—I couldn't piss it away on cigarettes and booze."

At eighteen, Bahre bought a truck built to carry four tons and drove to Westfield, Massachusetts, where he overloaded it with fifteen tons of concrete septic tanks. He hauled the tanks forty miles home and set them in holes for area contractors.

"It was a wonder I didn't kill myself," Bahre said, laughing. "You could hardly turn the corner."

In 1964, he visited Oxford, Maine, to race a car at Oxford Plains Speedway, a small dirt track. The owner was losing money and wanted out. Bahre bought the track, moved his family to the upper-class neighborhood of Paris Hill, and settled into the former home of Hannibal Hamlin, Abraham Lincoln's first Vice-President. He tore down many of the track's ramshackle outbuildings, erected new ones, paved the road course, and began running the show himself.

Thirty-five weekends a year, for twenty-three years, Bahre stood on a cement block in the middle of the track and acted as referee. His job was to decide whether a driver had moved illegally or raced with an overly large carburetor.

As the small track became a commercial success, Bahre's real estate business also boomed. He developed lakefront property and built some of the first malls in the area. He used money from the Farmers Home Administration—the same agency that had held his parents' mortgage—to build apartments for elderly and poor people. He gathered a group of area business leaders to form the Oxford Bank and Trust.

By the time Bahre sold the Oxford track in 1986, he had built it into one of the nation's best small tracks. But Bahre, by then a millionaire several times over, had his mind fixed on a grander vision—creating a top-rated speedway to run NASCAR events.

When Bahre first visited Loudon's Bryar Motorsports Park, he found a short track that area townspeople had long used to race motorcycles and go "mud bogging"—a sort of demolition derby in which drivers ram four-wheel-drive trucks into deep mud at high speeds. They usually have to be pulled out with a tractor.

But the motor park was near Boston and situated off Route 106, the main thoroughfare between Concord and the Lakes Region. Bahre, who had agreed not to build another speedway near Oxford, bought the Loudon track for $1.6 million and filed an application to expand.

The Loudon Planning Board approved the petition. Then, in the first of a series of protests that have dogged development at the track ever since, a group of residents sued the planning board. The board, they alleged, had broken its rules by waiving requirements and giving the proposed plans only a cursory examination.

Lawyers for both sides filed motions and countermotions to try to get the case thrown out of court. Months passed. Spring, and racing season, approached. Bahre had predicted the track would open in October and his plans were stuck in neutral.

So he invited the plaintiffs to discuss their concerns over dinner. In response to their worries, Bahre agreed to restrict the amount of beer sold at the track and the size of containers brought into the park. He also agreed to pay for what little could be done to muffle noise from race cars. The track was sunk eighteen inches into the ground and special sound-absorbing billboards were placed at either end of the speedway. Some of the track's noisiest events—drag racing, demolition derbies, tractor pulls, and mud bogging—were banned, as was racing after dark.

The plaintiffs withdrew their lawsuit and the expansion moved ahead. Bahre began building new grandstands: 55,000 seats, then 82,000—with hopes of perhaps 110,000 in all. Eventually, he captured two Winston Cup races, a rare prize.

Bahre has paid to widen part of Route 106 to smooth traffic snarls and laid millions of dollars worth of gravel to make parking easier for race fans. Critics in the area continue to object to noise and traffic—especially on Winston Cup weekends, when cars snake down the highway for miles.

But several of the predictions made when Bahre first opened the speedway have proven false. Development of hotels and restaurants along Route 106 has been slow, and Loudon's small-town charm hasn't changed much. Fears that the races would bring a deluge of "outsiders" were unfounded. Most of the hundreds of thousands of race fans who buy Winston Cup tickets years in advance and attend other weekend events are from New Hampshire and Massachusetts.

For his part, Bahre said the money he has made since opening the track has never been the sole point of his ambition. The fun, he said, is in taking risks and making projects succeed against all odds.

When he bought the track, NASCAR president Bill France Jr. told Bahre he had only a slim chance of getting even one Winston Cup date—a race the Bahres needed to make the speedway a success. But Bahre said he didn't worry the speedway would fail, despite France's discouraging words. "At least he didn't say no," Bahre said.

Dorothy Vaughan

She protected Portsmouth's past.

BY SARAH M. EARLE

T he penny-candy, milk-bottle charm of restored Portsmouth has never
found its way to Dorothy Vaughan's living room. Her shelves have collected none of the salt-kissed offerings of the sea, no funky trinkets
from downtown shops, no cultural treasures, nothing of the burgeoning high-
tech universe.

Yet, if all of these elements define Portsmouth, none define it so well as
Vaughan herself. And none can say so succinctly what she said to the local
Rotary Club forty years ago. In ruffled collar and cat's eye glasses, the ninety-
four-year-old slips easily into her 1957 persona, reciting portions of the brave

Dorothy Vaughan, at age
94, in 1999.
Ken Williams/Concord Monitor.

speech that stirred Portsmouth to its soul. "Do you want to wake up some day and find that you live on Main Street USA, and that you have nothing but bowling alleys and honky tonks and bars?" she asks, her cheeks pinkening against a backdrop of old books. More than a backdrop, actually, the books envelop the little woman, all but filling her living room, crowding every crevice and spilling out onto every available surface. A visitor may have to share a chair with a stack of old newspaper clippings or a town history. Vaughan makes no apologies. Sharing space with history, after all, is what she taught this city.

At mid-century Portsmouth resembled anything but the well-polished hub of culture, business, and tourism it is today. What's more, the city was about to part with the very riches that could save it.

The site of one of the earliest American settlements, Portsmouth grew from a wealthy lumber town to a vital trading port to New Hampshire's capital. The dual fists of trade and politics ensured the city power and wealth into the 1770s, when the workings of the American Revolution began to fray its edges. At the end of the war, with the capital moved inland and numerous trade routes disrupted, Portsmouth teetered on the edge of depression. Proving its resilience, the city reestablished its prominence in trade and quickly regained its wealth. But as hostilities with England and France continued, trade again faltered, and by the end of the War of 1812, had all but died.

Portsmouth turned its sights instead to shipbuilding and manufacturing. The Portsmouth Navy Yard, established by the federal government in 1800, began constructing ships for warfare and commerce, providing employment in both the maritime and artisan trades. The Navy Yard carried Portsmouth into the twentieth century, but without its former glory. The growth of textile manufacturing on the Merrimack River, along with the advent of the railroad in the 1840s, meant the demise of coastal trade.

This time, Portsmouth turned to beer to reclaim some of its prosperity. By the late 1800s, the city boasted three breweries, including one of the largest on the East Coast. Foundries, machine shops, and textile mills also popped up. Little maritime activity continued. The once thriving community of Puddle

Vaughan's work helped turn Portsmouth into one of New Hampshire's most picturesque cities.
Ken Williams/Concord Monitor.

Dock became a muddle of brothels, immigrant housing, decaying wharves, and a city dump. By 1907, the channel was completely filled in. "It was a kind of seedy, run-down part of town," recalls Tom Cocchiaro, communications manager for the Portsmouth Chamber of Commerce. The other side of town, where Cocchiaro grew up, wasn't much better. Human ideals would take the two sides in very different directions.

In the 1950s, federal urban renewal programs began sweeping the perceived dirt out of the corners of the country, tearing down "substandard" and inefficient buildings and replacing them with modern structures. Most Americans embraced the idea, not realizing until decades later how much they'd lost.

But the wrecking ball hadn't met the likes of Dorothy Vaughan.

During the 1950s, much of the northern section of Portsmouth was torn down in the name of urban renewal. Here, the campaign was met with less enthusiasm than in some cities, recalled former mayor Eileen Foley. "The people cried. It was really bad," she said. "I think it got people thinking."

But for Vaughan, thinking was never enough.

A young girl when she moved to Portsmouth with her family, Vaughan learned to drink in the history around her. When the city opened the historic John Paul Jones house as a canteen for servicemen during the war, she was determined to be a part of it. John Paul Jones had long been her hero, and she'd adopted his motto: "I have not yet begun to fight."

Indeed. Vaughan, only twelve, showed up at the canteen's doorstep, offering to help serve and clean up. They told her to ask her mother. Knowing that was one fight she wouldn't win, Vaughan found another way in. She started coming on Thursday afternoons to roll bandages for the Red Cross. She'd wrap furiously so she could finish her pile first and then steal a few minutes to look around the house. "That was the beginning of my falling in love with old houses," she said.

Blessed with a vision beyond her years and her era, Vaughan looked at the old houses lining the streets of Portsmouth, most of which had evolved into ramshackle apartment buildings, and saw beauty. "When I got here, I thought, oh, this is the most beautiful city I've ever seen," she said.

Vaughan's other love, books, deepened her love for old buildings, as she learned the city's rich history. After high school, Vaughan worked her way through the ranks at the city library, pestering her superiors to teach her what they knew, and applying for every position that opened. Every time, she was told she was too young, she was undereducated, that she wouldn't get the position. But most of the time, she did.

In 1956, Vaughan watched helplessly as a historic house near the library was torn down. Hearing of its pending demise, she had visited City Hall and pleaded with officials to save it. Her pleas fell on deaf ears.

As urban renewal set its sights on other historic houses, Vaughan decided she would have to talk a little louder. Still, when the opportunity came, she didn't exactly shout for joy. Vaughan's brother came home one evening, she recalls, and announced that he'd signed her up as the guest speaker for the next Rotary Club meeting. "In those days, women didn't go to the Rotary," she said. "I didn't like the idea at all."

But strong-willed brother beat out strong-willed sister, and Vaughan showed up to speak. "I think about it now, and I wonder how I did it," she said.

That night Vaughan looked out at the audience and saw the city manager and the mayor, among other bigwigs. She hesitated. After twenty-five years at the library, she'd finally gotten the job of head librarian and didn't want to ruffle any feathers. "I thought, I wonder if I really dare to say what I think," she said.

She did. "I said, 'People come here because we have all these beautiful houses, and we're tearing them all down,'" she said. "I told them, we've got to stop tearing down houses."

Those words changed the course of Portsmouth's history.

"She got people's attention," said Roberta Ransley, head librarian at Strawbery Banke, the re-created Puddle Dock village that evolved from Vaughan's efforts. "The early movers and shakers were the ones who started this whole process and brought us to where we are today."

"Dorothy came and said, 'We've got to save this city,'" Foley said. "After that, people realized we've got to keep what we've got."

"I didn't think they were listening, but they were," Vaughan recalled. "Everything took off from there."

That night, the Rotary Club set up a committee to save Portsmouth's heritage. With Vaughan at their helm, members took control over their city's fate. They visited historic villages in Sturbridge, Massachuetts, and Williamsburg, Virginia, for inspiration. Successfully changing a state law to permit restoration as part of urban renewal, they uncovered federal money that could be used for urban renewal. They turned old warehouses on Market Street into storefronts, beautified Prescott Park, and established a professional theater. With the government's blessing, they acquired thirty historic buildings in the south end of the city, arranged for the relocation of residents, and consolidated the houses into the Puddle Dock area. In 1965, Strawbery Banke opened to the public. The force was unstoppable.

Little by little, Portsmouth evolved from a blue-collar military mongrel to a

Sherburne House in Strawbery Banke, as it looked before the restoration efforts in the middle of the century.

Library of Congress photo.

cultured pearl of tourism, small business, and arts. "I guess you could say Portsmouth came to a cultural awakening," Cocchiaro said. On the waves of tourism came swarms of entrepreneurs, who saw Portsmouth's growing potential. The Seacoast Repertory Theater was born, and Prescott Park began offering outdoor concerts and plays. Businesses beat a path to Portsmouth and, rather than running roughshod over its history, saw an opportunity to blend in. Chains like Newberry's and Walgreen's gave way to unusual shops like Water Monkey Funky Outfitters and sidewalk eateries like Café Brioche.

Amid all these changes, Vaughan remained active in historic preservation. As the city learned to appreciate its heritage, her role changed from crusader to consultant. She became a fixture at city council meetings, and an adviser in the delicate blending of the new and the old. When the developer of the now prominent Sheraton Hotel came to the city, Vaughan gave him a walking tour of downtown, pointing out the historic gems that made it unique.

The presence of the navy yard, the Pease International Tradeport, and the city's seaside location mean it will always have a place on the map, Cocchiaro said. But without Vaughan and her compatriots, it would be showing a very different face to the world.

At the end of the twentieth century, the current of change continued to shape the city. The population hovered at 23,000. Tourism continued to grow. *Money* magazine regularly rated the city among the top ten best places to live in the United States. The redevelopment of Pease promised renewed commerce. High-tech industry courted the city for its chic, artsy appeal, bringing computer and Internet business to the worker-friendly area. Nearly twenty hi-tech firms made their homes in downtown Portsmouth, earning it the nickname the e-Coast.

Yet all the change sprung from the same passion to keep things the same. Today, residents and tourists alike will tell you why the city stands out. "It's old, but it's lovely. And I think that's how we'd like to keep it," Foley said.

"We just heard it was a really beautiful city with a lot of history," said Susan Haines, a visitor from Massachusetts.

Sherburne House as it looks today, the pride of Strawbery Banke.

Ken Williams/Concord Monitor.

And though the average tourist may never hear of Vaughan, she has not been forgotten for her part in that history. In 1965, she was awarded an honorary doctorate of humane letters from the University of New Hampshire. In 1968, she visited with Lady Bird Johnson at the White House. In 1987, she was listed among Charles Brereton's *New Hampshire Notables*. She has also received a lifetime achievement award from the National Rotary Club and a plaque from Strawbery Banke, crediting her with saving Portsmouth's waterfront neighborhood.

Vaughan keeps all of these mementos—the still-shiny plaque, the telegram invitation to Lady Bird's luncheon, the menu listing prosciutto and melon and filet of sole veronique—among her piles of treasured books.

But she hardly has time to dwell on them. These days Vaughan keeps busy serving as a hostess for the historic Wentworth Gardner House and doing research for a book about Portsmouth's first women settlers. She's also working with other historians to get the original state house moved back to Portsmouth from Concord. "I guess I just do what comes naturally," she said.

Tara Mounsey

She won a gold medal—and inspired a generation.

BY SANDY SMITH

The little hands stretch desperately over the railings, fingers wiggling in anticipation of a touch from their hero—a high-five would be almost too much to hope for. Yet as the hockey players file toward the locker room between periods, they extend their bulky gloved hands to the youngsters, who peer giddily into the tunnel until the final ponytail disappears.

Women have been playing ice hockey since the dawn of the twentieth century, but until the 1990s, most people figured the ponytails hanging below a helmet had to belong to a long-haired boy. Girls playing hockey? You must mean field hockey.

Mounsey practices in her uncle's backyard during a Christmas break from school.

Andrea Bruce/Concord Monitor.

All that has changed. When Tara Mounsey and her United States team-mates won the first-ever Olympic gold medal for women's hockey at the 1998 Winter Games in Nagano, Japan, it was suddenly all right for little girls to pick up sticks, to step on the ice with dark skates without toe picks.

"We were performing out there not only for ourselves, but for the sport of ice hockey and the future of women's athletics in general," said Mounsey, a defenseman on the Olympic team. "We were out there playing, and one of our main goals was to supply the United States and the whole world with role models for younger athletes."

That's something Mounsey didn't have when she began playing Concord Youth Hockey. When she slipped on that first tournament jersey at the age of five and a half, she had no way of knowing the impact she'd eventually have on hundreds of thousands of aspiring young athletes.

"We never thought it was anything out of the ordinary. We never knew where it would go," said Mike Mounsey, Tara's dad. "We just did it because it was what you did. You couldn't play other sports at five and a half, but you could play Concord Youth Hockey."

Maybe Concord was ahead of its time. While some of her future Olympic teammates were hiding their long hair under helmets or registering under false names simply to play hockey, Mounsey wasn't even the only girl playing with the boys back in the mid-1980s in Concord. Players like Stacy Boudrias, Stephanie Acres, and Sheila Killion were already donning Concord Youth Hockey uniforms, blending in—and fitting in—with the predominantly boys' teams.

Sure, there were occasional heckles from the crowd, but overwhelmingly, playing hockey with the boys was a positive experience for Mounsey and her family. In fact, according to her parents, when Mounsey began playing on all-girls' teams, the opposing girls took more cheap shots at her than did the boys.

Mounsey signs autographs at the Manchester Airport on her triumphant return from the 1998 Olympics in Nagano, Japan.

A. J. Wolfe/Concord Monitor.

The sport of hockey was always just that to the Mounseys: a sport, something to work hard at and have fun with. The thought of Tara as a pioneer didn't cross their minds. A few school districts in Massachusetts had already established girls' programs, and prep schools had been offering the sport to females for years. That Mounsey was playing didn't make her special.

How she was playing, now that's a different story.

The Mounseys, and the country, caught their first glimpse of things to come when Tara scored on an end-to-end rush to lead the New Hampshire Selects girls' team to the national Pee Wee championship. By that point, Mounsey was beginning to realize her potential.

Her first USA Hockey development camp, as a young teenager, in St. Cloud, Minnesota, stacked her up against the top players from around the United States. "At those camps, that's when you can tell if you've got what it takes or if you don't," Mounsey said.

She did.

In fact, Mounsey quickly became the first and only girl ever to make the Concord High School hockey team—as a freshman.

"When I made the Concord High team, I knew that was paving the way and giving some younger girls confidence," Mounsey said. "I think that just opened some doors and allowed younger girls to gain some confidence and see that someone could do something extremely challenging and succeed."

For Mounsey, however, gaining acceptance in a predominantly male sport and making the Concord High team were the easy part. The biggest challenges lay ahead.

Just before Christmas her sophomore year, Mounsey's hockey future lay crumpled on the blue line on the ice at Everett Arena. A blown-out knee forced her to miss the remainder of the season. For someone accustomed to playing and working out daily, the following months were harder to take than the championship loss the previous season. Mounsey threw herself into rehab as wholly as she did the game. But that set her back further. She developed tendinitis in her knee, and a second surgery kept her off the ice her entire junior season as well.

"I had a goal to win a state championship for Concord High. I had a goal to go to a Division I college and play hockey, a goal to win a gold medal in the '98 Olympics," Mounsey said. "I just felt like I would be a failure if I didn't stick it out."

Her return was worth the wait. She was named a captain her senior year, leading Concord to an undefeated championship season and earning herself state Player of the Year honors. A month later, she was named to her first U.S. women's national team at eighteen years old. A month after that, as the most highly recruited player in the country, Mounsey chose an Ivy League education and the opportunity to play for Brown University.

All the sacrifices—predawn skates, early nights, saying no to nights out with friends—were beginning to yield dividends.

"There were definitely things I didn't do growing up that other kids did," Mounsey said. "But as I got older, I'd choose to go to bed earlier so I could get up early and skate and work out before school."

It didn't take long for Mounsey to put her mark on the college game. She scored two goals with five assists in her debut—outrageous numbers for any player, unheard of for a defenseman. By the time the season was through, Mounsey was named a first-team all-star as well as Rookie of the Year in both the East Coast Athletic Conference and Ivy League.

The day the season ended, she headed to Lake Placid to join the national team in preparation for the World Championships and helped lead the United States to a silver medal, finishing just behind nemesis Canada. Moments after the grueling overtime loss in the gold medal game, Mounsey said: "We're almost there, and I think we'll get (the gold) when it counts."

Her words were prophetic.

"Tara's not only a great athlete but also a bright, articulate young woman. She's the kind of person who helps foster the positive image we try to embody," said Olympic coach Ben Smith. "You don't have to be at Brown and see all the kids huddled over the railings trying to touch her to know the impact she's had. Her eyes just sparkle through the mask. You can tell she cares about the sport and loves sharing it with others."

She cared enough to postpone her sophomore year of college to train with the national team for the Olympics. And when the pre-Olympic tour opened on her home ice, New Hampshire greeted Mounsey with an ovation that nearly lifted the roof off old Everett Arena.

Mounsey finished the tour as the top-scoring defenseman and the fifth-leading scorer overall, but in the next-to-last game before leaving for Japan, she twisted her good knee on a routine play. Mounsey vowed she'd be fine, that nothing would stop her from playing on the Olympic stage. But up to the day before the opening game, Coach Smith wasn't so sure.

Mounsey, pictured during the world championships in Canada in 1997.

Denise Sanchez/Concord Monitor.

When the United States took the ice against China, there was Mounsey, scoring a goal and assisting on another in a 5–0 win. Team USA went on to beat Sweden, Finland, Japan, and Canada to reach the gold medal game on February 17, 1998. Mounsey had racked up two goals and four assists through those five games, again leading U.S. defensemen in scoring, all the while playing on a bum knee.

To this day, she downplays the injury. "I was in pain, but not as much as it was made out to be. Everyone had bumps and bruises. It's kind of turned into this huge injury, like I was a hero because I was injured. But I didn't want that," Mounsey said.

Only Mounsey knows how she felt, but Coach Smith knows how he and the team felt. "She's such a competitor, and she demonstrated that to her teammates both personally and physically," Smith said. "You see the reaction she gets on the ice, but you don't know the admiration from her teammates and the coaches. It's felt by everyone in the locker room."

It's no wonder that even after Mounsey took a costly penalty, resulting in Canada's lone goal to make it 2–1 late in the gold medal game, Smith put her right back on the ice for the final minutes. And when the United States scored an empty net goal, the 3–1 victory was history. Mounsey and her 19 teammates had won the first Olympic gold medals awarded in women's hockey.

What came next is a blur. Mounsey and nine of her teammates appeared on *The Late Show* with David Letterman that night. There were parades and countless requests for appearances.

At home, she was immediately recognizable. Strangers in stores or walking down the street did double-takes. "What surprised me was all the boys waiting to have her sign autographs," said Sue Mounsey, Tara's mother. "It wasn't just the girls. Little kids will remember her like we remember Bobby Orr."

Her newfound fame was overwhelming at times, but Mounsey welcomed the chance to share her story.

"It changed for a while, as far as the lifestyle, having to do interviews, all kinds of appearances, and it's still like that to a point," Mounsey said in 1999. "But overall, I can honestly say it hasn't changed me at all."

Mounsey went on to study pre-med at Brown, with hopes of becoming an orthopedic surgeon. She put her education on hold again, however, in hopes of competing with Team USA in the 2002 Olympics in Salt Lake City.

"I enjoy the feeling that little kids are looking up to me and want to do something good with their lives, become a star hockey player or a star musician, just do something and stay out of trouble," she said. "I really value my position."

Sam Tamposi and Gerald Nash

They built New Hampshire's southern tier.

BY TIM MCLAUGHLIN

S am Tamposi Sr. and Gerald Nash lived by their word and launched multi-million-dollar development projects with just a handshake.

The next time you drive through Nashua and the rest of New Hampshire's southern tier, try to imagine fallow land, shuttered mills, and laid-off workers loitering along vacant storefronts. That image doesn't come easily, especially when you're tied up in commuter traffic and corporate head-liners such as Fidelity Investments, Anheuser Busch, Coca-Cola, Raytheon, Sylvania, and Honeywell stare at you in every direction. Tamposi and Nash lured scores of these firms, many from Massachusetts, to New Hampshire by

Nash (left) and Tamposi on the cover of *Country Lifestyles* magazine in 1990.

260

selling them land or swiftly developing factories and office buildings for their workers.

And when they weren't wheeling and dealing real estate, Tamposi and Nash played kingmaker. State representatives, governors, U.S. senators, and presidents spanning three decades owe debts to the two men from Nashua.

But in the 1950s, their hometown and the rest of the state reeled when major employers closed their textile and shoe plants and migrated south for cheaper labor. The economic exodus edged Nashua dangerously close to becoming a ghost town.

But a Friday night poker match nearly forty years ago served as a pivotal moment in Nashua's emergence as a center for economic development. That's when Sam Tamposi, the son of a Romanian immigrant, met Gerald Nash, a fourth-generation box maker. Tamposi was a Dale Carnegie graduate and a plunger at the card table. Nash was a detail man and more circumspect. But both men knew what hard work was and how to sell when nobody was buying.

"We hit it off immediately," recalled Nash, whose longtime business partner died of cancer in 1995.

During their heyday in the 1960s and 1970s, Tamposi and Nash developed 120 acres of commercial and industrial land per year, or about half of the state's economic growth during that period. On a handshake, they developed a 125,000-square-foot building for Digital Equipment Corp., which moved in before signing a lease. As Nashua grew, so did the surrounding communities of Hudson, Merrimack, Amherst, Hollis, and Litchfield.

Former governor Walter Peterson credits Tamposi and Nash with playing a major role in turning a region on the brink of decay into a suburban hotbed of technology and high-paying jobs. Today, one in five of the state's manufacturing jobs are in Nashua, Hudson, and Merrimack.

"They were important to all of New Hampshire," said Peterson, who grew up next to Nash and was a high school classmate of Tamposi. "They were both frenetic, hard-driving kind of guys who had a lot of confidence."

There were critics too. In the 1980s, as the real estate boom crept northward, residents warned local politicians *not* to turn their communities into mini-versions of Nashua, with its traffic jams, chain retailers, and roadways galore. "That's the last thing we want to be," one man told the Concord Planning Board in 1988. "They've paved over all the land down there."

But Tamposi and Nash didn't just sell land. They sold New Hampshire, its tax advantage over Massachusetts and the work ethic of its residents. They were golden long before hipsters started using the word to describe everyday occurrences. Admirers called Tamposi "King Midas."

Nash offers a different comparison. "I liken land to wine. After you squeeze the grapes, you put it away, you age it, and it gets more and more valuable," he explained. "We had a good ability at looking at land and seeing its value in the future."

Nasi Tambose, Sam Tamposi's father, emigrated to the United States in 1907 when he was sixteen years old. Born in Avdella, Macedonia, he grew up in a territory where the borders constantly changed. He was considered a Vlach, a mix of Bulgarian and Romanian. Ethnic differences in that region could be bloody and fatal: Turkish soldiers murdered Nasi Tambose's father. After coming to America, Nasi Tambose moved his family from New York City to a farm in Nashua. Born in 1924, Sam Tamposi grew up baling hay, milking cows and caring for vegetables. His destiny wasn't farming, though. He was a born salesman whose credo was "Hustle is the name of the game."

Indeed, Sam Tamposi could sell. His first deal was a $2 junk car he sold for $10, according to his oldest son, Sam Tamposi Jr. He sold everything from airplane rides at Nashua's airport to Electrolux vacuum cleaners door-to-door. When other salesmen quit at dinner time, Tamposi knocked on doors late into the evening. Tamposi earned $1,000 his first month selling vacuum cleaners. The feat earned him a trip to the Waldorf-Astoria.

In the mid-1950s, his native Nashua was losing its economic velocity. In one fell swoop, Textron shut down, leaving 1,500 workers scrambling for jobs. About that time, Tamposi entered the real estate game, investing his life savings in an abandoned building. Space back then could be had for twenty-five cents a square foot.

Tamposi's first development project was a building for McCallister Scientific in 1959. A few years later, he met Nash at the poker match.

Like Tamposi, Nash grew up selling. As a child, he bought a metal wagon from his sales of Larkin Soap. He sold fireworks in the summer and sold popcorn balls to Works Progress Administration workers for a nickel apiece during the Depression.

When he got older, Nash worked in his father's paper box factory and made twenty-five cents an hour. His father was a businessman from the old school. "His word was his bond. You did the right thing. You kept the truth," said Nash, who learned his father's philosophy while accompanying him on business trips.

Nash and his partner were the engine of the southern tier economy.
Courtesy of Gerald Nash.

Before meeting Tamposi, Nash dabbled in real estate, but most of his time was spent at the Nashua Paper Box Co., where he was a part owner. After selling his stake to his brother Ralph, Nash joined Tamposi full-time.

When making a deal, Tamposi and Nash answered to no one but themselves. They snapped up land and developed buildings on speculation, which means they did not have tenants signed up before construction began. "We weren't afraid to own a building," Nash said. "We didn't bet anything we couldn't back up."

Both men had a knack for looking at a piece of raw ground and seeing its possibilities. Once settled on a site, they financed their plans through a combination of their own equity and bank financing. Once they established a track record of success, lenders were eager to finance their projects.

It wasn't unusual for them to have four or five projects going simultaneously. In all, they developed about 120 commercial buildings.

"Sam and I, when we were developing in our prime, could borrow from any bank in New Hampshire," Nash said.

Once in the door, Tamposi and Nash introduced prospective clients to mayors and the governor. This sort of treatment, and the promise of a new office building in less than four months, appealed to out-of-state businesses used to red tape in Massachusetts. "They named the price. We got it done fast," Nash said. "We knew everybody and got the projects going."

Tamposi wasn't somebody who enjoyed working with details. He looked at projects in broad strokes. After a project got going, Nash said it was usually his job to watch over the construction.

"We had our differences," Nash said. "We'd yell at each other. We kept separate offices for when one of us was miffed we weren't rubbing elbows. It makes for better relations."

Their relationship also allowed for either one to freelance without the other. One such deal came in 1963 when Tamposi announced the development of the New England Automotive Center, a consortium of about a dozen dealerships in one location. The idea was novel and controversial. Nashua downtown merchants opposed Tamposi's project because it would move several dealerships off Main Street. The group went to court and won an injunction against Tamposi's project. He ignored the court order, however, risking his own capital by moving forward with the project.

Tamposi fought his opposition by going door-to-door asking neighbors personally to support his plan. He also convinced Detroit auto makers to back his development. In the end, Tamposi won, creating the first auto village in the country. The concept has become a standard in the industry.

A major disappointment for the men came in the early 1970s when they unveiled a proposal for a massive mixed development project in Merrimack. The planned urban development of 3,500 acres called for a self-sustaining community including retail shops, housing, schools, and a fire station.

"It would have been like Reston, Virginia," Nash explained.

Opposition was fierce. Partly because of Tamposi and Nash's industrial projects in Merrimack, the town's population nearly quadrupled from 4,000 in 1960 to 15,400 in 1980. Critics said the developers weren't interested in the environment or orderly growth. They argued that a vote for the project would be a vote for Central Park muggings, more traffic congestion, more crime, and no birds, Sam Tamposi Jr. recalled. The critics won out.

Nash and Tamposi changed their tactics. They sold 950 acres of the land to Digital Equipment Corp. Those office buildings now are occupied by Fidelity Investments. And piece by piece the would-be master-planned community became a thriving enclave of office and industrial development.

But Nash and Tamposi's idea did not die at the hands of the Merrimack Planning Board. Instead, they squirreled it away for another time in another place.

In the early 1960s, Tamposi and Nash started assembling land in Citrus Hills, Florida, which featured rolling terrain of watermelon fields and forests seventy miles north of Tampa. As Nashua boomed in the 1970s, the developers waited patiently for their Citrus Hills plan to bear fruit.

Meanwhile, the men enjoyed their wealth and influence. They helped elect their friend Walter Peterson governor in 1969. They were confidants of Barry Goldwater, Gerald Ford, and Richard Nixon. In the 1980s, they lunched with Ronald Reagan and George Bush. In the 1990s, Nash counted Bob and Elizabeth Dole as his close friends. He thinks Elizabeth would make a good president.

"We both thought you should be involved in politics," Nash said. "You have to back up what you like."

In 1977, Tamposi was invited to become a limited partner in the ownership of the Boston Red Sox. Warren Rudman vouched for his credentials.

Tamposi became a serious baseball fan and started making trips with the team. He struck up a relationship with slugging legend Ted Williams. The Splendid Splinter loved to fish and had a favorite spot not far from the land Tamposi and his partner were accumulating in Citrus Hills.

After a tour, Williams became a spokesman for the project and eventually built a home there. The first development on the 4,000 acres came in 1982. Five years later, the dream of a master-planned community was well under way. Nashua wasn't faring too badly either. *Money Magazine* ranked the city as America's Number One place to live.

Tamposi and Nash were rich men who still got jazzed creating deals. Asked about a 1979 magazine article that put his net worth in excess of $20 million, Tamposi told a reporter, with a wink, "Well, that was several years ago."

"Money became secondary to making deals," Tamposi Jr. said. "He liked seeing other people succeed. He had a lot of partners who did well. He always liked to see people improve themselves."

Elizabeth Titus Putnam

She founded the Student Conservation Association to improve and protect the national parks.

When Elizabeth Titus Putnam was a sophomore in college, she read a magazine article about the sorry state of America's national parks. That's all it took to launch an idea that became a lifelong crusade. Putnam's senior project was a plan to match crews of young people with conservation projects that meager national park budgets couldn't cover. She was introduced to a former National Park Service official, and the Student Conservation Association, now headquartered in Charlestown, New Hampshire, was born.

Elizabeth Titus Putnam is responsible for maintaining and improving national parks.
Courtesy of Student Conservation Association.

From its founding in 1957 through the turn of the century, 35,000 people volunteered through the SCA. In 1999, that meant more than a million hours of volunteer time for national parks and other organizations. Some students worked on four-week summer crews; some did yearlong internships. After fire devastated Yellowstone National Park in 1988, the SCA brought in 600 volunteers over the next three summers.

In 1993, Hurricane Hugo prompted a similar effort in the Florida Everglades.

From Putnam's perspective, the strength of the program remains the commitment of its volunteers. "It's the most wonderful feeling when you see your fledgling baby, now forty-three years old, in the hands of such absolutely wonderful people," she said in 1999. "I feel blessed."

Robert Rines

He founded New Hampshire's only law school.

By the end of the twentieth century, the term "renaissance man" already sounded old-fashioned. That is, unless it was attached to the name Robert Rines.

Rines was a lawyer, a physicist, an author, a composer, an educator, an inventor—and a serious Loch Ness Monster investigator. So when you learn that he set out in 1973 to start a brand-new law school specializing in patent law in a Concord barn, somehow it doesn't sound far-fetched. More important, it worked.

The Franklin Pierce Law Center definitely started out as a countercultural institution. Students included a handful of scientists and doctors, some students looking for a nontraditional legal education, and some who had been turned down by traditional schools. Students grew vegetables on school property. Books were donated from the Supreme Court and from companies that

Among Rines's many inventions: the Franklin Pierce Law Center.

Ken Williams/Concord Monitor.

were downsizing. Rines scraped and painted secondhand furniture for the school, with the help of his in-laws.

"Everybody felt part of the spirit of it," Rines said. "We became fast friends."

And they were serious, too. By the 1990s, Franklin Pierce had become one of the country's top institutions to study intellectual property law, outranking Harvard, Stanford, and Columbia. "We are," said a professor at the 1999 graduation ceremony, "the little law school that could."

Derek Owen

His stone walls stand the test of time.

For much of the twentieth century, there was little use for the stone walls erected by the earliest settlers of New England. They stood in the way of telephone lines, of new highways, of progress. They marked old farm boundary lines that didn't matter anymore with factories, banks, and housing developments buying up the land. If they were in the way, stone walls were knocked down.

Derek Owen of Hopkinton, a builder and teacher, helped change all that.

Stone walls may be part of New Hampshire's town-green-and-white-steeple history, but they are also attractive and useful. By the 1970s, they were

Derek Owen repairs a wall he built in Concord.

Ken Williams/Concord Monitor.

popular again. Owen has built them in Hopkinton and all over Merrimack County. He's built them in Vermont, Connecticut, and Maine. When the Smithsonian Institution wanted to celebrate New Hampshire culture in 1999, Owen built one in Washington.

"Stone walls have proven the test of time," Owen says. "Concrete hasn't. We like to think it will last. It should—we grow stones in New Hampshire."

Dudley Dudley, Ron Lewis and Nancy Sandberg

They defeated Aristotle Onassis's plan to build an oil refinery on Durham Point.

Ron Lewis broke the story in a tiny local newspaper. Nancy Sandberg led the citizen group in opposition. Rep. Dudley Dudley backed them up with State House politicking. And in the end, small town America had beaten the richest man in America.

In the 1970s, when oil prices were high and the lines for gasoline were long, Aristotle Onassis proposed building the world's largest oil refinery at Durham Point. He had the support of Gov. Meldrim Thomson, who had promised to "drill in the mountains and drill in the valleys" to find oil in New Hampshire.

Aristotle Onassis (right) chats with Gov. Meldrim Thomson in 1973. Onassis had proposed a $600 million oil refinery on Durham Point.
AP/Wide World Photos.

And he had the support of William Loeb, publisher of the *Union Leader* of Manchester, which rolled out the red carpet in a headline the day Onassis arrived: "Welcome to the two Big Os, Oil and Onassis."

But the voice of opposition was stronger. And when the Legislature finally voted on a bill granting the state authority to approve the refinery despite overwhelming local opposition, Onassis lost – big time.

"I was young enough at the time to think the right side won most of the time. And so I did have that confidence," Dudley said, marveling at her victory twenty-five years later. "People could say that could have been arrogance. I don't know. But I knew that we were in the right."

Guy Chichester

In the battle against Seabrook, he was an inspiring leader.

BY STEVE VARNUM

Until the Clamshell Alliance, the fight over the licensing and construction of the Seabrook nuclear power plant was a nice clean one.

It was argued by nice clean lawyers in nice clean suits. They gathered in nice clean buildings to trade piles of nice clean documents. The public, to the extent that it knew about the project at all, aired its concerns in nice clean columns of newsprint.

Truth is, says Guy Chichester, there was no fight. It was a mismatch: poorly financed citizen groups against a small army of industry bureaucrats and government regulators. The reports were highly technical, with highly adaptable conclusions. State and federal licensing officials who opposed the project were replaced by those who moved it along.

"It was always an exercise in making the paperwork fit the licensing process. That's all it ever was," says Chichester, who was president of one of

Chichester was among hundreds of anti-Seabrook protesters in the 1970s.
Jimi Allen/Concord Monitor.

273

those citizen groups, the Seacoast Anti-Pollution League. The Clamshell Alliance shifted everything. In the summer of 1976, Chichester huddled among anti-nuclear activists plotting strategy around picnic tables and living rooms all over New England and taking their message to meeting halls, streets, and the construction site.

From then on there was a fight, and it wasn't a nice clean one. It looked like hand-drawn placards, sounded like songs and slogans, felt like the tired shoulders of police officers dragging sagging bodies onto buses, and smelled like hundreds of people jailed for two weeks in National Guard armories.

The Clams didn't stop construction of Seabrook Station, but they crippled it. Only one of two planned reactors ever went on line, with overruns of more than $5 billion that led to the bankruptcy of Public Service of New Hampshire, the state's largest utility.

The Clams' efforts, multiplied by the individuals and groups they educated and energized, crippled the industry as well. The Seabrook protests, along with the Three Mile Island accident in Pennsylvania three years later, turned popular opinion against nuclear power. As a result, no nuclear reactor ordered since 1973 has been completed.

Seabrook was a seismic shift in the way we look at nuclear power. And at the center of the quake stood Guy Chichester.

Chichester came late to political activism, in his late thirties, but was born into political awareness. He grew up in Queens, son of a New York City fireman and a telephone operator, both of whom were union members. His family instilled the importance of participation and political action. City politics was discussed constantly.

He remembers going with his aunt and grandmother to vote when he was still a young boy. They went behind the curtain, pulled levers, then went home and waited for whatever was going to happen next.

"This was a very mysterious process . . . but it was important baby, it was important!"

A self-proclaimed "newshound," Chichester says as a young man, "I did all the things you don't do in a bar—discuss religion and politics.

"I always went with plenty of information and was able to convince people. Turn them around, you know? And turning one vote around is like two votes. The guy who was going to get the vote doesn't, and your guy does."

He paid close attention to the forces shaking American culture in the 1950s and 1960s: in particular, the juxtaposition of the nonviolent civil rights movement, exemplified by Martin Luther King Jr., and the violence it was met with.

When Chichester returned from a four-year Navy hitch and got into carpentry, his quiet, agricultural Long Island was changing rapidly, and not for the better. Farms were plowed into housing developments, and the infrastructure of the small towns couldn't keep pace.

He and his wife Madeline moved east to Stony Brook, and the development was right behind them. "We were always running away from the land shark," Chichester says. By the time their kids were in school, they couldn't go to work or the grocery store without being clogged in traffic.

As a kid, he'd spent summers in Downeast Maine with his grandfather, in a house with no electricity or running water and "air conditioned plumbing." They picked blueberries, fished for "tommycod" on Penobscot Bay, and waited for the supply wagon to come from Blue Hill every two weeks.

"We had wonderful, wonderful times there. I loved that part of the world," he says.

So when the land shark chased them clear off Long Island in 1970, they landed in Center Rye, New Hampshire. "This felt like old Long Island to me," he says.

Chichester heard it when Aristotle Onassis wanted to put an oil refinery on Durham Point, and he heard it when Public Service of New Hampshire wanted to put its nuclear reactor in Seabrook, not far from his new home. The big lie.

"They tell you it's going to lower your taxes, provide good stable employment—and they overblow all of the projections enormously," he says. "In the case of the refinery, they said we wouldn't be subject to OPEC, we wouldn't be subject to people cutting off our oil supply. . . . New Hampshire would get gasoline and heating oil first.

"Always it's the jobs, the taxes, it's the candy shop of benefits that they hold out to people. And of course it's all bull———. The jobs as often as not are held by people who don't live here, they come from somewhere else. They just add more pressures onto the taxpayers when they get here."

The first big lie that energized Chichester was President Richard Nixon's "secret plan" to end the Vietnam war. As a local organizer for George McGovern in the 1972 presidential primary, he got Politics 101: Get the voter list, call every name, and offer rides to the polls. In Rye, Raymond, and Exeter, McGovern nipped rival Edward Muskie. McGovern left New Hampshire not with a win, but with momentum that propelled him to the nomination.

"I have a big belief in the ability of people to get information and use it wisely in that process. I think that's what real democracy is all about," says Chichester. "You give people information, you give them a fair kind of reading on what it's all about from as many angles as possible. They'll be able to figure out which way to go."

In the midst of a successful fight against Aristotle Onassis's oil refinery proposal, a representative of the Seacoast Anti-Pollution League had come to Rye with a message: "If you guys really want something to worry about, do you know they're building a nuclear power plant down in Seabrook?"

The proposal had burrowed through a maze of governmental agencies for years, but had barely cracked the public consciousness.

Even if it had, most people probably would have favored it. After a decade of Arab embargos and oil spills, nuclear power was widely viewed as a cheaper, cleaner—even safer—energy source. And after Hiroshima and Nagasaki, there was something in the American psyche that hungered to use this fearsome new energy for good.

But there was much the public didn't know. "They were setting the American people up as guinea pigs," Chichester says. "Because (the government) understood that radiation is a killer, and that it was not well understood, and that the technology was new, and that no one could predict what would happen with it. And that there would be accidents and that people were going to be hurt, made sick, and killed.

"And that it was all going to be controlled in secret by an agency (the Atomic Energy Commission) whose mission was to develop the nuclear power industry."

He began working with the Seacoast Anti-Pollution League in January 1975 after reading an AEC report that projected thousands of casualties in the case of a nuclear meltdown and radioactive release. What was worse, he thought, was that the government seemed to shrug at that possibility.

Chichester didn't. He became SAPL's president.

SAPL was not anti-nuclear at the time. Its official concern was mitigating the environmental and other problems the plant could cause. Chichester knew this open-mindedness was only a strategic position for some members, their ticket into the process.

He saw that as a trap. By not opposing the project, he thought, they were helping advance it. Within months the group came out against the nuke.

The need to educate himself about nuclear power quickly put him in touch with activists with more radical ideas than SAPL was entertaining. One, an organic farmer named Sam Lovejoy, had cut down a weather tower at the site of a proposed nuclear project in western Massachusetts that was later canceled.

A film was made about Lovejoy's nuclear war, and Chichester brought it to a SAPL meeting. In it, social critic and historian Howard Zinn observed that nearly every progressive law is 180 degrees different from the one it replaced, and that only when citizens rebel against the entrenched order and injustice are those laws changed. He described civil disobedience to force such change as an honorable democratic tradition.

"That was about all I needed," said Chichester. "I had been thinking about, how do we get people in the streets? I didn't know really how. I was not quite ready yet." What had been missing were the moment and the opportunity. "Now I could see that I got enough right here and this is the moment."

Chichester was determined to move the opposition faster, farther than others in SAPL were comfortable with. He had already been involved in leafleting customers of a bank whose directors were involved with PSNH. He had helped hoist a demonstrator onto a 120-foot pole on the Seabrook site, where he stayed for three days in the dead of winter.

In summer of 1976, with representatives of grass-roots anti-nuclear groups from throughout New England, he founded the Clamshell Alliance and became its first spokesman.

The Clam philosophy drew from the teachings of King and Gandhi. "The people in a just cause are the equal of any government in terms of a great contest, if they will conduct themselves in nonviolence and directly confront the government until the job is done," says Chichester.

A Chichester-drafted statement of purpose was accepted. Its bottom line: Through direct action and civil disobedience, the group would prevent Seabrook from being licensed and operated and work toward the shutdown of all nuclear power plants in New England.

Seabrook was the focal point because it wasn't licensed yet and because it was in the realm of a certain pro-nuclear zealot. "We could count on a gross overreaction from Mel Thomson. And we were excited by the prospect," he says. "So Seabrook became IT."

It was too much for some of SAPL's directors, who feared his actions might compromise their legal intervention. Chichester resigned, and the no-nukes cause got an impassioned spokesman. Many among the several thousand who demonstrated against the plant, who invaded the construction site, who got arrested, and who remained environmental and political activists more than twenty years later say it was a Chichester speech that spurred them to action.

> Give the world the best you have
> and the best will come back to you.

Chichester calls it the family motto. It hangs, cross-stitched by Madeline, in the corner of their kitchen in Center Rye where he warms organic vegetable soup in a microwave oven on a muggy afternoon. Outside, salt breezes stir the air.

He has been a full-time political activist, consultant, family cook, and housekeeper for about twenty-five years now; Madeline, a lighting specialist, brings home the regular paycheck. In those years Chichester has won some, lost some, and history will judge the rest.

The work has meant time spent away from his family, time in court and time in jail. Chichester was working at a Clamshell command center and wasn't among the 1,414 arrested in the giant 1977 Seabrook demonstration, but has been at least a dozen times since. He was arrested in 1990 after chainsawing a Seabrook siren pole and acquitted in 1993 after arguing that the New Hampshire Constitution gave him the right because he had no other redress to stop Seabrook.

With eleven others, he was jailed for five days last year after trespassing during a protest at weapons manufacturer Lockheed Martin Sanders in Nashua. He has been arrested in every New England state and at the Pentagon.

All part of the work, he says. "If you're working in a just cause and have to make certain sacrifices, you sleep soundly at night," he says.

"What will come back to you is peace of mind. And that, you know, is gold."

Pierre Hevey

His credit union, the first in the country, served Manchester's French mill workers.

BY NANCIE STONE

Gilberte Brosseau was only a child on Manchester's West Side when the nation's first credit union was born, but she remembers payday and the line of workers rushing home to do their banking.

"The mills closed at 5 or 5:30, and they would come up the hill like ants," Brosseau said in an interview taped in 1994, when she was eighty-nine. The workers were hustling toward her living room, headquarters of St. Mary's Bank.

They were hustling toward the hope of a better life. At the turn of the century, Manchester and its mills represented opportunity to the French Cana-

Pierre Hevey established St. Mary's Bank, the nation's first credit union.
Diocesan Museum, Manchester.

dians from Quebec who built Brosseau's neighborhood. But the river that powered the industry was also a line of demarcation between the established commerce of the city and the newcomers who settled the West Side. To build a strong community, immigrants needed capital, and Manchester's banks stood across the Merrimack River, a distance not only of miles but also of prejudice.

"It was difficult in terms of language barriers, cultural barriers," said David Deziel, St. Mary's vice president of marketing and member services. "No bank had what we would call a branch (on the West Side), so at the very least it was inconvenient."

In St. Mary's parish, Monsignor Pierre Hevey, the leader of the community as well as the church, heard of the credit union movement—people's banks—that had gathered strength in Europe. In 1907 Hevey introduced the idea to other leaders in his community, and within a year, St. Mary's Bank—La Caisse Populaire Ste. Marie—opened for business.

New Hampshire became the first state to pass a law relating to credit unions so that St. Mary's could incorporate. Though new to the United States, the concept of credit unions had taken hold in many European countries, beginning a half-century earlier. Groups that otherwise wouldn't qualify for credit created cooperative banks where decisions were made by members. A membership fee earned the right to join, set up accounts, or apply for farm and small business loans.

"That's a common thread in the history of credit unions," Deziel said. "They served the needs of underserved groups and people ignored by the mainstream institutions."

St. Mary's Bank had modest beginnings. Officers were volunteers. Joseph Boivin, Brosseau's father and St. Mary's first president, volunteered the family parlor as its headquarters. Advertising consisted of a sign in the living-room window.

Since Hevey wanted children to learn to save, he talked up the idea at the parish schools. Soon children were ringing the Boivins' doorbell on the way to school, proffering their nickels or dimes.

The bank's safe was a locked box that Brosseau's mother fretted about keeping in the house. Every so often a trusted member of the credit union took the money to a safer place, probably one of those banks across the river.

Her family sacrificed dining-room chairs to the comfort of waiting customers, then installed a bench in the hall. Evening meetings in her father's office, filled with cigar smoke and laughter, woke her up. During St. Mary's first year, 212 people paid the $5 membership fee so they could open accounts and borrow money. By the end of the century, St. Mary's Bank served 32,000 members throughout the state and held assets of $340 million, New Hampshire's second largest credit union.

"We still ask for that $5 membership," Deziel said.

For Hevey the credit union filled a larger vision for his parish. Hevey had come to New Hampshire from Quebec with a missionary's zeal, following his countrymen to a land that was considered a Protestant bastion. Hevey was not just a keeper of the Catholic faith but, as a leader in the community, also wanted to protect and foster the French Canadian culture, said Monsignor

Wilfrid Paradis of Manchester, who has written a history of the Catholic Church in New Hampshire.

"Hevey probably thought they would be able to continue life somewhat isolated to preserve language and faith," Paradis said. "They wanted to keep those two things that made them individual."

Hevey arrived in Manchester in 1882 to minister to St. Mary's parish. He set out to create the institutions that bind a community.

"As a person he was sure of himself and assumed quite an authority," Paradis said. "That was the style of the clergy, but he had a bit more of it." By the time of his death in 1910, Hevey had rebuilt St. Mary's church after a fire that destroyed the original wooden structure. The brick church still stands on the hill above the Merrimack and Manchester's mill buildings.

Hevey established the hospital that is now Catholic Medical Center a few blocks south of the church. He opened schools for girls and boys, bringing nuns from Canada and brothers from Europe to teach. He established the convent where the sisters lived. He opened two orphanages and started a nursing home for those at the other end of life. He established a cemetery. In all he began twenty-five institutions, one of them the credit union.

"What he was trying to do is make the French Canadian community sort of self-sufficient, well organized, educated in the faith, taking care of the needy," Paradis said.

For decades St. Mary's Bank had no ambitions beyond the borders of its neighborhoods. The common language was French, and loans stayed local, a grocery store on one block, a shoe store on another. Individuals could borrow to build a house for their family, perhaps one of the triple-deckers that still line West Side streets.

Borrowers and lenders were neighbors and friends, making the credit union a cooperative venture for the community's success or failure. "You knew literally you were taking that (loan) from your neighbor," Deziel said.

After six or seven years Brosseau's family got its parlor back when St. Mary's Bank rented a building a few blocks down the street. In 1916 the bank hired its first manager. By 1923 the credit union had $1 million in assets, and in 1930 it built its first bank headquarters, a marble-faced building that later succumbed to urban renewal.

St. Mary's main bank office now sits within view of Brosseau's living room, at the base of the hill that mill workers once climbed to reach her house. Not until the 1980s, when it opened a branch downtown and another at the northern end of Manchester, did St. Mary's look beyond its heritage as a neighborhood credit union.

"It was a question of philosophy and values for the board of directors," Deziel said. "They felt they ran a credit union as originally intended, a very small cooperative for a certain group of people in a certain location, and no one raised the question, 'Should we spread the good news?' "

Eventually, St. Mary's came to call all New Hampshire its community and provide the services you would expect of any bank. But unlike banks whose shares are traded in the stock market, St. Mary's shareholders are its customers.

"It sounds like a subtle difference to say the credit union customer is the owner, but it affects all decisions," Deziel said. "The goal is not to create huge payoffs for shareholders."

By the end of the twentieth century, St. Mary's was reaching out to new groups of consumers, such as Manchester's growing Spanish-speaking population. Although customers could still use French in the bank or request it at the ATM, some tellers also spoke Spanish.

In 1999, St. Mary's dedicated $650,000 to helping the Manchester Neighborhood Housing Service provide financial education and loans to families purchasing their first houses.

"We were founded by a group of people that immigrated, encountered language and cultural barriers, came to town and got entry-level positions," Deziel said. "Those are our roots, so that's our mission: to help similar groups."

Lotte Jacobi

Some of the most memorable black-and-white images of the century were hers.

BY NANCIE STONE

Albert Einstein, Eleanor Roosevelt, Robert Frost. Chances are, if you re-member a photograph of these people, the image belongs to Lotte Jacobi.

She captured many of the famous people of the twentieth century in black-and-white photographs that took formality out of portraiture to reveal personality. At a time when photographers used set poses and studio props to convey social status and character, Jacobi carried her equipment and lights to her subject. She talked and listened and drew people out until they relaxed in front of the lens.

Jacobi took some of the most well-known photographs of the century.

Courtesy of Gary Samson.

"She helped free photography from being bound to the studio," said Gary Samson, a longtime friend who met Jacobi in the 1970s when he made a film about her. "Lotte was committed to revealing the person in front of the camera."

Born in Prussia in 1896, Jacobi fled Nazi Germany in the 1930s and came to New York City. She spent the last three decades of her life in Deering, New Hampshire.

Behind the camera she waited for those moments when her subjects were most themselves.

She accompanied Einstein when he sailed near his home on Long Island and photographed him pulling his boat from the water, his pant legs rolled up his calves. A year later, she photographed him in Princeton and caused a stir with her picture of him wearing a leather jacket. Not suitable for such a great man, she was told. She visited Frost in Vermont on a sweltering summer day, arriving rumpled and hot and finding him just as uncomfortable. Her appointment was short. But Frost, a man known for an acerbic nature, enjoyed the visit so much that he canceled his other appointments.

As they walked around his farm, Jacobi brought her camera and captured him with his hand outstretched to make a point.

"The advice she gave is to be ready to take that photo. Don't be so caught up in technique," Samson said.

Although Jacobi is best recognized for her portraits, her collection of more than 45,000 negatives includes landscapes, flowers, scenes of Deering and Hillsboro, cityscapes in Europe and New York, and people she met on her travels, which included a trip to Tajikstan and Uzbekistan in the 1930s. She

Jacobi's photographs took the formality out of portraiture.
Courtesy of the Lotte Jacobi Archive, UNH.

invented the art of photogenics, putting abstract images directly onto photo-sensitive paper.

Jacobi was the daughter, granddaughter, and great-granddaughter of photographers who ran a respected studio in Prussia. She began taking photographs with a pinhole camera she made when she was fourteen.

Her father moved the Jacobi studio to Berlin when Lotte was a young woman. She studied theater and cinematography, as well as photography. At one time she hoped to be an actress. Instead she pursued her fascination with the stage by photographing the personalities of Berlin's flourishing theater life in the 1920s and 1930s, among them Lotte Lenya, Peter Lorre, and Kurt Weill.

In the 1930s the Nazi party came to power and began closing businesses owned by Jews. Jacobi knew her family would have to leave Germany. In 1935 after her father died, Jacobi, her son from her first, brief marriage, and her mother came to New York, where they had extended family.

"She was not known in the states at all and had to struggle in the beginning," said Beatrice Trum Hunter, her daughter-in-law.

In a biography, *Lotte Jacobi Berlin New York,* authors Marion Beckers and Elisabeth Moortgart write that Jacobi was hampered by the personal tone of her photography, which was not appreciated in the United States. There was also the difficulty of breaking into the structured system of selling photographs to the media.

Many of the subjects of her portraits were fellow expatriates, who offered her introductions to other potential customers. Jacobi wasn't shy, and she used her camera as a way to meet people.

One such connection brought her to a reception for Eleanor Roosevelt, whom Jacobi admired. In the receiving line Jacobi told the first lady she wanted to take her picture. Roosevelt drew back. She hadn't always been pleased with pictures taken of her. A friend rescued the moment by telling Roosevelt that Jacobi was well known in Europe and a refugee—a fact that caught Roosevelt's interest. She later called Jacobi, said she had only a short time to pose, but then stayed later. One of the photographs became her official White House portrait.

Self-portrait, Berlin,
Germany, circa 1930.
Courtesy of the Lotte Jacobi
Archive, UNH.

In New York, Jacobi's son, John, married Beatrice Trum Hunter and converted a summer home in Deering into a guest house, where the family could live year-round. When Lotte Jacobi's second husband died and her apartment building was demolished to make way for Rockefeller Center in New York, she gave up the city and moved to Deering, living with her son and daughter-in-law for five years before buying a nearby cabin.

In Deering she came into her own. Jacobi was always an ardent supporter of democratic principles and individuality. In New Hampshire her voice carried, at Deering's town meeting, in the art associations, and in the Democratic Party, where she was a delegate to the national convention.

She defended photography as art, not a mechanical process. At a meeting of the New Hampshire Art Association she stood on a table to make her pitch that photography belonged in its shows. When she discovered that photography had been omitted from the exhibit of another New Hampshire art organization, she went to battle, although she had no plans to submit her own work.

"In ten minutes she had created a firestorm. She called grant agencies, and they brought pressure to bear," Samson said. "Lotte cared about photography enough that she didn't want to see it demeaned."

Jacobi did not hoard her talent any more than her opinions, welcoming other photographers to her home. She would spend an afternoon reviewing a student's work, giving it serious attention. She was sharp and direct, but she treated her students as equals.

"She said that you can't live without art. That is very much a part of life as breathing or eating," Hunter said.

Jacobi was passionate about her friendships, but once she wrote someone off, she never looked back and never forgave. She didn't care about money, and in New York she had to be told to charge more for her photographs. She never threw anything away, even saving the ticket she bought to sail to America. Decades later she called the Cunard Line to cash it in for a trip back to Europe.

She didn't drive a car until after she came to Deering, and despite lessons she was a menace on the roads. She preferred to call on her "magic carpet" for transportation: friends whom she invited to take her wherever she needed to go. Jacobi would promise an hour's trip but detour her way into an entire afternoon.

"She made people feel it was a privilege," Hunter said.

By the time she moved to Deering, it was known that commissions followed her requests.

Samson met her when the University of New Hampshire proposed making a film about her. "She was thrilled about that," said Samson, who now manages the university's Photographic and Instructional Services. "She wanted to be remembered for her work."

Jacobi, who photographed in black and white only, objected to filming in color. As a compromise, Samson proposed using color film but producing the piece in black and white if she insisted. He drove the finished film to Deering with trepidation. "She said, 'Oh, my God, I'm glad I didn't talk you into doing this in black and white,'" Samson said.

The trust that developed eventually led Jacobi to give her collection of negatives, prints, and papers to the university. The Library of Congress had offered to take them but warned it couldn't catalog them for ten years, Samson said. "Lotte said, 'Well, I'll be dead by then,'" he said.

In 1985 Jacobi's son died of cancer, a blow that Samson marks as the beginning of Jacobi's physical decline. She became forgetful and didn't eat right. She scorned help. Eventually she moved to a senior center in Concord. She died in 1990 and is buried in Deering.

Jacobi's legacy is her commitment to photography as a creative art that could capture the complexity of her subjects. "She really got to the soul, the inner being of the person," Hunter said. "In many of her good portraits you do feel you are looking at the inside of people."

Amy Beach

At the turn of the century, she was the country's top female composer.

BY NANCIE STONE

At the turn of century, when serious music was the province of men only, Amy Cheney Beach, a Henniker native, changed that tune. She became the country's foremost woman composer and one of the most popular composers of her time.

Amateur pianists formed Amy Beach Clubs in her honor. Symphonies across the United States—New York, Boston, Philadelphia, Chicago, St. Louis, Los Angeles—performed her orchestral pieces. A jubilee in Washington, D.C., honoring her seventy-fifth birthday devoted two nights to her work.

She was the first American woman to compose a symphony. At twenty-five,

A child prodigy, Beach became the nation's top female composer.

Courtesy of the University of New Hampshire.

she was the first woman to have work performed by the Handel and Haydn Society in Boston. And she was a virtuoso pianist who performed her compositions with orchestras in the United States and Europe.

"She is an example of someone in a pretty repressed time who became a role model," said Peggy Vagts, head of the music department at the University of New Hampshire. "There were few women composers . . . and not many women performers."

Beach composed in the Romantic style popular in the late 1800s, a music typified by lush harmonies and long melody lines. Women of that era were expected to compose songs. Beach's first major piece was a grand mass, completed when she was twenty-two. To undertake such a project revealed Beach's determination, ambition, and confidence.

"It's over an hour long. It's huge," Vagts said. "Any composer, male or female, would only write with the expectation you will get a performance."

The Handel and Haydn Society premiered the mass three years later.

Beach saved the many complimentary reviews that followed, and these are now part of the Milne Special Collections and Archives Department at the University of New Hampshire's Dimond Library. Music critics almost apologized for their praise. "When a young woman of nineteen, whose life has no public or professional purposes, but is passed in domestic quietude, sets herself to a great task in any art, and completes it at twenty-two, one cannot but note this with respect," began one unidentified columnist. "Especially is this the case if she chooses that art in which, as the authorities are agreed, it has been virtually impossible for women to accomplish anything independent and original—the art of music."

Newspapers described Beach as medium in height, stout—round and rosy, said one paper—with violet-blue eyes and brown hair that she pulled back into a bun. Her bearing was serious, but her rare laugh was hearty.

She was born in 1867 in Henniker. Her mother was a pianist and singer; her father was a paper manufacturer and importer. The stories of Beach as a child prodigy were repeated in newspapers across the country as respect for her work grew.

According to those accounts, Beach could sing whole songs on key by the time she was a year old and could improvise harmony to her mother's soprano before she was two. She identified musical keys with colors and so would ask her mother to play the pink song or the purple song. She played music by ear as soon as she was allowed at the piano at age four. Once when she was asked to play a piano that was tuned improperly, she transposed a Beethoven piece by a half-tone to correct for that.

During a stay in California with her mother, she used her perfect pitch to transcribe bird songs for a professor who was writing a book on the subject.

She began performing publicly at age seven, playing piano compositions suitable for adults. When Beach was eight, her family moved to Boston, where she attended private schools and received formal instruction in piano. She never received training in composition. At thirteen or fourteen she wrote the conductor of the Boston Symphony Orchestra asking if she could study with him and was told to learn on her own by transcribing musical scores. She did.

She made her debut as a pianist at sixteen and played with the Boston Symphony Orchestra at seventeen.

At eighteen she married. Harry Harris Aubry Beach was a prominent surgeon who was twenty-four years her senior. Because of his position in society he did not want his wife performing except for charity, and encouraged her to turn to composition. She wrote under the name Mrs. H. H. A. Beach.

In all she composed 150 pieces, including her *Gaelic Symphony,* the first by an American woman, and an opera. All but three of her works were published.

Harry Beach died in 1910, Amy Beach's mother only a few months later. Beach went to Europe to recover and eventually returned to performing, soloing with European orchestras. She came home in 1914 as World War I began.

Critics now introduced her as "the greatest woman composer in the country and one of the best in the world."

Beach moved to New York City. For the next decades, she performed during the winter season and composed during the summers. For fifteen summers she worked at MacDowell Colony in Peterborough.

Although Beach kept a diary from 1926 until a few weeks before her death, her writing reveals little about her. In tiny, crabbed lines she records weather, walks and meals, the visits of friends, new dresses, and times of journeys.

Even with friends she maintained the reserve of a Victorian lady about personal matters.

Beach was unflagging in her efforts to promote her music, keeping up a steady letter-writing campaign urging conductors, singers, and pianists to perform her work. One diary entry that Vagts recalls read, "I am half killed with letter writing."

In a 1918 article titled "To the Girl Who Wants to Compose" for *The Etude* journal of music, Beach wrote: "There is music which uplifts us to a point far above and beyond the mere emotional plane. . . . (Music) may be not only the creation of an art form, but a veritable autobiography, whether conscious or unconscious."

The University of New Hampshire keeps a collection of material related to Beach.

Ken Williams/Concord Monitor.

Her financial success enabled her to donate the proceeds of one song, "Ectasy," to rebuild the MacDowell Colony after it was damaged in the 1938 hurricane.

Toward the end of her life she suffered from congestive heart failure. She was too ill to attend the jubilee that celebrated her seventy-fifth birthday. The last entry in her diary was on November 5, 1944, when she wrote, "Not feeling well." She died December 27.

By the time of her death her style of music had begun to fall out of favor. It was overly sentimental compared to the innovative styles of twentieth-century composers.

"In a sense that is fair criticism, because it is true," Vagts said. "In another sense she was perfectly happy with the language of music in the later 1800s, and she stuck with it."

A renewed appreciation of that style in recent years and the women's movement in the 1970s revived interest in Beach. A new biography, *Amy Beach, Passionate Victorian,* was published in 1998, and UNH hosted aconference and concert on Beach and her contemporaries.

John Swenson

He was the Granite State's most successful quarryman.

These days, when people refer to New Hampshire as the Granite State, they think they're saying something about our character: Granite, as in tough and strong, steadfast and true. Granite, as in hard to deal with. Sometimes they mean granite-headed, as in our refusal to do what the rest of the country thinks is right. Sometimes they even mean granite-hearted.

But for much of the twentieth century, when people referred to New Hampshire as the Granite State, they were really just thinking about rocks. That's because New Hampshire was one of the premier places on the planet

John Swenson's company has survived more than 100 years.

Courtesy of Swenson Granite.

The CBS Building in
New York was built in
part from Swenson
granite.
Courtesy of Swenson Granite.

for cutting, polishing, and finishing granite. Concord granite, known for its fine texture, was the standard by which all others were measured.

At the center of it all for three decades was John Swenson, the state's most important quarryman, a Swedish immigrant who came to town, learned a trade, started a business, outlasted his competitors, and created an empire that endures today.

When Swenson died in 1918, the *Concord Monitor* took comfort only in the fact that his sons would continue his work: "Few men of his generation have contributed as much to the industrial upbuilding of the city of Concord as the late John Swenson, a self-made man of many friends and a national reputation for ability and integrity, who carved for himself from Concord granite a career, a fortune and a business employing hundreds of men at good wages."

Ken Burns

His films popularized American history.

If Americans in the 1990s had a keener understanding of their history than those before them, Ken Burns of Walpole deserves much of the credit. Broadcast on public television, his giant-subject documentaries have taught us about the Civil War. Baseball. Jazz. Woman suffrage. Lewis and Clark. Thomas Jefferson.

His work has brought both acclaim—millions of viewers, three Emmy awards, two Oscar nominations—and criticism. In the process, American history has become his story.

"He's captivated by the story, the historical story, and its importance to the nation and what it says about who we are and therefore what we might become," said Dayton Duncan, another well-known Walpole resident and longtime friend of Burns.

To Burns, though, the story is only half the story. "What I've tried to do is

Ken Burns, at home in Walpole.

Ken Williams/Concord Monitor.

make documentary not merely the exposition of something that's already been arrived at, a form of journalism, but a form of art as well. I'm more interested in that. I'm not a historian. I'm a filmmaker."

And what's a filmmaker doing in rural New Hampshire? Burns was born in New York City, grew up in Ann Arbor, and then, partly because he could make movies more inexpensively, landed here. "Tom Paine responded, 'Wherever there is not liberty, that's where I shall make my home.' I wish I could say that the reason I'm in New Hampshire is because of that. It's not. I was borne here irresistibly by lots of forces in and out of my control. It's beautiful here. It's a way."

Sandy Davis, Sylvia Greenfield, and Nancy Clark

They witnessed a revolution in the treatment of mental illness.

Sandy Davis, Sylvia Greenfield, and Nancy Clark started their nursing careers at the state's psychiatric hospital in Concord in the late 1960s, a time when hundreds of patients checked in with little hope of ever checking out. Their jobs included cooking up giant vats of eggs and oatmeal and supervising patients as they did the hospital's cleaning. The psychiatric treatment meted out could be crude, even shocking by the standards of the late 1990s.

And everything was about to change.

"There is a general agreement at the present time among politicians of different persuasions, professionals in the field, citizens and especially the patients who are victims of the situation that the New Hampshire Hospital is in

Nancy Clark sits in the greenhouse area of New Hampshire Hospital, where she is director of rehabilitative services, in 1999.

Robin Shotola/Concord Monitor.

a deplorable state and change is barely needed," a study commission concluded in 1972.

The result: a new philosophy of "deinstitutionalization." A system of community-based mental health services. And a new state-of-the-art hospital that was used not as a warehouse but as a brief stopover point for patients in the midst of crises.

For Davis, Greenfield, Clark, and dozens of mental health professionals like them, their workplace changed. Their work changed. But their ethic stayed the same:"We always said, think of that as your mother being here, your sister being here," Greenfield said. "How would you want them to be treated?"

Larry Gilpin

He directed WMUR-TV's rise to prominence.

For much of the twentieth century, the biggest news source in New Hampshire was the *Union Leader* of Manchester. In the 1990s, that changed. As its advertisements made clear, more New Hampshire viewers got their news from WMUR-TV than from any other news source. Give Larry Gilpin, the general manager, a big dose of credit.

When Gilpin arrived at Channel 9 in 1985, it was still a small-time operation. He expanded the station's news coverage, setting it apart from the Boston market with a focus on New Hampshire. He built a palatial studio in Manchester and extended the station's reach to the North Country. With the changes came clout that had previously gone to the newspaper—particularly during the presidential primaries of 1996 and 2000—and a national reputation. "For the purposes of presidential politics," wrote the *St. Petersburg Times*, "there is virtually no other station in America."

Throughout, Gilpin remained the man behind the curtain, anonymous to the station's viewers and guarding his privacy from the curious press. His colleagues described him as smart, personable, humble, and direct, and then, respecting his wishes, stopped. Said Julie Campasano, the station's program director: "He's our little secret now."

Frank Chappell and Warren Hoyt

They guarded POWs in the northern woods.

BY SARAH M. EARLE

s his old friend rages, cursing the Republicans through a mouthful of breakfast and gesturing wildly with his croissant, Frank Chappell just smiles, feigning interest in the fog outside the window.

Anger, conflict, confrontation—they are weapons that have never suited him. Not even in Camp Stark, fifty years ago, when someone placed a gun in his hands and made him a guard over 200 German prisoners.

"I didn't like being a guard," said Chappell, remembering the World War II prison camp where he spent two years of his youth, just up the road in the town of Stark. "Guarding someone with a gun—I just didn't like that."

So it was Chappell who taught the prisoners the song "Don't Fence Me In," a chorus that floated through the forests day after long day. It was Chappell who organized soccer games between the guards and the prisoners.

And it was Chappell who, without ever laying a hand on the prisoners,

Warren Hoyt (left) and Frank Chappell were guards at the Stark POW camp during World War II.

Andrea Bruce Woodall/Concord Monitor.

298

dealt them a deeply wounding blow. Late in the war, the camp received a film-strip that was circulating through prison camps around the country. German footage confiscated by the British, it showed glimpses of the Holocaust taking place across the globe from this quiet village camp.

Mustering all his reserves of force, Chappell herded the prisoners into the mess hall and made them watch the actions of their countrymen. "Some of them didn't want to go in," Chappell said. "I had to bring a club in the barracks and bang on the bunks."

As the Germans watched the black-and-white images of emaciated Jews, piles of corpses, and firing squad slaughters, "You could hear them hollering and talking in German. . . . 'It can't be, it can't be,'" Chappell recalled.

But it was. And the Germans who left Camp Stark in the months to come took those images with them. "They couldn't get over it," Chappell said. "But it was something that they needed to see . . . I don't think their feeling and attitude about Germany was ever the same after that."

Chappell knows the power of an attitude. Or perhaps, conversely, it never occurred to him to hate the people he found himself guarding—people who were by definition the enemy.

Either way, the memories he carries with him now are as bright and guileless as his actions as a man of twenty-five.

On this sun-glazed morning, Chappell is running errands near his home in Berlin, just miles from the old prison camp. He picks up a croissant and a small coffee at Dunkin' Donuts and stops by the apple-green house of his friend Warren Hoyt. His buddy of fifty years greets him from his living-room couch, where he's struggling to get up on a pair of crutches—last week he took a fall down the stairs. Chappell finally tugs Hoyt to his feet and helps him to the kitchen table. Chappell drapes his coat and hat on a chair beside a sighing woodstove and sits down. Hoyt pours himself cream from a pitcher painted with a boy in lederhosen, a girl in braids, and some faded German phrase. And the memories—memories owned now by precious few—play at random.

"What was the name of that German cook?" Chappell asks. "Oh, I can't remember."

"He was a good cook."

"Oh, I guess he was. You ought to taste the pork roast he made." There was pork roast at Stark. There was beer and candy and warm beds. And there was kindness.

Midway through the war, in response to pressure from England, the United States opened 500 camps across the country to relieve England of about 400,000 prisoners of war. New Hampshire's only prison camp, cloistered in the northern woods, Camp Stark opened in the spring of 1944 in a converted Civilian Conservation Corps complex. The goal was to produce pulpwood for the nearby paper mill, which the war had stripped of manpower.

Chappell, who came to Stark as a sergeant after a bout with malaria sent him home from training, remembers watching the first prisoners arrive. "They were all marching and they were singing some kind of a song," he said. The singing never stopped. The Americans learned the Germans' music, the

Germans learned theirs. Prisoners and guards captured rabbits, raccoons, even a bear in the woods, and made pets out of them, posing together for pictures. At Christmastime, the prisoners made gifts for the guards' children. And the Americans shared their peanut-butter candy with the Germans.

That's not to say life at Stark was easy. The prisoners worked long hours in the woods felling trees. Relations among the diverse group of Nazis, anti-Nazis, and Communists were sometimes rocky. The long rows of barracks, if adequate, were indeed stark. And the quiet nights found the prisoners longing for their homeland and wondering about the safety of their families.

But on top of these unavoidable hardships, the prisoners never endured cruelty or abuse at the hands of their captors. Stark, like most American prison camps, became known for its fair treatment of prisoners.

Beyond that, in Stark the boundaries between soldiers, prisoners, and townspeople could not stay up. Chappell was not alone in his quiet acceptance of the prisoners, his gradual friendship with the men he could have justified hating.

During the war, as other countries abandoned their Geneva Convention commitment to humane treatment of prisoners, America made it a point to stick to its. With a "do unto others" philosophy, the country hoped to secure proper treatment for its own soldiers captured overseas. It also hoped that its reputation for benevolence would motivate Germans to surrender.

That may have been the case for many of the prisoners in Stark. The first group that came had been captured in Normandy, after surrendering to the British.

"A lot of them told me afterwards, they were glad that they did," Hoyt recalled. Chappell and Hoyt remember little about the political strategies that shaped the camp. They reminisce, instead, about the people. "They were a good group," Chappell said. "Most of them were very easy to get along with."

As it turned out, most of the prisoners at Stark were not Nazis. The large group that had surrendered in Normandy consisted mostly of ordinary civilians, forced into service. "One told me one day, 'I don't want no trouble. I just want to go home,'" Hoyt said.

Chappell chuckles, remembering the way the Germans tried to shirk their sawing duties and their knack for getting into mischief.

One day, checking the barracks during roll call, he detected a strong smell of cabbage. He followed his nose all the way to the latrine.

"And do you know what they were doing? They were bootlegging," Chappell said. The prisoners had been given seeds and were allowed to grow vegetables in their barracks. They had mixed a concoction of cabbage and potatoes and other scraps and stored them in containers in the latrine. "I tried to keep it quiet . . . I was trying to keep the peace," Chappell said. He even tasted a little of the brew, after confronting the prisoners about it. "Oh, it was bad," he said. "I had to run back and get my mouthwash."

Eventually, worried that the moonshine would be discovered and the prisoners shipped to another prison, Chappell convinced them to dump the stuff. Forty years later, that moonshine gurgled up through the cracks again, in stories swapped between prisoners and guards at German-American friendship day. In 1986, Dr. Allen Koop, a Dartmouth professor who wrote a book about the camp, and several townspeople organized a reunion of Camp Stark alumni. Five former prisoners traveled to the tiny village, where a freshly painted church and rows of orange pumpkins greeted their arrival. Chappell picked out familiar faces, now lined with age, as guards and prisoners toured the site of the camp, now just an overgrown clearing. At a huge welcoming ceremony, they sang songs in both their mother tongues.

The Germans there proved that the fond picture Chappell paints of the camp is no illusion.

"In any war, the enemy is always a bad man, and the other ones are the good man," ex-prisoner Gerhard Clauss told the *Boston Globe* at the reunion. "I would say, eventually something like cooperation developed."

"We were treated correctly, no problem there," ex-prisoner Hans Wenzell told the *Caledonian-Record*. "If anyone said they weren't treated right, I wouldn't believe them. It was no Holiday Hilton, mind you. We were treated fairly, the food was good, we had no problems . . . Let me tell you, if we had been ill-treated I wouldn't be here today, would I now?"

People with ties to the camp come to visit Stark all the time, according to Madeleine Croteau, a long-time resident who helped organize the reunion, and a subsequent one in 1996. She remembers one woman who came a couple of years ago, looking for people who remembered the camp. Her father had been imprisoned there, she told Croteau, and she felt drawn to the place. She remembered her father's stories of a school bus that used to drive by the camp everyday. The kids would all lean out the windows and jeer—until one day, when the bus driver drove the bus right up to the fence and stopped it. "Those Germans started singing songs to those kids," Croteau said. "And from that day on, there was no more jeering."

"People come all the time to look people up," Croteau said. "They want to see the place and touch it. I know there was a magic. But probably in my lifetime, I'll never know what it was."

Chappell can't quite describe that magic either. Today, he is one of just a handful who remember Stark firsthand. But even with the wisdom of age and hindsight, he doesn't try to define the impact the little camp may have made.

Others have tried. "The reason for the war, as far as most Americans were concerned, was to restore peace," Koop wrote. "And peace meant not only the cessation of hostilities but also the replacement of Nazi tyranny by a peaceful and democratic Germany. In many ways, Camp Stark anticipated this. Its men and women, Americans and Germans alike, became war heroes by becoming peace heroes, reaching out to each other in decency across barriers of nationality and war."

Hartmut Lang, a representative of the German government and speaker at German-American Friendship Day, said, "The experiences of those former prisoners of war are not forgotten. I'm sure they have contributed substantially to the image the average German has of the average American. It is the image of the fair and quietly decent American. This image, I assure you, is alive in Germany."

As for Chappell, "I just never forgot it," he said. "That's all."

Thomas Williams

He raised the standard for writing fiction in and about New Hampshire.

BY ALEC MACGILLIS

You won't find Leah, New Hampshire, on the crumpled map in your glove compartment, but if you've lived in the state long enough, you probably know roughly where it is. Chances also are you haven't heard of the man who founded the fictional town by that name, Thomas Williams. But you've more than likely read something by one of his former writing students at the University of New Hampshire, a group that includes John Irving, Alice McDermott, and Ursula Hegi.

In a region densely wooded with writers and writing teachers, Williams, who died in 1990 at age sixty-three, rose a bit higher than the rest. Countless

Countless writers have set their plots in New Hampshire, but few have stayed as true to their fictive hometowns as Thomas Williams did to Leah, where almost all of his stories take place.

Courtesy of Instructional Services, Dimond Library, UNH.

writers have set their plots in this state, but few have stayed as true to their fictitious hometowns as Williams did to Leah, where almost all of his stories take place. Dozens of other local authors have supported their writing habit by teaching. But few invested as much in their day job, however discouraging it may have been at times, as Williams.

Like other writing teachers, he joked that by instructing young authors he was only creating competition for himself—but that didn't keep him from coaxing his students to success that sometimes surpassed his own.

"Tom was instrumental in getting me to believe in my own writing," Irving said. It was Williams who urged Irving to attend the Iowa Writers Workshop after graduating from UNH, and who helped Irving sell his first story while he was still in Durham. The two stayed in touch for years afterward; Irving named Williams's wife the godmother of his first son.

"Tom remained my sternest critic," Irving said. "He took everything I wrote to task, but always in a constructive manner. The success of my fourth novel, *The World According to Garp,* notwithstanding, Tom never let my popularity get in the way of his criticism.

"I simply respected no one's opinion of my work as much as I respected his."

Williams's high standards for his students were exceeded only by those he set for himself. What one notices first about his writing is its meticulous attention to detail; those who knew him say he wrote numerous drafts longhand before committing anything to type, and it shows. Reading him takes time, not because his work is difficult, but because one wants to take as much care with the language as its creator clearly did.

In the short story "Goose Pond," Williams intricately describes a scene that in reality passes in a flash: the encounter between a doe and a newly widowed man who has gone to the woods for solace.

> He saw the face of the deer beside a narrow tree, and for a moment there was nothing but the face: a smoky brown eye deep as a tunnel, it seemed, long delicate lashes, a black whisker or two along the white-shaded muzzle. The black nose quivered at each breath, the nostrils rounded.
>
> Then he began to follow the light brown line, motionless and so nearly invisible along the back, down along the edge of the white breast. One large ear turned slowly toward him. It was a doe, watching him carefully, perfect in the moment of fine innocence and wonder—a quality he suddenly remembered—the expressionless readiness of the deer.

The same setting is succinctly described in his foreword to the story collection *Leah, New Hampshire:* "In the fall the deer are the color of the spaces between the trees." For Williams, using words with precision was not just a matter of personal preference but a kind of obligation for the serious writer—especially one who worked in New England. In a 1986 essay in the *New York Times Book Review,* he argued that the region's best writers, from the Puritans on down, had shared a "sanity, even temper, humor, and coolness" that called for a clear-eyed appraisal of the world around them: "I see in (New England) an injunction to use language very carefully, to resist the ordinary consistencies of diction and thought, those automatic responses that obliterate what is darker—the real reason for these words."

Like other writers who became identified with the state—Robert Frost and Donald Hall, for instance—Williams was no native. He spent the first ten years of his life in Minnesota, then moved to New York City with his mother after his parents' divorce. In 1940, when he was fourteen, he and his newly remarried mother moved to Lebanon. After the mild-mannered Midwest and the cosmopolitan city, the unvarnished Upper Valley town unsettled the young teenager.

Williams's first impressions of the state are easily discerned in his 1966 story "The Snows of Minnesota," one of three stories he published in *The New Yorker*. In the story, a boy recently arrived in Leah from the Midwest finds that "his classmates talked with hard, dry voices, and said words like 'modren' for 'modern' and 'idear' for 'idea.' They put r's where none belonged and left them off where they should have been, and had strange, stiff ways of moving, as though they were being watched by enemies. The school playground was nothing but hard dirt and worn tree roots that came to the surface and froze, helpless under the grinding feet of the children."

In the end, the boy in the story overcomes his homesickness for Minnesota by building a tremendous cave for himself inside a tall snow bank in the backyard—only to see it ruined.

Despite his difficult debut, Williams remained in New Hampshire, leaving only for a two-year stint in the Army and for graduate work at the University of Chicago, the University of Paris, and the University of Iowa.

In 1958, he joined the English faculty at UNH, where he had earned his bachelor's and master's degrees. By that time, he had already published his first of eight novels, *Ceremony of Love.*

And he had already dug his roots into the state. In 1954, he and his wife, a nurse from Vermont named Elizabeth Blood, built a cabin on the slope of Mount Cardigan in Alexandria. It was an impressive feat, their daughter Ann Williams recalled: Abjuring power tools, the young couple cut logs with hand saws, stripped them down, mixed cement in a wheelbarrow, and topped it all off with a shed roof.

The Williams family spent most of its vacations at the cabin, which expanded with time. And Alexandria became, along with Lebanon and Durham, the third major piece in the composite that made up the fictional Leah. In Williams's stories, Cardigan became the ever-present Cascom Mountain.

It was also to Alexandria that Williams went for comfort in the last year of his life, when he succumbed to lung cancer.

"That last summer he'd say to me how happy he was with his life; what more could he want than to look out at the mountain and the animals crossing the field he'd cleared down below?" said Ann Williams, a writer herself, living in San Francisco.

While Williams became converted to the virtues of New Hampshire, he would always regard it with the critical eye of an outsider. In his foreword to *Leah,* he wrote that the state "can be cruel, especially to its poor, or sick, or old. In its public, or collective, stance, it can act as a skinflint and a buffoon among its neighbors."

But, he continued, "Its people, however, like most Americans, can be decent and generous if, for a moment, they forget dogma, forget 'conservatism' and sanctimony, and the myths of an imaginary history. To me Leah quite often seems to be a real town in an imaginary state I have to prove over and over again in order to believe in its beauty and its paradoxes."

In the same foreword, Williams tells the reader what his Leah is like: "Around the town, on old asphalt and dirt roads, are tar-paper shacks, and moldy house-trailer slums; in New Hampshire the brush and the trees grow quickly and screen these places from those whose theories, political, economic, and aesthetic, would be damaged by too much ugliness."

It's another damning description of the state, but it's not entirely representative of the town that emerges in the story collection, which was published after Williams died. There are relatively few house trailers in Williams's Leah; his rendering of the state is less stark, less "nitty-gritty," as Northwood writer Rebecca Rule puts it, than that of other New Hampshire chroniclers like Russell Banks and Ernest Hebert.

Most characters in Williams's New Hampshire are sensitive and reflective; one learns about them more from lengthy descriptions of their inner thoughts than through dialogue, of which there is relatively little.

There are plenty of hunters and fishermen in Williams's stories, but they are no macho warriors, crowing over their catch. In "Goose Pond," the widower kills the doe with his bow but takes little satisfaction in it: "If he were twenty again he would be happy. To have shot a deer with a bow—he'd be a hero, a woodsman, famous in Leah. How it would have impressed Mary! She would have said little about it—she went to great lengths never to flatter him; her compliments had been more tangible, seldom in words. He must think of something else. The world was too empty."

In his best stories, Williams exhibits an extraordinary understanding of characters in situations quite unlike his own. He wrote about the widower in "Goose Pond" when he was in his twenties. Some of his most affecting stories are about children; in addition to "The Snows of Minnesota," there is "The Voyage of the Cosmogon," in which a boy steeps himself in a Star Wars-type show to escape a depressing home life. Read now, the story is a startlingly timely depiction of a disconnected teenager.

At times, Williams's sympathy for his characters is so tangible that, compared with more ironic fiction of recent decades, it seems to edge toward sentimentality. Irving, for one, rejects this label, arguing that Williams "took risks with emotional material in storytelling. Some critics call a writer sentimental for even attempting to move a reader emotionally, but it is sheer cowardice on a writer's part not to seek the emotional reaction. . . . You either show the readers something that tears their hearts out, or you presume intellectual superiority to such an aim and don't write from the heart."

By the same token, it would be inaccurate to call Williams old-fashioned. His 1975 novel *The Hair of Harold Roux,* which won the National Book Award, is highly experimental, a folding of several stories inside one another.

One of the ironies in Williams's strong regional identity was that he was so little known in the state he wrote about, even as he racked up several national writing prizes. "If you asked our neighbors here, they wouldn't have heard of him, while in the literary scene in New York, they had," said his widow, Elizabeth Williams.

Her husband did not hold his relative anonymity against local residents; in fact, he sought out their company. "He was very comfortable with people interested in the outdoors; he was able to have a relationship with someone who never read a damn book in their lives," she said.

Where Williams still retains his fame is among his former students, who glowingly recall his rigorous classes. Williams, they say, was that rare writing instructor who was demanding without being pedantic and encouraging without being easy to please. Most of the class time was spent discussing students' stories; of each submission, he would ask, "Is this a story?"

For Rebecca Rule, having Williams once answer "yes" to that question in discussing a story of hers was "one of the most incredible moments of my life. By his standards, that was a tremendous accomplishment."

Rule recalled Williams's ability to zero in on the strengths of a student's story; he once suggested she reduce a lengthy description of a bathroom in one of her stories to one line, "The hair curled in the sink."

Reading *The Hair of Harold Roux,* whose main character is an English teacher, one gets a sense of how frustrating Williams often found teaching. Elizabeth Williams said her husband often wished he could have devoted himself entirely to writing.

Yet writer Donald Murray and poet Charles Simic, who also taught at UNH, both recall passing Williams's office and seeing him inside, poring over students' stories, marking everything, down to stray commas.

"He took their work very seriously and treated them with professional respect. He didn't kiss off students like some teachers do," Murray said.

The frustrations of the writer's life didn't keep Williams from encouraging his daughter Ann, who took his class one year. Now that she's published some stories and is working on her first novel, Ann Williams wishes her father were still around to coach her.

Not that he left her empty-handed. As it turns out, he bequeathed her a geography. "I also had a mountain in my stories, but he thought my name for it was silly sounding, and he said, 'Why don't you just call it Cascom?'" Ann Williams said. "So I did, and before I knew it, it infected me. Now I use 'Leah' and all the rest."

Bob Montana

He created Archie Comics.

BY JONATHAN FAHEY

It started like this: A family is moving into the neighborhood, and a freckle-faced, red-headed boy is showing off for the new girl-next-door—a charming blonde named Betty—by standing on the seat of a speeding red bike. "It's just a matter of skill, that's all," he says, smugly.

His eyes are closed, his arms folded.

Betty is hooked.

"Hyah. M'name's Archie," he says.

With that, Archie Andrews was born. Since then, he has worn bell-bottoms, spoken like a beatnik, worn plaid shirts, flowered shirts and, mostly, a v-neck sweater with a big letter "R." He has been seventeen-going-on-eighteen for nearly sixty years, running around Riverdale High, chasing Veronica, being chased by Betty, relying heavily on his friend Jughead's loyalty (if not his advice), and parrying with his rival, the reviled Reggie.

A photo of Montana in his studio hangs at the Meredith Historical Society.

Ken Williams/Concord Monitor.

Archie and his universe were sparked in December 1941 by Bob Montana, a graduate of Central High in Manchester who lived much of his life in Meredith. When Montana died in 1975, he left a wife, four children, and some of the most recognizable comic characters in history.

Mark Cohen, a cartoon art historian from California, says Archie became one of the best-selling comics of all time precisely because it was so familiar. "It had characters that people could relate to," he said. "It had rivalries and insecurities and everything that kids are going through, and it comes across is a funny, palatable way."

Montana was working at MLJ Comics in New York drawing superheroes when publisher John Goldwater declared he wanted a strip about a normal teenager. Montana said he had just the thing.

Did he ever. Archie debuted as a supporting strip inside a comic book devoted to a superhero called *The Shield*. The first book dedicated to the Riverdale High gang was published in 1942, as Montana was entering the armed service.

During the war, Archie's popularity grew, and just before Montana was discharged he was given an offer to syndicate Archie. It started running daily in twenty newspapers. It ran daily for the next thirty years in as many as seven hundred.

While MLJ Comics, which soon changed its name to Archie Comics, continued publishing monthly comic books, Montana produced the daily and Sunday strips with the help of an assistant.

Jeff Cuddy of Hooksett helped Montana for thirteen years, from the early 1960s until Montana's death. Cuddy inked and lettered the sketches that Montana sent him from Meredith and then sent them on to New York.

Cuddy attributes Archie's success in part to its timing. "The thing that made Archie so well-liked," he said, "was not only that he was humorous, but people were fed up with violence and war, and Archie was such a positive thing."

Cuddy met Montana after finishing a mural that Montana had sketched on the wall of a deli in Manchester. Montana liked the results and called Cuddy a few months later to ask if he wanted to work with him. "He was very fussy

Archie, Veronica, and Jughead have changed little over the years.
Courtesy of the Montana family.

about the work," Cuddy said. "But Bob was a great teacher and he was very patient. We really had fun.

"He had a terrific way of drawing. Every little face was a portrait."

Montana had the ability to evoke very physical comedy—sight gags, for example—on a flat page. He also wrote a laugh every day.

Montana's daughter Lynn thinks Archie's popularity is based on its simplicity. "They are archetypes," she said. "There's part of Archie and Reggie in every boy, and there's parts of Betty and Veronica in every girl. And Jughead is the fool, and he's the wisest one."

Archie may be the archetypal teenager, but with one significant twist: He's got two attractive young women vying for his attention.

Generations of boys agonized over whom to prefer: arrogant, wealthy Veronica or earnest, homegrown Betty. This was never about looks—Cuddy says they were drawn the same: both strikingly well built, with different color hair. It was about style, about personality, about fantasy.

Girls, Lynn Montana said, are posed with a similar, if somewhat less stirring dilemma. "Veronica is who every girl wants to be," she said. "But really, they are Betty."

She says the strip was as much for adults as for children. It was a depiction of teenage life, but because Montana was drawing and writing about high school, Archie recalled for older readers the best of their school years. At the same time, it offered preteens a glimpse of the future.

Joe Mannarino was just such a kid. Mannarino, an Italian immigrant, has a special tie to Archie and to comic books in general: They taught him how to read.

At least for the moment, Archie has chosen Veronica over Betty.
Courtesy of the Montana family.

"As opposed to every other kid's parents," he said, "my mother didn't throw my comic books away because she knew how much they helped me."

Mannarino has been collecting since he was eight. He owns more than 15,000 books and runs an auction house in New Jersey. "People think that comics have a negative influence, when, in my opinion, it's the opposite, " he said. "What people learn to do is read between the panes. It's good for the imagination.

Mannarino said that although the retail price of a *Pep #22*—the issue in which Archie first appeared—is "only" $10,000, one in mint condition would fetch $20,000 to $25,000 at auction.

In the first episode, after thrilling Betty with his bicycle trick, Archie eventually slips up (of course). He puts his head through a precious portrait and breaks a priceless vase, getting him in trouble with Old Man Cooper if endearing himself further to Betty.

For years, Archie has been getting himself in similar pickles: inviting Betty and Veronica on the same date or trying to sneak into someone's pool—usually ending up where he's not supposed to be.

Montana's penchant for slapstick and the one-liners that punctuated his strips were informed by a childhood on stage. His parents Ray Coleman—the Great Montana—and Roberta Pandolfini were vaudeville performers. Bob Montana was born in California and grew up on the road, performing rope tricks and singing with his sister.

"Cartoonists are frustrated actors who pantomime through cartoons," Montana said in a 1959 interview. He started his pantomime on paper at age four, when he started drawing to entertain himself during trips.

After vaudeville died at the hands of the Depression, the Montana family moved to Boston. Montana's father died when Montana was thirteen, and his mother moved the family to Haverhill, Massachusetts, where they lived for three years before moving to Manchester. And shortly after high school Montana landed a job at MLJ.

After World War II, Archie was nearly an instant hit.

Courtesy of the Montana family.

Once Archie was established, Montana moved to Meredith with his wife, Peggy Wherett, whom he had met in the service. The family lived for extended periods abroad. "He was adventurous," Lynn Montana said, and it helped keep the comic strip fresh.

He raised horses, chickens, and sheep on his farm on Meredith Neck. He grew vegetables. He sailed on Winnipesaukee, skied, hiked, went scuba diving, all of which, in some form or another, made it into the strip.

Although Montana was somewhat private—he gave few interviews—he was always active in the Meredith community. He wrote a musical called *Mutiny on the Mount* about the *M/S Mount Washington,* and he talked at schools. In the 1950s, he bought a 1920 Ford Model T and painted it red to resemble Archie's rig. He installed a fire pump in the radiator so it would spout water, and he carried a revolver with blanks to simulate backfires. He dressed up as Archie, costumed a friend as Jughead, and paraded around at the Sandwich Fair.

With a strip every day, he was always on the lookout for ideas. Montana's children could earn a quarter if they came up with one. He read magazines and music to keep up with the times. Most of all, he looked around.

And sometimes, the real-life people Montana met ended up as cartoons in his strip. "He liked bringing citizens into the things he did," Lynn Montana said.

This has resulted in some dispute over whom the Archie characters are modeled after. Haverhill, Massachusetts, newspaper articles claim they came from Haverhill High. Manchester accounts say the same about Central High. People in all the places Montana has lived—Meredith, New York, Italy, England, and Mexico—have recognized themselves in his strips. And this, ultimately, is what made Archie resonate so broadly. Everyone sees themselves in Archie or Reggie or Veronica or Betty or, best of all, in Jughead.

"I always thought Bob was Archie," Jeff Cuddy said. "He was a prankster. He liked a practical joke."

Montana *was* part Archie, as are most of us. He admitted as much once, when he called Archie and Jughead's pranks "a personification of all the things I tried to get away with in school."

"He was a very kind person," Cuddy said of Montana, "but he had a twinkle in his eye."

Arthur Walden

From Wonalancet, he and his dogs journeyed to the bottom of the earth.

BY SARAH M. EARLE

Somewhere in Antarctica, in some life-void crevice or cleat of ice on the unworn tread of Earth, lies the heart of one New Hampshire legacy. There is no grave or marker; perhaps nothing is left. Just the memory of a big yellow dog named Chinook who drew his last breath from the Antarctic wind. The wise-faced mongrel who died in that wilderness carried a new sport to his hometown, fathered a famed breed, and pulled one New Hampshire man into history.

Of course, history has to be about the man. Dog heroes fit few genres besides children's books and television series. But were Arthur Walden alive

Arthur Walden and Chinook in Wonalancet before their last Antarctic adventure.

Courtesy of the Tamworth Historical Society.

today, he would certainly defer honor, the way he did when he returned from Admiral Richard Byrd's famed South Pole expedition.

An old road that winds through Tamworth bears Chinook's name instead of Walden's. And those who remember the quirky adventurer inevitably remember his dog. "My mother, who is ninety-five, remembers him riding through town, and Chinook was always on the seat beside him," said Joan Casarotto, president of the Tamworth Historical Society.

In the cluster of towns around the tiny village of Wonalancet, everyone has heard stories of Walden and his dogs. Some remember his noisy kennels, his big Stetson hat, his dog sled rides and his practical jokes. A few remember when his name—and Chinook's—hit national newspapers.

In 1928, Walden, a veteran adventurer and sled dog hobbyist, caught wind of Byrd's ambition to fly over the South Pole. "Walden, though beyond the age considered maximum, was in a fever to go," Marjory Gane Harkness wrote in her book, *The Tamworth Narrative*.

Walden, fifty-eight, took a train to Boston to meet Byrd and, competing with 3,000 other applicants, secured a spot on his team. A few months later, Walden and his dogs headed to the bottom of the world, where they helped Byrd chart new Antarctic territory and fly over the South Pole for the first time in history.

The honor lives on in his hometown. "He put Wonalancet on the map," Casarotto said.

But Walden's accomplishments stretch far beyond Wonalancet.

In 1890, Walden came to New Hampshire from Minnesota to visit his father's summer home. At the urging of the lovely and lively Kate Sleeper, a distant relative nine years his senior, he stayed. But not for long.

Just before the great gold rush, the twenty-three-year-old Walden followed his own rushing heart to Alaska. There, he and a companion built a wilderness cabin and lived off dried salmon and reindeer moss. But "what fascinated Walden most about Alaska was the lack of roads and the use of sled dogs," the *Carroll County Independent* reported. The trip "set the course of his life, stimulating his love of adventure, his knowledge of survival in an unforgiving environment, and his love and appreciation of working dogs."

On his return to New Hampshire, Walden acquired four St. Bernard puppies and trained them in tandem hitch. Increasingly fascinated, he voyaged again to Alaska and returned with another dog, a direct descendant from Robert Peary's Greenland huskies.

In 1902, Walden married Sleeper and settled at her Wonalancet farm. His second love, Chinook Kennels, was soon born, and he quickly became a novelty around town.

"Arthur Walden . . . had come on the quiet intervale scene as a rather flaming figure," Harkness wrote. "His exploits and pranks were widely quoted . . . a horse, for instance, would be taken out and harnessed wrong end to, while its owner was indoors courting in the kitchen."

Determined to develop the perfect sled dog, Walden tried breeding. The union of a St. Bernard mix and one of the Peary husky descendants produced a litter of three, which Sleeper, a Rudyard Kipling fan, dubbed Rikki, Tikki, and Tavi. Walden's keen eye soon fell on Rikki, a floppy-eared yellow pup who proved exceptionally intelligent. He renamed the dog Chinook, in honor of a dog he'd left behind in Alaska, and fell boyishly in love with the animal.

So close were the pair, it is said, that one could read the other's mind. Walden had already rejected the whip for verbal commands and hand signals, but with Chinook he rarely needed even those. "The affection between him and Walden was a beautiful thing to see," Harkness wrote. "One sensed that each knew and understood the other perfectly, and it was Walden's rare boast that he never needed to give Chinook an order." Here was his perfect sled dog.

Walden bred Chinook to German and Belgian shepherds, producing a slew of dogs that resembled the hundred-pound wonder. Meanwhile, he practiced his sled-driving skills by giving rides all over town. "This team was an utterly delightful innovation in the intervale at that time," Harkness wrote. "And every girl or woman given a ride in that sled had the thrill of her life."

The Walden farm, already a popular vacation resort for upper-class travelers, began attracting sled-dog hobbyists and fans. Walden participated in dog-sled races around Canada and New England. In 1924, he helped organize the New England Sled Dog Club to promote the exciting new sport. Still operating and racing today, the club credits Walden for its birth.

But those big yellow dogs did more than win races. The team helped bring electricity to Wonalancet by hauling equipment over areas inaccessible by road, setting up the first hydroelectric plant in Carroll County. Walden's team, led by Chinook, also became the first dog-sled team to reach the top of Mount Washington.

"Against perishing winds in a blizzard, Chinook showed himself the remarkable dog he was," Harkness wrote.

Only one greater test awaited.

No one can say for sure what possessed Walden to leave Wonalancet for a desolate world unmarked by human feet. Any memoirs from his trip were

When Walden returned from the Antarctic, townspeople wanted to rename the road that linked Tamworth and Wonalancet in his honor. He asked them to name it for his dog instead.

Max Becherer/Concord Monitor.

destroyed in the fire that also took his life in 1947. A few smoke-singed photos show Walden posing with Chinook, the dog's paw in his lap, or riding behind a row of Chinook-looking dogs.

But schoolchildren still read about the trip that helped make Walden famous.

Already a decorated and celebrated hero for his flying techniques and Arctic expeditions, Richard Byrd set his sights on Antarctica and the South Pole in 1928. Winning a spot on the team, Walden returned to Chinook Kennels to prepare a team of his own. "For one long winter, the quiet of Tamworth was shattered by the howls of more than 100 dogs," William Fennell wrote. Walden hired three young men to help him train his noisy clan and accompany him on the expedition. He filled out his team of "Chinooks" with malamutes and huskies from other farms. In August 1928, the crew left Boston Harbor in a rusty old ship, the *Eleanor Bolling*.

When they hit New Zealand, Walden and his dogs were packed onto the main expedition ship, *The City of New York,* and proceeded to Antarctica. As the ship nudged the Ross Ice Shelf, Walden surely listened in on Russell Owen's morse code message to the *New York Times*: "This day we have carried the American flag further south than it has ever been before."

Anchored on the Discovery Inlet, the ship spilled out its load of men and dogs, who were greeted by the "natives," flocks of emperor penguins. The odd birds fended off the dogs' curious sniffs with flipper slaps to the nose.

A few days later, the team hit the Great Ice Shelf and, just beyond it, a little basin just right for setting up camp. Byrd dubbed it "Little America" and ordered the team to unpack. As Byrd began his test flights for his trip over the South Pole, Walden, his men and his dogs hauled in the supplies that would help colonize the little community.

Always surrounded by the yips and howls of his dogs, Walden was apparently less tolerant of his human companions. With Byrd's permission, he and another team member built their own separate hut. A crate that had held an airplane engine became their cabin, and a gasoline drum burned seal oil for heat. There, Walden endured Antarctica's crippling cold and four-month nighttime.

But he was no hermit. One night, twenty-two people crammed into his cabin for a party, where, far from prohibitionist America, the "medicinal" liquor flowed.

In October, Walden's teams of dog sleds headed south to lay down supply depots for team member Laurence Gould's geological expeditions. Gould's team followed in another train of sleds, exploring yet uncharted territory.

Meanwhile, Byrd prepared for his pioneer mission. And on November 29, 1929, he became the first person to fly over the South Pole.

In his book *Little America,* Byrd wrote, "Had it not been for the dogs, our attempts to conquer the Antarctic by air must have ended in failure." Nor did Byrd overlook Walden. "On January 17th, Walden's single team of thirteen dogs moved 3,500 pounds of supplies from ship to base, a distance of sixteen miles each trip, in two journeys," Byrd wrote. "Walden's team was the backbone of our transport. Seeing him rush his heavy loads along the trail, outstripping the younger men, it was difficult to believe that he was an old man."

On one occasion, Walden's whole team went through the ice. On another, jumping a crevasse, the team veered and tipped over and Walden found himself pinned beneath the sled. "Without a word, he scrambled clear, righted the sledge, started the dogs, and resumed his steady trot," Byrd wrote.

During the geological expeditions, the going sometimes got so tough, Carter wrote, that the men got into the harnesses with the dogs and helped pull. Whether Walden bowed under a harness, Carter doesn't say. But the act shows the primitive bond that developed between man and beast in this hostile land.

Ironically, these instinctive bonds were often snapped in the name of practicality. At the end of expeditions, the teams often had to kill the oldest and weariest of the dogs in order to make a successful return trip. "This is cruelty to animals, but this is a hard land, and there is no other way," Gould wrote.

The deepest of those bonds, too, would be broken out in the wild. During their first days in Antarctica, Walden put the semi-retired, twelve-year-old Chinook in the harness to limber him up and help transport supplies. After being taken off the harness, he lagged behind, and when the team reached the base, he had not returned. Hours of searching turned up nothing.

Walden sensed what had had happened. A day or two before, he had had to rescue Chinook from a losing fight with three young huskies. He believed the dog became heartbroken over losing his dominance and resigned himself to death. The night before his disappearance, Chinook woke Walden up twice by placing his paws on his face, the same way his father had the night before he died. "Perhaps that was his way of trying to tell me goodbye," Walden later said.

Byrd called the incident "perhaps the saddest during our whole stay in the Antarctic."

The following spring, an explorer came across what looked the marks of a dog's feet on a crevasse shelf. But no one would ever know whether they were Chinook's.

The log cabin that Walden called the Antlers Team Room is still used by his relatives in Wonalancet.

Max Becherer/Concord Monitor.

There is no grave for Walden's best friend. But Chinook and dogs like him are memorialized in the little town that sent them to the bottom of the world.

When Walden returned, townspeople wanted to rename the road that linked Tamworth and Wonalancet, Walden Highway. Walden declined but told them if they wanted to honor him, they could name the road Chinook Trail. A sign bearing a drawing of Chinook still marks that stretch of road. In 1935, Byrd, who went on to lead four more Antarctic expeditions, dedicated the memorial that now stands in front of the old Chinook Kennels. It reads, "Admiral Byrd Memorial to All Noble Dogs whose lives were given on dog treks during the two expeditions to Little America, Antarctica, to further science and discovery."

Walden lived out his days tinkering around the Wonalancet kennels and farm. He built windmills and wheelbarrows and dug complex systems of fish ponds; he told stories about his adventures, his quirky sense of humor intact. He liked to tell about the time he misplaced his favorite sweater. After a five-week trip to Antarctica, he said, he returned to find he had the sweater on. "There was no way of telling," he said.

In 1947, Walden died after pulling his wife from their burning house. Katherine slipped into a coma, and died several months later, never knowing he'd saved her.

But the kennels lived on. Before his departure to Antarctica, Walden hired Milton and Eva Seeley to work at the farm. They eventually bought Walden out and began breeding a new line of Alaskan malamute now known as the Kotzebue line.

The dogs became wildly popular, and Eva "Short" Seeley became a celebrity in her own right. In 1932, she raced in demo dog-sled races at the Lake Placid Olympics.

The New England Sled Dog Club secured itself a place in New England sportsmanship, and Seeley's dogs accompanied Byrd on two more Antarctic expedition. During the war, some of the dogs were sent overseas to work on search and rescue teams.

In the 1940s, the Chinook line of dogs was sold to a Maine kennel, where it eventually dwindled to just eleven dogs. In 1966, the *Guinness Book of World Records* declared Chinooks the rarest breed of dogs in the world. In the early 1980s, several dog breeders rallied behind the breed and established the Chinook Owners Association. Today more than four hundred purebred Chinooks are registered with the United Kennel Club.

One kennel, Great Mountain Chinooks of Westbrook, Maine, writes, "We strive to stay true to Chinook's original purpose by creating what we believe to be the quintessential working Chinook, a total dog, with magnificent drive, praiseworthy confirmation, and superior intelligence."

Walden would approve.

Helenette Silver

Her book on New Hampshire wildlife became the bible of conservationism.

W hen Helenette Silver died in 1990, wildlife was at its strongest ever in New Hampshire. Deer populations were increasing, and the moose herd had rebounded from near extinction to nearly 9,000. In some measure, Silver's research was responsible for the animals' good fortune.

In the 1950s, as the state awoke to its role in managing wildlife, Silver set about documenting the entire history of New Hampshire's wildlife populations. Her 1957 book, *History of New Hampshire Game and Furbearers,* offered wildlife officials an unprecedented view of how the age-old struggle between man and beast had played out so far in New Hampshire. It described Native American hunting trips along the Merrimack River, the fur trading of early white settlers, and the age-old controversy over managing the deer population.

Forty years later, the research was still relevant: Biologists looked to her work for guidance on issues from deer digestion to woodcock mating habits.

"You look back at more than 10,000 years of human existence in New Hampshire, not that much has changed," said Eric Aldrich, spokesman for the state Fish and Game Department. "I think that's what Helenette helped show us."

Warren Rudman

He was a politician who spoke his mind.

When Warren Rudman announced he was leaving the U.S. Senate, he was neither a discredited nor a played-out politician. In fact, he was the most effective representative New Hampshire had dispatched to the Beltway in a generation. His name was synonymous with ethics in government, along with a well-publicized indifference to personal advantage or the biases of his party.

Rudman was at the center of most big fights of the Reagan and Bush administrations. His Gramm–Rudman Act was the era's first serious attempt to bring crushing federal budget deficits under control. He helped investigate

Rudman was known for speaking his mind in the Senate.
Concord Monitor.

the Keating Five favor-trading scandal. He was vice-chairman of the panel examining the Iran-Contra imbroglio. He convinced his colleagues to confirm his longtime protégé, David Souter, for a seat on the U.S. Supreme Court. And he spoke his mind—criticizing the religious right, wasteful military projects, and Ronald Reagan's irresponsible budgeting.

Throughout, Rudman expressed near constant frustration with Washington gridlock. "This place is ninety-nine percent frustration and one percent exhilaration," he told a reporter in 1985. "It's hard to live on that one percent."

Seven years later, not much had changed. "I've had about all of that place I intend to put up with," he said. And so he quit.

Elizabeth Yates

She taught generations of children about black history.

Amos Fortune came to this country from Africa as a slave at the age of fifteen. Forty-five year later, through his work as a tanner and carpenter, he bought his own freedom. Later, he bought the freedom of four others, and when he died, he left a small sum to the public school in Jaffrey, his adopted hometown, to use "in any way it sees fit to educate its sons and daughters."

At least as important as the legacy of his bequest is the legacy of his life well lived—as told in Elizabeth Yates's book *Amos Fortune, Free Man*. In 1951, the book won the Newbery Medal, the highest accolade in children's

Elizabeth Yates at Gibson's bookstore in Concord, 1999.

Ben Garvin/Concord Monitor.

literature. And for nearly fifty years, the book was used to teach children about black history in New England—not only the sons and daughters of Jaffrey but those throughout New Hampshire and the nation.

"He was called Mr. Fortunatis by his friends because he seemed to bring good fortune to those who knew him," Yates said in 1999. "All I can say is that dear man has brought an awful lot of good fortune to me. And I don't mean in shekels. I mean in my relationships with children."

Virginia Colter

In a troubled time, she was a voice for nonviolent protest.

On July 13, 1968, as war waged in Vietnam, two U.S. soldiers came to Concord armed with a small arsenal of captured Viet Cong weapons They were met by a white-haired lady, armed only with words of pacifism.

Virginia Colter thought the State House exhibit glorified killing. Calmly and firmly, she persuaded the soldiers to move on to Maine, the next stop on their itinerary.

"I don't believe in war as a solution, and they have a military point of view," she said that day.

Colter inspired anti-war activists across New Hampshire.

Ken Williams/Concord Monitor.

The incident was one of many in Colter's effort to the war in Vietnam. She worked for peace candidate Eugene McCarthy in the Democratic presidential primary. She participated in anti-war protests, making sure her younger colleagues were respectful of the local police officers. She organized a vigil to mourn the local men who died in Vietnam. And she opened the Peace Center in Concord, which became a hub of anti-war activities—from planning demonstrations to counseling youths on how to avoid the draft.

"She was 50 percent of the peace movement in the area," said fellow activist Lois Booth of Canterbury. "The rest of us were the other 50 percent."

Betty Hill

An alien encounter catapulted her into celebrity.

BY SARAH KOENIG

The military investigator walks square-shouldered up the street of the New Hampshire town. He stops at a house and knocks at the door. It opens and a tall blond woman appears in the threshold.

That's when Betty Hill turned off *The X-Files,* never to watch it again. A five-foot brunette, Hill did not like to see herself—or her world-famous story—exploited by Hollywood.

That's her job. The grande dame of alien abductees, Hill is about as shy as a circus barker, as jolly, and as engaging.

Disregard for now that the senior publicist at *The X-Files* is pretty sure there never has been an episode based on the Hill case. Accept for the moment that Hill sees UFOs more frequently than some of us see Honda Civics. To talk to Betty Hill is to suspend certain Earth-bound assumptions.

The 1961 case of Betty and Barney Hill was the nation's first bona fide

Betty Hill, in 1999.

Ken Williams/Concord Monitor.

alien abduction story. Carl Sagan called it the first of its kind in the modern genre. The case was painstakingly chronicled by John Fuller in *The Interrupted Journey,* which was made into a movie, *The UFO Incident,* starring James Earl Jones.

The case involved a torn and stained dress, strangely scuffed shoes, a mysterious hand-drawn map, and, most intriguingly, two missing hours that would be accounted for only years later through medical hypnosis.

"What made it so prominent was that it was so well documented, so from the standpoint of the public consciousness, it became the most important case," said John Mack, the Harvard Medical School psychiatrist and author of *Passport to the Cosmos: Human Transformation and Alien Encounters.* "I don't think anybody has debunked it effectively."

Perhaps the Hills' most convincing evidence that they were not crackpots was the Hills themselves. She was a social worker and he worked at the post office. They were active in social and political causes, and were responsible, loving parents.

According to Peter Geremia, director of the state chapter of Mutual UFO Network and a friend of Betty Hill's, the last thing the Hills and the doctor who treated them wanted was to become UFO freaks. "The abduction scenario at that time was something that the nut cases were talking about," he said.

Seth Shostak, an astronomer with Search for Extraterrestrial Intelligence, a research group in California, agreed the Hills' utter respectability was what catapulted their story into the mainstream. "They were more or less Mr. and Mrs. Front Porch, after all," he said.

It was September 19, 1961, and the weather report predicted a hurricane along the New Hampshire coast, so Betty and Barney Hill cut their long weekend short and headed back to Portsmouth in their 1957 Chevrolet Bel Air.

They stopped at a restaurant in Colebrook, where Betty ate a piece of chocolate layer cake and Barney ate a hamburger. At 10:05 p.m. they were back on Route 3 heading toward the White Mountains.

The sky was clear, and just past Lancaster Betty noticed a bright light close to the nearly full moon. As it got closer and brighter, she pointed it out to Barney, a World War II veteran who knew something about planes. He assumed it was a satellite, perhaps off course.

Their dachshund, Delsey, was getting antsy, so they pulled over to let her out. Betty took binoculars from her car. Fuller described the moment this way: "Betty put the binoculars up to her eyes and focused carefully. What they both were about to see was to change their lives forever, and as some observers claim, change the history of the world."

Afterward, Barney was disinclined to discuss what he had seen, but Betty did so in a letter to the National Investigations Committee on Arial Phenomena. "We did see several figures scurrying about as though they were making some kind of hurried type of preparation. One figure was observing us from the windows . . . and seemed to be dressed in some type of shiny black uniform," she wrote. "At this point my husband became shocked and got back in the car, in a hysterical condition, laughing and repeating that they were going to capture us."

Barney drove wildly in an effort to escape. Past Franconia Notch they left Route 3 and headed down a smaller road.

Betty Hill said she was more curious than afraid at the time. "I understand something's going to happen and I don't know what it is, but I'm ready for it. At that point I rolled down the window and waved hello to the craft," she said, laughing into the crook of her arm. "I was sure it was a flying saucer, but I didn't say so."

Suddenly a cluster of beings blocked their way. Barney stopped the car but could not restart it. The men came toward them.

For almost three years, their memories would stop at that scene, only to pick up sometime later that night, when they found themselves driving south near Ashland.

The next day, Barney, a fastidious dresser, noticed the tops of his shoes were badly scuffed. Betty's dress was ripped and covered with powdery pink stains. There were shiny spots on the car trunk that caused a compass to flutter.

Against Barney's wishes, Betty told her sister about the incident. On her sister's advice, she reported it to Pease Air Force Base, which took the sighting seriously. According to Pease records, officials there, too, had logged an "unknown" at about 2:00 the same morning.

Only after investigators visited the Hills did they realize their trip had taken at least two hours longer than it should have. They remained haunted by the feeling that something unexplained had happened to them. Betty had recurring nightmares.

In February, the Hills began making pilgrimages to the White Mountains to try to retrace their route. They were unsuccessful, but they did meet many people in the region who had seen strange lights and flying objects. "Actually, that was just the beginning," Hill said of the initial encounter.

Betty Hill grew up in Kingston, the oldest child of liberal Irish-American parents. Her mother was a labor organizer and her father worked in a Haverhill, Massachusetts, shoe factory. At a time when even fewer minorities lived in New Hampshire than now, she was taught tolerance.

She remembers being six years old and ringing the doorbell of the house across the street, where an interracial couple lived. When the black wife answered, Betty stroked her hand, fascinated. As a student at the University of New Hampshire, she befriended a black girl her dormmates shunned.

A divorce and several business ventures later, Betty earned her social work degree and took a job with the state department of child welfare. She married Barney, who was black, in 1960. Asked if they were targets of racism, Betty laughed. "It was wonderful, because it screened out all the people we didn't want to associate with anyway."

The Hills were well regarded in the community. They were active in politics, helped set up programs for the poor, lectured about civil rights, and held official positions with the NAACP.

Their public lives continued more or less as usual after their UFO encounter, but by 1964 their psychological anxiety still had not abated. Barney had an ulcer that was not responding to treatment. He missed work, and both were depressed.

Eventually they were referred to the Boston office of Dr. Benjamin Simon, a psychiatrist who specialized in hypnosis. The conversations that transpired during their trances became a permanent chapter in the annals of ufology.

Fuller made liberal use of the tape recordings of the hypnosis sessions, which revealed episodes of rapture and terror.

Geremia has listened to the tapes. "It's enough to make you not sleep at night," he said. "There's one particular portion, when Barney is reliving what happened, really reliving every moment, and he lets out a screech on that tape that's absolutely bone-chilling."

After months of hypnosis, a fantastic story emerged. Simon could not entirely dismiss or accept the results; he did not think they were lying, but he attributed their story to some kind of shared fantasy.

The Hills recounted that they were taken on board by beings whose eyes were disproportionately large and slanted. Betty said one of them spoke English, though not very well.

They were medically examined—flakes of skin scraped off Betty's arm, her reflexes tested, and a needle inserted in her navel. Although it does not appear in Fuller's book, Mack reports that a semen sample was taken from Barney.

When they finished with her, Betty asked the "leader" where he was from and he showed her a complicated cosmic map, which Betty later drew. She asked for proof of their visit and he gave her a book written in strange symbols, but then changed his mind and took it back.

"I recognized the importance of what was happening," Hill said. "I knew these were astronauts from another solar system. I told the leader, 'This has been the most wonderful experience of my life,' and that I really appreciated meeting him and would he please come back because I had a lot of friends who would like to meet him."

She and Barney, who died of a stroke in 1969, never did see these aliens again, but soon people all over America wanted to meet the Hills. Someone had leaked their story to the *Boston Herald Traveler*, which played it on the front page for almost a week. One day Betty Hill found dozens of reporters at her doorstep. "My first concern was, how was the state going to take this?" said Betty.

Her bosses were supportive. It was 1965, and the existence of UFOs and extraterrestrial life was a possibility admitted even by the U.S. government.

"A lot of that interest came from the government. Not so much because they thought alien craft were buzzing all over the countryside, but because they wanted to find out if there were Soviet aircraft they didn't yet know about, for example," said Shostak, the California researcher.

Official commissions consisting of scientists and military experts were set up, and by the late 1960s they had come to the conclusion that national security was not at risk from these unknowns.

The extraterrestrial debate was alive in academia as well. Elizabeth Bilson, director of a space research center at Cornell University, joined the astronomy department in the early 1960s, when Carl Sagan was investigating UFO stories.

"It's true that at that time there was a wave of belief, even among scientists," she said. "It wasn't ruled out, for example, that on Mars there is some more important life than just microbes or bacteria. . . . And Mars is not so far away. If it were true, that there was really intelligent life there, it was not at all outrageous to think they could visit with us."

If the nation's intelligentsia took the issue seriously, so did average people. Even today, polls consistently show that roughly 50 percent of Americans believe in UFOs. Every year, thousands of people say they have been abducted.

Although Betty Hill now says she never hesitated to talk about her encounter, and that the press attention did not ruffle her, a letter she wrote to her mother explaining why she and Barney had agreed to work with Fuller tells a different story. "In the beginning we felt this was our own personal experience, and believed there really was not any great public interest," she wrote. "We were fearful for we believed that we would face scorn, ridicule, and disbelief."

After book's publication in 1966, the Hills went on a book tour that took them to television and radio studios all over the country—a circuit Betty would continue to travel until her retirement in 1991. She appeared on F. Lee Bailey's televised *Lie Detector Test* (and scored well), sat next to astronauts, scientists, and movie stars on programs like *The Merv Griffin Show,* and gave lectures alongside Sagan and members of the crew of *Star Trek.*

The Hill story gained steam. A noted astrologer became convinced that Betty's hand-drawn star maps corresponded to some recently discovered stars. The procedure of amniocentesis was introduced years after Betty reported having the needle inserted into her navel as a "pregnancy test."

Meanwhile, the Hills, and later Betty alone, began to look for—and to find—UFOs. For fifteen years, she said, she organized a secret network of ufologists whose members included policemen, retire military officials, reporters, and other professionals. She claims to have more than 250 photographs of UFOs. To this day she sees them, sometimes flying over her house in Portsmouth, or hovering above her yard, where her cats and chickens roam.

And she became interested in the scientific aspects of the field. "Anybody can tell a weird story," she said. "I want people to get beyond the experience and into the proof."

Hill retired from the UFO circuit because she was "bored, bored, bored," she said. She got annoyed with fakers, whom she believes she can identify, and wanted more time for her own projects, such as her 1995 book, *A Common Sense Approach to UFOs.* It included passages such as, "Sometimes, I am asked if I think Big Foot might travel around on-board UFOs. Basically my answer is no."

Hill does not regret her abduction experience, but it still causes her confusion. "The only thing I wish they'd tell me is why the heck they were here," she said.

Although her group worked "undercover with the government, you might say," she does not want the government to admit UFOs' existence. "Because people will say, 'Shoot 'em! Get rid of 'em!'" she said. "We're Americans. If we don't like it, we kill it."

In the mid-1980s, Tom Elliot, a television producer from Waltham, Massachusetts, was one of the many ordinary, educated people who joined Betty's expeditions. More than ten years later, he still had no explanation for the purplish glow on the railroad tracks they visited near Exeter, or the pyramid of lights that hovered overhead.

"I saw things I can't explain, but I guess my main problem is I can't make the jump that because it is something interesting, it must be from 'out there,'" he said. "I'm one of those people who think she's sincere. I don't think she's making it up. But I don't know why she believes what she believes."

That is the consensus of many people who know Hill, including Geremia and Mack; she is committed to the truth, they say, but her version of it is not necessarily theirs.

That doubt does not concern Hill. As she wrote to her mother in 1965 about *The Interrupted Journey,* "We hope the publication of this book will enable the reader to judge for himself and to decide if this is illusion, hallucination, dream or reality. Love, Betty and Barney."

David Souter

An enigma in public, he became a powerhouse on the U.S. Supreme Court.

BY BURTON HERSH

When George Bush nominated David Souter to fill the U.S. Supreme Court seat of retiring liberal William Brennan in August of 1990, leading politicians scratched their heads. Souter presented an enigma.

Three years earlier, Ronald Reagan's doomed effort to confirm Robert Bork had provoked the most bitter partisan exchange in the Senate since Watergate. Bork's voluminous writings and his opinions from the circuit court ultimately suffocated his prospects, and Bush had no interest in a replay.

So it looked in the summer of 1990 as if the best thing about Souter's record was how many pages remained blank. Next to a noisy, dogmatic lion of the bench like Bork, Souter struck official Washington as a rabbit—a pasty, bloodless clerk programmed to shun publicity and avoid committing himself.

"I can assure you that he has no skeletons in his closet," Souter's mentor, Sen. Warren Rudman, told Bush. Rudman's reputation for probity made Bush

David Souter in 1990, after his nomination to the U.S. Supreme Court.
Ken Williams/Concord Monitor.

inclined to listen; another close administration adviser, White House Chief of Staff and recent New Hampshire governor John Sununu, had appointed Souter to the state Supreme Court in 1983 and helped in 1989 to boost Souter onto the U.S. Court of Appeals for the First Circuit.

Souter had moved up quietly through the chairs, yet there was virtually no paper trail for anybody to track him by—no controversial law review articles, few speeches, any decisions handed down constructed so narrowly around the facts of each case that Souter's own prejudices were impossible to extrapolate. By 1990 the activist Reagan appointees had left the Supreme Court approaching deadlock over a number of contested precedents, led off by concerted efforts to roll back the consensus on abortion and affirmative action. Powerful factions on both sides intended to squeeze out of Souter some kind of commitment as to how he expected to vote once these inflammatory issues resurfaced.

But Souter wouldn't tell. Two years earlier, his name had been bruited around as a Supreme Court possibility; months earlier he'd undergone the mandatory investigation that opened the way for his First Circuit appointment. By 1990 Souter was feeling bruised and a little pessimistic, not sure any seat was worth so exhaustive an invasion of his privacy. Politely, if firmly, Souter had declined before the Senate Judiciary Committee to commit himself on *Roe* v. *Wade* or any other subject. "I won't take a litmus test," he insisted to Rudman. "I'll discuss judicial philosophy with them, but I won't go down there and be compromised. I won't discuss how I might rule in future cases."

Around Washington, a figure as reticent as Souter appeared unfamiliar to the point of alarming. Where could you find another Republican so indifferent to his perquisites? Souter drove a car so old and rusted out that the passenger's side door had to be opened from the outside. He lived in a peeling farmhouse in East Weare, rumored for some years to lack electricity. His quarter of a century of legal practice plus his time on the bench had allowed him to build up a net worth of $621,252.41—undoubtedly enough to sustain him halfway through the next millennium.

At fifty, David Souter had never married. Speculation made the rounds. The fact was here, too, Souter was a throwback, an old-fashioned heterosexual bachelor. He appreciated his own company, enriched by a good book or Bach on the phonograph.

This suggested to some that Souter was a loner, a "hermit." Such was a total misreading. Although he obviously picks them carefully, Souter has accumulated over his career a range of friends so dedicated and admiring that, in describing his talents, they have to watch themselves not to sound infatuated.

The son of an assistant bank manager, Souter was a good enough student at Concord High to move along to Harvard College, where he is best remembered for forming an "eating club" called the Daryrumple Society. He won a Rhodes Scholarship to Oxford and reportedly belonged to a crowd that regularly got back from their nights of boozing so late that they required a ladder to make it over the locked gates.

At Oxford, as at Harvard Law a few years later, Souter's reputation spread quickly as an inspired mimic and impressionist, a wit with a dry, up-country style, and a storyteller likely to become the center of any gathering. "No one I've ever met is more fun at a party," one classmate remembers.

After law school David Souter moved back in with his parents in Weare and became an associate at the law firm Orr and Reno in Concord. The prospect of a life bent over other people's trusts soon palled; in 1968 he enlisted as a staffer in the state attorney general's office. Two years later, Rudman was appointed attorney general and made Souter his deputy.

Almost immediately, Souter was the one everybody looked to whenever a case got tangled. Rudman found Souter "a slight, soft-spoken man who projected an air of immense self-confidence." Respect deepened into friendship, and by the time Tom Rath joined the office in 1972 he found himself in the position, according to Rudman, where often "his job was 'to go to lunch with Warren and explain what David was saying.'"

By that time, solidarity was important. In 1972 Gov. Walter Peterson's middle-of-the-road regime gave way to that of the right-wing fire-eating Gov. Meldrim Thomson. Thomson was chockablock with initiatives, a good many patently against the law. The operative principle here involved advancing the governor's interests but never functioning blindly as the governor's private advocate.

Rudman—and, before long, Souter, who replaced him as attorney general in 1976—contrived to preserve objectivity. When Thomson attempted to jam through a slipshod permitting process preparatory to building the Seabrook nuclear plant, or extend legalized gambling around the state, or mandate the invasion of individual citizens' tax files, the governor found himself blocked by his own attorney general. Insofar as each of these efforts would have to be backed up by elements of law enforcement, Rudman and then Souter felt justified in mounting energetic opposition, and almost always prevailed. "There were a number of fiery moments before the Executive Council whenever the governor and the attorney general went head to head," Rath remembers.

Other proposals Souter felt it to be incumbent on him to support; a number would haunt him throughout his Supreme Court hearings in 1990 and reappeared throughout his Meldrim-made-me-do-it line of defense. On behalf of Thomson, Souter backed the imposition of a literacy test on voters as well as the governor's quirky decision to fly flags at half-staff on Good Friday. Souter maintained that filing racial breakdowns of state employees would "institutionalize quotas" and referred to affirmative action as "affirmative discrimination." While attorney general he alluded in a brief to abortion as "the killing of unborn children." He prosecuted the pickets at the Seabrook plant hard and defended the state's imprisonment of more than 1,400 of them.

Wilbur Glahn, Souter's deputy, went through the motions of defending these periodic shows of force by the governor before the First U.S. Circuit on appeal, where they were routinely struck down. "When I was in the A.G.'s office it was filled with a lot of pretty liberal young guys who didn't agree with anything Meldrim Thomson represented," he recollects. But whatever the authentic motives, enough of the language survived to make Souter squirm a decade and a half later.

In 1978, prodded by Rudman, Souter accepted an appointment to the Superior Court. He advanced in 1983 to the state Supreme Court, where he assumed an unselfconscious intellectual dominance, parsing issues in his meticulous, cerebral way that left little for colleagues to oppose. Critics on the left would claim to discern a pattern too friendly to prosecutors, too insensitive to minority rights and "questionable police behavior" as applied to picketers at Seabrook and other protesters at "society's short end."

What kept coming through, Rath insists, was "an unfailing, unflagging allegiance to the rule of law. He is a conservative in the classic sense, in that the role of government is delimited by what is assigned to it by its people. It does not have any intrinsic authority of its own. He reads laws and cases in a straightforward fashion and does not interpret." To this Rudman adds that out of respect for "stare decisis (the Latin term for judicial respect for precedent) he would never vote to overturn" a landmark decision, "knowing what turmoil that would cause in our society." If it ain't broke, don't fix it.

Rudman's observation was intended to explain Souter's eagerly awaited swing vote when the moment came to contest *Roe v. Wade*. Other clues were starting to abound. Restless on the New Hampshire bench, Souter took up a position, ultimately president, on the board of Concord Hospital, where abortions were routinely performed, and became an overseer at Dartmouth Medical School. He sailed and took long hikes, often by himself, or attended Episcopal services in Hopkinton. Much of the time he sat alone and read, his ramshackle Cape Cod in Weare so tumbled with volumes that Souter himself would joke that the place "looked like somebody was moving a bookstore and stopped."

The call to Washington in 1990 seems both to have energized and unnerved Souter.

Throughout his many hours of examination before the Senate committee he kept himself agreeable, responsive, firm in his determination not to get into areas—abortion especially—in which he had never ruled. He was undeniably deeply versed in the law. Hour by hour he overcame the initial impression around the capital made by such blunders as his statement that his greatest accomplishment on the state bench was to persuade the Coast Guard to forsake its claim to patrol Lake Winnipesaukee.

Despite Ted Kennedy's opposition and the widely circulated statement by Kate Michelman of the National Abortion Rights Action League that this vote represented a "dangerous leap of faith," Souter passed onto the U.S. Supreme Court by a vote of 90–9.

Souter's positions his first few months on the bench appeared to reinforce the apprehensions on the left that he would fall in automatically behind the conservative bloc spearheaded by William Rehnquist and Antonin Scalia. While disagreeing with a decision permitting the state of Oregon to deny Indians the right to employ peyote in their religious ceremonies, Souter dismayed moderates by concurring with the Scalia majority in *Rust v. Sullivan* in reaffirming the government's right to restrict what doctors in federally financed clinics could divulge, especially concerning reproduction, to female patients.

The stunner came in April 1992. After a series of conclaves with recent Republican appointees Anthony Kennedy and Sandra Day O'Connor, the three issued a joint opinion that backed up the long-standing conclusions of Harry Blackmun and John Paul Stevens and reaffirmed *Roe v. Wade.* Crafted principally by Souter, the hard-nosed analysis observed: "For two decades of economic and social developments, people have organized intimate relationships and made choices that define their views of themselves and their places in society, in reliance on the availability of abortion in the event that contraception should fail. That ability of women to participate equally in the economic and social life of the Nation has been facilitated by their ability to control their reproductive lives."

Souter's implications were unequivocal: Abortion must remain in place largely to back up birth control. The right to privacy superseded every community imperative.

Conservatives were shocked. After having assured his friends that Souter was a "home run" for their cause and that he personally had "very detailed assurances" that Souter was reliable on *Roe v. Wade,* John Sununu was personally affronted. U.S. Rep. Chuck Douglas decided that Souter was fundamentally a "statist," uncomfortable with either asserting a new right or reversing an established precedent, willing to "sanctify something just because somebody who is long dead may have gotten it wrong." After having introduced Souter around and sponsored him on the Judiciary Committee, fellow New Hampshire Republican Sen. Gordon Humphrey observed sadly that "in retrospect, Souter's jurisprudence leaves a lot to be desired, from my point of view."

Later that year, an identical coalition declared unconstitutional the recital of religious prayers at public school graduations. By 1994, judicial historian David Garrow would observe in *The New York Times,* Antonin Scalia's repeated barbed references to Souter in opinion after opinion made it plain that Scalia realized that "he has decisively lost the struggle for the intellectual leadership of the Court to someone who was not supposed to be a major player."

By the end of 1995, lamented Bill Buckley's *National Review,* David Souter had "voted consistently with the liberal wing of the Court—as, this year, on federalism, term limits, affirmative action, racial gerrymandering, school desegregation, and religion." With his repeated dissents, even against a temporary majority, jurists and scholars agreed, Souter was deliberately "paving the way for a court in which his current dissents become the majority opinion." His increasingly influential style of libertarian moderation was more damaging, according to the conservative scorekeepers, than decisions by Clinton appointees Stephen Breyer and Ruth Bader Ginsburg.

It depends, of course, on how you define conservative. In 1997 William Brennan, the plainspoken liberal to whose seat Souter succeeded, died at the age of ninety-one. The two men had become close friends, and Souter gave one of the eulogies at Brennan's funeral. The influential justice, Souter remarked, had set a standard that would continually challenge future courts to prove him wrong: "Only the Lord can know when the court and the country will come to terms with Justice Brennan's reading of the American Constitution."

Meanwhile, clearly, anytime the court attempts to make law rather than interpret it, New Hampshire's emerging David Souter has made it plain enough how formidably he intends to stand his ground.

Pamela Smart

For the media, her murder trial was a drama "to die for"

BY SARAH KOENIG

The jurors had just convicted Pamela Smart of first-degree murder, and a few of them were in tears. Judge Douglas Gray spoke to them in private. He told them the media would be after them, offering them book and movie deals. And his part, he added, should be played by Clint Eastwood.

The comment caused widespread indignation. There is no place for levity when sending a twenty-three-year-old woman to prison for the rest of her life, many complained.

In fact, Gray's role was played by a lesser star, although Helen Hunt was cast as Smart for the TV movie—the same one in which Channel 9 reporter Bill Spencer of Manchester played himself.

Smart's murder trial created an international media frenzy.

AP/World Wide Photos.

The Pamela Smart trial was the most highly publicized in New Hampshire history and ranks as one of the country's most notorious televised trials. Its tawdry narrative pushed its way into popular culture through newsprint, television cable lines, true-crime book jackets, and, finally, movie scripts. Audiences couldn't get enough.

It began in 1990, the tale of a pretty, ambitious, twenty-two-year-old newlywed who had an affair with a fifteen-year-old Winnacunnet High School sophomore, Bill Flynn. With help from a couple of friends, Flynn shot Smart's husband, Gregory Smart, execution-style in the condo the couple rented in Derry. Slowly the shocking murder story unraveled to implicate the grieving widow, who was accused of convincing the boy to kill her husband in exchange for a future with her. Ultimately the boys confessed and testified against Smart, who was sentenced to life in prison for first-degree murder, conspiracy to commit murder, and witness tampering.

Smart landed in prison in Bedford Hills, New York, where she continued to fight for release. "I have, and continue to, maintain my innocence," she wrote in 1999. "I only accept responsibility for having had an affair with Bill Flynn, for which I am deeply regretful."

If the coverage satisfied the public, it also caused some judicial, journalistic—and even societal—soul-searching. Smart filed a petition for habeas corpus in U.S. District Court in Concord, based on the argument that pretrial publicity—frequently compared to a Roman circus—tainted the jury, and that Gray failed to safeguard the jurors, and Smart, from that prejudice.

"Who made it the soap opera it became? Who?" asked Smart's mother, Linda Wojas, remembering the many inaccuracies printed about her daughter, who she believes is innocent. "You'd see something in the paper or on TV that was wrong, and you'd want to yell, 'Hey! Everybody! It's not true! Wait!' But nobody cares. They got their sound bites, their quotes, and they're done. But the damage is done. Always, the damage is done."

Smart's case was not particularly meaningful from a legal point of view. It set no groundbreaking precedents, tested no new scientific methods of gathering evidence. Rather, it had what producers of both news and fiction knew to be the delicious details of marketability. And the story broke at a time when the technology to deliver those details had ripened to match the public's huge appetite for true crime.

WMUR-TV in Manchester aired the trial live every day, bumping advertisements and soap operas in favor of record-setting ratings. "It couldn't have been scripted or cast or directed better if it had come out of Hollywood," said Jack Heath, the station's news director at the time. "In fact, the movie paled in comparison."

Coverage of the Smart story began like that of any local murder—locally. Gregory Smart's killing, on May 1, 1990, looked like the result of a robbery gone bad and was followed as such. A month later, three teenagers—Bill Flynn, Patrick "Pete" Randall, and Vance Lattime—were arrested. The story did not take off nationally until the police established that Pamela Smart had been having an affair with Flynn, a student in the school district where she worked.

Feeding the story was the perception that Smart was Flynn's teacher.

Smart was not a certified teacher, although she did work with Flynn on one or two extracurricular projects.

"It had sex, it had violence, it had youth, it had the older woman concept. It had the flavor that you see generally on daytime TV," said Mark Sisti, Smart's lawyer at the time. "Within about a week we were fairly sure it was getting more attention than it should have. It took on a life of its own." By August, the nation was paying attention; by September, *Hard Copy* had paid a key witness, sophomore Cecelia Pierce, $1,000 for her interview on its show "Scandal at School: One Girl's Secret."

(By the end of the trial, Pierce would get an additional $300 from *A Current Affair* and $100,000 for a movie contract with Once Upon A Time productions. She was not the only one to cash in: One juror made recordings of her thoughts and tried to sell them to the defense attorneys for $25,000; another juror sold an article to the *Boston Globe,* reportedly for $15,000.)

Gregory Smart's parents appeared on *Donahue*. By the time jurors showed up at the Rockingham County Superior Court for the trial's opening day, they had a hard time finding parking spots. Reporters had arrived representing Italian, Australian, and Japanese media.

According to Stephen Brill, who started *Court TV,* the trial's popularity was not surprising. "Trials are the most dramatic form of nonviolent combat we have," he said.

As the case wore on, the most salacious details of Smart's life became common knowledge. She liked heavy metal music and was a Van Halen fan. Her puppy was named Halen, and Smart allegedly asked Flynn and Randall not to kill Gregory Smart in front of the dog and not to get blood on the sofa. She and Flynn had watched the steamy movie 9½ *Weeks* and recreated some of the scenes in her bedroom. She had given him a picture of herself posing suggestively in a bikini—a photo that still can be found on "The Pamela Smart Resource Center" on the Internet.

The press gleefully contrasted these details with what they saw in court, commenting profusely on the bows in Smart's hair and on her shoes, on her color-coordinated business suits and controlled demeanor. Headlines dubbed her "Ice Princess" and "Maiden of Metal"—a moniker she originally earned as host of a radio show at Florida State University.

Local residents were hooked, too. Michelle Franz ran the Seabrook Village Video store at the time. Suddenly 9½ *Weeks* was a hot rental, she remembered. "We had a TV in the video store that showed movie reviews," she said. "People would come in and ask us to put the trial on instead. It was the topic of conversation. It became a part of people's lives."

Residents in Derry and on the Seacoast sat riveted to the coverage in beauty parlors and restaurants. "I heard of students taking time off from classes to watch," said Paul Maggiotto, who prosecuted the case. "I think it gave people a real education in the court process."

The Rockingham County courthouse was small, and seating was limited. The court began to issue tickets—30 a day—to accommodate the public. Spectators lined up, sometimes as early as 4:30 A.M., to get a ticket for the 9:30 proceedings.

At Winnacunnet High School, then-Superintendent Jim Weiss said, "there was a feeding frenzy from day one." He had been on the job for about a month when he looked out his window and saw two dozen police cars pull up to arrest Smart.

"My frame of reference was local papers, not *The Washington Post* and *Paris Match* and *The London Times*," he said. The district hired a media consultant to help handle the press. Several reporters had to be thrown off school property.

Adding to the media intrigue was the case's central character, Pamela Smart, whom many believed was herself a deft manipulator of the press. Not long after the murder, Smart issued a plea on Channel 9, asking for any information the public might have about her husband's murder.

Smart had a degree in communications and theater and aspired to be a television reporter. Her role model was CNN anchor Bernard Shaw. During the initial investigation, Smart kept in touch with reporters and the police. Once convicted, she gave her first interview to *Primetime Live*'s Diane Sawyer. Wojas said her daughter was tricked into that early Channel 9 appearance by Spencer, who came to their door saying he had information that Gregory Smart was involved with drugs. Pamela Smart agreed to the interview in an effort to dispel the drug story, which she said was false.

Author Joyce Maynard, who lived in Keene at the time, remembers seeing Smart's televised appeal. "It looked like every performance of every other grieving person on television," she said. "It was as if life was imitating television. . . . When I saw that, I didn't say, 'Oh, she did it,' but I did think, 'This is a television person.'"

Maynard eventually published *To Die For,* a novel about television culture inspired by the Smart case. The book was made into a movie starring Nicole Kidman. In the book, the Smart-like character, Suzanne Maretto, is eventually killed by a hit man posing as an ABC producer.

Ken Englade, a true-crime writer who published the first book about the case, *Deadly Lessons,* also thought Smart and her mother worked the media. He lives in Albuquerque, New Mexico, and, nearly a decade after the trial, said he'd recently seen a "Free Pam Smart" bumper sticker on a car. It probably got there thanks to Wojas, who began a nationwide campaign after her daughter's conviction. She organized a fund-raising cookout that drew supporters from as far away as Florida, and a Friends of Pamela Smart newsletter. Years later, donations from supporters helped pay for the correspondence law courses Smart took in prison.

The enormous publicity—more than 1,200 newspaper and magazine articles—meant the public began taking sides. People showed up at the courthouse with signs saying Smart was innocent. At Winnacunnet, the socioeconomic rift between students from "have" and "have-not" towns widened, said Weiss, the former superintendent; the kids involved with the murder were from Seabrook, one of the poorest towns in the district.

Smart's lawyers appealed the case, saying the jury could not help but be influenced by the avalanche of media coverage. The defense had tried to get a change of venue and later asked Gray to sequester the jury, which he eventually did after the second day of deliberations.

"That poor kid didn't even have a chance to go to the bathroom without the cameras following," said Sisti. "It was an insult to the judicial system. That media attention couldn't have helped anyone. She was guilty before the trial started. They were sitting back, waiting, salivating for her fifteen-year-old lover to take the stand, like hungry wolves."

The Boston Herald advertised a call-in number for readers to register their guilty and not guilty votes, and published the results before the trial ended. Channel 9 ran a half-hour special called "Anatomy of a Murder." Wojas believes it was impossible for even well-intentioned jurors not to be affected by the coverage. A transcript from a tape made by one juror reads, "I feel like I'm really exposed to the press. . . . I mean, even before I go to scratch my nose or anything, I think about, 'Oh God, how many pictures are they going to get of me scratching my nose.' And so this has turned out to be a whole lot more stress than I have ever, ever imagined it could ever be."

Smart was found guilty after three days of deliberations.

When Smart reappeared in Gray's courtroom in 1997 for a hearing, he banned cameras from the courtroom. "Why? Because life is a learning process," he told a reporter.

In New Hampshire, press access is at the judge's discretion, and some are more accepting of cameras than others. Although legal observers say no sweeping changes occurred in New Hampshire courts as a result of the Smart trial, they say lawyers and judges alike have thought twice about their dealings with the media since the case.

Professor Albert Scherr of the Franklin Pierce Law Center in Concord said New Hampshire attitudes about cameras in courtrooms have shifted since the early 1990s. "It's defined by people's reactions to O. J. Simpson. Prior to O. J., it was defined by Pam Smart," he said.

Scherr said the Smart case "brought New Hampshire crime reporting into the electronic age," with mixed results. The media, in particular the TV media, began to pay more attention to trials, "and probably there was an improvement in coverage in the sense that more aspects of any particular case were looked at," he said. But that also has meant coverage "even if those aspects weren't there or particularly interesting. So it started to distort things," he said.

A decade later, Englade said if Smart's case broke today it probably would not get the coverage it got in 1990. "The twenty-four-hour news cycle is something that didn't exist in Pam Smart's day," he said. "So this had a big impact." And his book, he added, would probably not have been written—and perhaps not the one by Stephen Sawicki, *Teach Me to Kill,* with the especially lurid cover.

"True crime is really in the toilet," he said. "O. J. killed it and JonBenet finished it off. Most of the big writers are getting out of it. The public has said, 'ho hum, another murder.'"

Anna Philbrook

She was the state's top expert and advocate for children's mental health.

As public events go, groundbreaking ceremonies don't usually come with much drama. But when the state broke ground for the Philbrook Center for Children's Services in Concord in 1969, it was the day Dr. Anna Philbrook's dream came true.

Philbrook was the state's first licensed child psychiatrist. From the moment she began working for the state hospital in 1933, she was New Hampshire's fiercest promoter of mental health services for kids. She believed children needed to be treated differently from adults. She believed they needed their own clinics and residential treatment centers. And she believed there was hope—that children could be saved from a life of mental illness.

For years, Dr. Anna Philbrook lobbied for psychiatric services for kids. The state broke ground for the Philbrook Center for Children's Services in 1969.

Collections of the State of New Hampshire.

In public life, making your dream come true generally means convincing cautious lawmakers that it's worth the investment. Philbrook's genius was her ability to wring compassion from a miserly legislature for the good of the kids she knew—and the ones who would come along in the future. "I have worked with so many youngsters who feel they're nobody. They live in a world of anger, fear, bewilderment—they long to be somebody," Philbrook once said.

In the care of Dr. Anna Philbrook, they were.

Maxine Kumin

She won the Pulitzer Prize for poetry in 1973.

Maxine Kumin's view most often included the woods, fields, and wildlife of Warner, and her poetry gave timelessness to a corner of New Hampshire. But from a hemlock weighted with snow, Kumin could whisk readers to refugees leaning under their burden of bedding and children. Such writing earned her the Pulitzer Prize in 1973 and many honors since.

"Her strengths are derived from her connection to place and nature," said Carole Oles, a fellow poet. "A poet whose life and work are intimately interwoven."

Oles and other poets credit Kumin's example and encouragement for opening larger horizons in their own writing lives. And for many younger women

Maxine Kumin at her home in Warner, 1999.
Ken Williams/Concord Monitor.

writers, she legitimized subjects by her mastery of them in her work: family, women's physicality, politics, environment, and her identification with her patch of New Hampshire. "Kumin's work was part of a sea change in American culture," said Robin Becker, who teaches at Pennsylvania State University. "It suddenly seemed to me things were possible for women to do, to think, feel, speak.

Don Foudriat

He helped clean New Hampshire's waters.

By 1971, it was no secret that New Hampshire's biggest waterways were polluted. Industrial pollution flowed from mills and tanneries straight into the Merrimack River. Partially treated sewage from Laconia fouled the water further north. But it was in that long, hot summer of 1971, when Lake Winnisquam wasn't clean enough for safe swimming for even a single week, that the cries of environmentalists became loud enough to catch the attention of state politicians.

"Things started to change when businesses dropped off because fewer people were vacationing here," said Don Foudriat of Sanbornton, who had been complaining about the water for years. "People started feeling the pinch, and that's when officials woke up to the fact that we were destroying not only our beautiful waters but our local economy and a major source of revenue for the state: tourism."

Foudriat's concern for Lake Winnisquam helped clean New Hampshire's waters from north to south.

Ken Williams/Concord Monitor.

Foudriat was among numerous local residents who alerted the media, lobbied politicians, and drew the federal government's concern. The result of their efforts: a $70 million cleanup that started in the Lakes Region and ended up helping all the way into southern New Hampshire. The Winnipesaukee River Basin Program included wastewater collection facilities and a massive treatment plant in Franklin. Not the stuff movies are made from, perhaps, but an improvement dramatic enough to change the quality of life for new generations of boaters, fishermen, swimmers, and wildlife.

Don Foudriat

Francis Grover Cleveland

He founded the nation's oldest surviving professional summer theater.

When Francis Grover Cleveland started the Barnstormers Theater in 1931, the players really *were* barnstormers. Their productions opened in Tamworth on Mondays, traveled throughout the week to Sandwich, Conway, Wolfeboro, and even Poland Springs, Maine, before coming back for a final Saturday night show in Tamworth. The next week? A new show, a new trip.

After World War II, the roving stopped, but the grueling schedule continued: eight productions in eight weeks each and every summer, a pace that was once a standard summer stock routine but, by the end of the century,

The Barnstormers' first-ever production, *The Ghost Train,* was performed in 1931. Ed Goodnow (right) directs Francis Cleveland, as the stationmaster, and an unknown actress.

Courtesy of The Barnstormers.

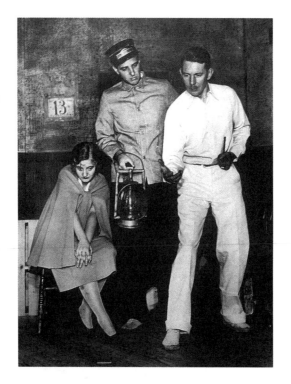

extremely rare. Audiences appreciated it, coming back week after week, season after season.

Cleveland, who once acted on Broadway but didn't like New York, explained his success like this: "It's a reasonable assumption that we are doing something right. There is no doubt that we have esprit de corps. We work together and no one nitpicks. But most of all, I think we approach our work, agonizing as it frequently is, with gaiety, bounce, and a certain humility."

Francis Grover

Cleveland

Jigger Johnson

A North Country log driver, he could brawl, curse, and drink with the best of them.

BY JIM GRAHAM

Albert Lewis Johnson was not a politician, industrialist, humanitarian, or scholar, yet sixty-four years after his death his name still commanded respect around the old mill towns and spruce-covered mountains of New Hampshire's North Country.

He was a lumberjack. And his gritty, hard-driving style on and off the job made him a legend.

"The further up the Androscoggin you go, the tougher they are. And I was born above the headwaters!" he liked to boast.

Jigger Johnson's career as a lumberjack spanned the turn of the century, when New Hampshire's rivers served as watery highways, floating massive amounts of timber from North Country forests to sawmills as far south as Connecticut.

Courtesy of Bob Monahan.

They called him Jigger Johnson.

Last of the great logging camp bosses, Jigger could out-work, out-fight, out-drink, and out-cuss any man who ever hefted a peavey. He had only two days of formal schooling his entire life—he lost his books the first day, and the teacher was out sick the second—but he delivered an impressive spoken resumé whenever he arrived at a new logging operation.

"I can run faster, jump higher, squat lower, move sideways quicker, and spit further than any son-of-a-bitch in camp!"

Anyone who doubted him was in for a brawl. Likewise for anyone who called him Albert. Or talked back to him. Or was slow on the job.

But for all his hell-raising, Jigger's legacy endures because he was also one of the era's best-loved, most-respected woods bosses. His knack for pushing men to exhaustion day after day was equaled only by his reputation for treating them fairly, paying them handsomely, and keeping them well fed and entertained. So when other camps typically ran short of men late in the season, Jigger's crews stayed on until the last log was sluiced into the sawmill.

That made him popular not only among loggers and their families (many of whom depended on the wages they sent home), but also among the lumber barons who made fortunes stripping New Hampshire's hills clean of virgin timber.

"He could walk into saloons in Berlin and North Stratford and recruit a crew of brawling lumberjacks to go with him to drive logs on the Nulhegan, the most dangerous tributary of the Connecticut," reported Robert Monahan, a longtime friend who wrote about Jigger for the April 1957 issue of *New Hampshire Profiles* magazine. "He probably would have to lick a dozen of them just to prove who was best man, which was a quaint custom of the time. He could do it, too."

Jigger's career spanned the turn of the century, when New Hampshire's rivers served as watery highways, floating massive amounts of timber from remote North Country forests to sawmills as far south as Connecticut. The work was back-breaking, dirty, cold, miserably wet, and deadly dangerous. It was done primarily in the bitter winter months, when heavy logs could be dragged more easily over snow and ice, and completed in the spring, when snowmelt turned normally small tributaries into torrents high enough to float logs.

Remembered most for his off-the-job antics, Jigger actually spent the bulk of his hard life mastering his craft, from cutting and delimbing trees with a double-bitted ax to accurately estimating the value of harvestable timber on an entire mountainside to dancing across tangles of treacherous, slippery logs twisting, bobbing, and rolling down through miles of rushing white water.

"Many people who saw the riverman only in his worst moment—that is, in town after he was in, unkempt, drunk, roaring, and fighting—forgot or never knew that those moments of violent relaxation form only three weeks out of fifty-two in the man's hard life," wrote logging historian Robert Pike. "It was pretty apparent that a riverman was strong in the back, but most people thought he must be weak in the head. This was not true."

Long before political correctness, computer software, and Hollywood action-adventure movies, Jigger was unabashedly a plain and simple man's man. An original. A crackerjack of a lumberjack.

"Jigger also was almost the last of his race—that race of men who cut a swath of timber from eastern Maine to western Oregon and yelled like crazed devils every spring, when the drive was in and they were released from the savage woods for a few days, as they pounded the bars in Bangor, Saginaw, St. Paul, and Seattle," wrote Steward Holbrook in *Holy Old Mackinaw: A Natural History of the American Lumberjack.*

"Some of that tribe, as in Jigger's case, were killed physically by civilization; as for the others, civilization has mowed them down spiritually—removing the high, wild color from their lives, ironing flat their personalities, and reducing them to the status of proletarians."

The state's last logging drive occurred in the summer of 1915, beginning near Mount Tom in Crawford Notch. The drives were stopped because they damaged river ecosystems and because the more lucrative logging markets moved west after the White Mountains' most valuable forests were clear-cut, leaving entire mountain ranges here virtually barren.

The forests have grown back in New Hampshire since then, and modern logging practices dictate that trees be harvested more gently, with techniques and equipment that allow the woods to recover at steady, sustainable rates. Most loggers also undergo extensive safety training, while professional foresters planning timber harvests often have master's degrees.

Jigger was born in 1870, in the farming and logging town of Fryeburg, Maine, near Conway and just south of Evans Notch and its famous logging camps. Little is known about his boyhood, except that it did not last long. At age twelve, he left home to become a logger and never returned.

A cook's helper, he set about making a name for himself when a logger twice his size mouthed off to him. Though camp custom forbade talking at the table, the belligerent logger, suffering from a hangover, would not be quiet.

"Jigger dutifully told him to shut up, prompting the elder man to jump the boy and push him to the floor where he pounded him. Jigger hugged the big drunk close, set his keen young teeth into an ear, and hung on," according to a 1983 profile in *The Mountain Ear,* a weekly newspaper in North Conway.

"When some of the crew pried the pair apart, a good hunk of the ear remained in Jigger's mouth. In honor of the young 'cookee's' grit and vigor, the crew passed around a hat and bought Jigger a fine new red woolen shirt to replace the one torn in the scrap, and a full pound of B&L Black, a favorite chewing tobacco of the time."

The origin of Jigger's colorful nickname remains a mystery, though several sources say loggers bestowed it upon the boy because of his small size. Others say it was because he drank heavily throughout his life. (A bar in Plymouth is named for him.)

In either case, while Johnson attained Paul Bunyan stature in lore, he was actually dwarfed in size by most of the men he led—and fought. Only five feet, six inches tall, he never weighed more than 160 pounds.

"His small size and great strength were what fooled many otherwise smart men," Monahan said. "He was actually as quick as a wildcat."

Jigger's most legendary barroom brawl occurred at a hell-hole called The Line House, a saloon on the international boundary between Quebec, Beecher

Falls, Vermont, and West Stewartstown, New Hampshire. The bar was a favorite among log drivers who worked the waters of the upper Connecticut River.

According to Monahan, during one particularly tough log drive, Jigger worried the logs coming down river would be easily snagged, creating a dangerous, costly logjam when they hit the rapids at the falls. So he forbade his two-dozen men to leave the river for a drink and a warm seat next to the Line House woodstove.

But the lights of West Stewartstown proved too tempting, and when Jigger found most of his crew gone off to drinking, he blew up like 160 pounds of dynamite. He stormed into the bar and grabbed a peavey—a stout, long-handled pole with a steel spike and pivoting hooked arm on the end, used to roll logs. Then he began swinging.

"Men went down like wind-felled pines," Monahan recalled. As his crew ducked out and scrambled back to camp, the bar's bouncer stepped forward.

The bouncer, a gigantic French-Canadian named LaPoint, threw Jigger to the floor and started kicking him with steel-spiked, or "calked," boots, which loggers wore at the time. Bleeding and bruised, Jigger managed to crawl along the floor until he could grab hold of LaPoint's stamping legs. With a quick heave, Jigger lifted the brute off his feet and shoved him onto the barroom stove.

"The stove wasn't red hot, the way some tell it," reported Jumbo Hilliard, a logger who was there. "But it was damn well warm, and Jigger held LaPoint there until he howled like the very devil, and we could smell meat frying."

The brawl ended, with a kerosene lamp smashed over LaPoint's head and his clothes on fire, when other loggers finally separated the two and smothered

Johnson poses outside his cabin in Passaconaway.

Courtesy of Bob Monahan.

the flames with a blanket. The scars left by the spiked boots on Jigger's back were common enough in those days that they were called "loggers' smallpox." He was covered with them over most of his body, though his head was unscathed—testimony, old-timers said, to his ability to keep his head out of harm's way.

It was still well before midnight when Jigger returned to camp, and he worked his men mercilessly for nearly eighteen hours straight.

By all accounts, Jigger was as hard-drinking and foul-mouthed as he was hard-driving.

"One of Jigger's greatest contributions to the logging industry was the virile and amusing profanity he always had on tap," wrote Holbrook, who logged with Jigger in 1910. "He could and did damn a person or thing in a manner that made the Pope's excommunication sound like a recommendation of character."

"Unfortunately, because of its phallic and other anatomical references, little of his bluest and best billingsgate can be reproduced," Holbrook wrote.

Repeated stories of his drinking indicate Jigger was almost certainly an alcoholic, or at least a serious binge drinker. In his day, though, such terms had not yet been invented, and hard drinking was a respected rite around logging camps.

"His drinking abilities passed all belief," Holbrook wrote. "He actually drank everything from clear grain alcohol to canned heat, and from horse liniment to painkiller; that is, everything except champagne and cocktails, both of which he held to be injurious to the stomach and kidneys."

The end of large-scale clear-cutting and log drives came too soon for Jigger, who struggled to make a way for himself in the fast-paced years after World War I, when it seemed the entire country transformed itself into a modern industrial power run by electricity and machines in factories, instead of brute strength and sweat in the outdoors.

Though several accounts say he had two daughters, there is no record of him ever marrying, spending much time with family, or living in a house with running water and electricity. Ultimately, he found modern life all too complicated.

And that probably made his drinking worse.

"It was only when circumstances forced him out of the logging camps, and into the ways of civilization, that he took the first step toward the grave," Holbrook wrote.

His slow decline started in the 1920s, when the pulpwood industry took a dive and Jigger was forced to find another trade. Well into his fifties, he was glad when old logging friends landed him a job as a fire lookout on lonely windswept posts atop 4,832-foot Carter Dome and 3,475-foot Mount Chocorua.

Jigger was a competent, alert fire spotter and was known to regale hikers with colorful tales while offering them water he packed up daily on his back. But when it rained and there was not much to do, he drank firewater instead and reported seeing winged eels, bats, and other strange phenomena. As much as U.S. Forest Service officials liked Jigger, they had to fire him.

He found work as a caretaker at an exclusive private game preserve but lost that job when his homemade still—which distilled a potent beverage he called "eagle sweat"—blew up and burned the lodge down. He then turned to his friend Monahan, who put Jigger to work at a Civilian Conservation Corps camp on the Wild River, near Gilead, Maine.

Jigger proved immensely popular with the younger, city-bred men of the CCC, the Depression era program that put unemployed young men to work in the nation's wilderness areas. But the camp's regimented hygiene standards and required nightly book study did not agree with Jigger, who was apt to disappear on drinking sprees.

Let go one last time, Jigger took to the woods by himself. He became a fur trapper and built a crude cabin on National Forest land near Douglas Brook in the Passaconaway area. Pelts of lynx, bobcat, mink, muskrat, weasel, fox, and the most valuable prize—fisher—provided him with enough pocket money to maintain his hardscrabble lifestyle.

"As a trapper, Jigger was something of a one-man Hudson's Bay Company," Monahan wrote.

Once, Jigger used a deer carcass to lure two bobcats to the base of a tree he had climbed and then pounced on them and bagged them, live, with his own hands. The cats were worth more alive (about $50 each) than as pelts, and one was sold to the University of New Hampshire, which wanted a wildcat for a mascot.

The end finally came in March 1935, when Jigger went to Conway to celebrate after having sold a lynx pelt for $100. Awakening the next morning, he realized he had not checked his trap line in the past twenty-four hours—as required by state game laws. Knowing the local conservation officer was around, Jigger rushed to hire a driver who could take him to a point where he could set off on snowshoes.

Accounts of what happened next vary. According to most, the driver went too fast and the car slipped on the ice on West Side Road and sideswiped a telephone pole just as Jigger opened the door to jump out. But one tale still told in the North Country said Jigger was leaning out the window to vomit after an all-night binge and hit his head on the pole.

A few hours later, Jigger reached the end of his own long trail.

"There, by the grace of God and of assorted genes, walked a man among men," Monahan wrote. "And there, too, as only a few of us who knew him intimately realized, was as gentle, kindly soul as one could meet. He was the roughest and finest character who ever set foot in the timberlands of the Northeast."

Some thirty years later, the Forest Service named a campground after him on the Kancamagus Highway, near where he trapped.

Judson Hale

As editor of Yankee *magazine, he became the booster of the backwoods.*

BY ALEC MACGILLIS

Far from the boundaries of New England, thousands of Americans still daydream in the colors of a fall maple and to the tune of a ringing village church bell. For many locals, the region may be losing its charm with every new shopping strip, but elsewhere the myth of New England is alive and well.

A good part of the credit goes to the publication that has served as New England's propagandist for the last sixty-five years, New Hampshire-based *Yankee* magazine, and its editor of thirty years, Judson Hale. Sixty percent of the magazine's 700,000 subscribers live outside the region; if one has any

Judson Hale poses with a stuffed chicken from his museum. The bird came from a Littleton farmer who created an unsuccessful museum of stuffed farm animals; Hale bought the treasure for $10.

*Ken Williams/*Concord Monitor.

356

doubts about the influence *Yankee* has on their perception of New England, just listen to them.

One issue moved a California reader to write in with memories of "feeling invincible in a big Pontiac convertible driving out the Mid-Cape Highway, with the radio playing Patti Page's recording of 'Old Cape Cod.'" Responding to an essay in the magazine by the late Jane Kenyon, a reader from Galveston, Texas, wrote, "Her prose took me back to the awesome beauty of Mount Washington." A reader in Umatilla, Florida, wrote the magazine asking for advice on how to turn beeswax candles into furniture polish.

For these readers and thousands like them, the little monthly magazine has come to resemble a letter from home, redolent of mom's kitchen and dad's pipe.

It is no accident that the magazine's rise in popularity has coincided with New England's slowed population growth and corresponding loss of political heft. The more people moved from the region to the Sun Belt and the West, the greater the market for *Yankee's* brand of nostalgia. The magazine has become the newsletter of the New England diaspora.

"It's not terribly surprising it's so widely read outside the region. It's a touchstone of stability—the town green and all that," said University of New Hampshire history professor Robert Maciecski. "It's addressing the exodus from New England. There are a lot of transplants across the country, and it's a way for them to keep their roots."

Central to *Yankee's* selling of the New England mystique has been Hale, who joined the magazine in 1958 and became its executive editor in 1970. Hale is an embodiment of the magazine and the regional image it projects, a "Yankee" in all senses of the word: outdoorsy, literate, possessed of a dry sense of humor and a head of hair as white as an albino rabbit.

Hale's role in shaping the New England aura would be significant enough if it were confined to his editorial work at the magazine, located in a cluster of red buildings on Dublin's Main Street. He is widely credited with helping make the magazine a more professional publication than it was at its founding in 1935 by Hale's uncle, Robb Sagendorph.

What has made Hale all the more pivotal in shaping attitudes about the region, though, is that he's strayed so far beyond it. Every year, he goes on a national tour to promote the *Old Farmer's Almanac,* which his family also publishes. From time to time, he can be seen on television talk shows, playing the quirky New Englander before a national audience. He's written two books on the region, including a memoir, *The Education of a Yankee.*

For many Americans, Jud Hale is to New England what Garrison Keillor is to the Midwest. How accurate a fit that is depends on how you define the region—and how you define Jud Hale.

As much as he might seem the classic New Englander, it's hard to pin down just what part of the regional stereotype Hale represents. On the one hand, he was born into an old Boston Brahmin family, with a professional opera singer for a mother. On the other hand, he spent much of his childhood in remote Vanceboro, Maine, where his parents started a school in the mold of German philosopher Rudolf Steiner.

He went to boarding schools from the third grade on, attending elite Choate in Connecticut, then Dartmouth. Like those most red-blooded of blue-bloods, though, he managed to get himself thrown out of college for bad behavior that he says included vomiting on a dean and his wife. He did a three-year stint in the Army as a tank commander in peacetime Germany before being allowed to return to Dartmouth for his diploma.

Having been turned away from New York publishing houses for his lack of experience, Hale came calling to his uncle, Sagendorph. Asked how he got into the magazine, Hale doesn't blink: "Nepotism."

He arrived in Dublin in 1958 figuring he'd spend at most a year before escaping back to New York. Instead, he fell under the spell of his uncle's venture, which was just taking off for good.

It was 1935, in the depths of the Depression, when Sagendorph launched the magazine with the help of his wife Trix's inheritance in her family's hometown of Dublin. Declaring itself the "monthly magazine for Yankees everywhere," the magazine set out with the following mission, described in its debut issue: "the expression and perhaps indirectly the preservation of that great culture in which every Yank is born and in which every real Yank must live."

In its early years, the magazine was packed with text, long essays by correspondents from around the region and much fiction and poetry. Issues in the first two decades included pieces like "How to Create Better Understanding Between City People and Country People," a lament about the spread of billboards, and a roundup of unsolved New England murders.

Typical was a piece by one Faith Baldwin, a newcomer to New England: "I have learned that the Old Guard consists of those who can trace their ancestry a hundred years or more in the village and have very little use for 'outsiders.' But what is an 'outsider'? I was told recently that the influx of outsiders was resented by the natives. Yet the speaker had lived here but eight years and was not of native stock!"

The magazine's look started to change after World War II as it learned to profit from the postwar boom. Its pages became filled with ads from mail-order firms, which saw the magazine as a homey forum to shop their wares; the magazine now included a "West Coast letter" from a transplanted New Englander and a "House for Sale" section, with monthly features of handsome New England homes on the market.

Meanwhile, its circulation took off, thanks in part to a steep rise in gift subscriptions; no longer did Hale have to make up letters to the editor from readers for a lack of real ones, as he did when he first came to the magazine.

Overseeing this expansion until his death in 1970 was Sagendorph, an Abe Lincoln look-alike who cast himself as the curmudgeon, to great effect. Hale recalled bringing in a Girl Scout troop to view the office, only to have his uncle bark, "Make sure they don't steal anything!"

According to former managing editor Tim Clark, Sagendorph created for himself the role of the "professional New Englander." It is not so easy to peg his successor, Hale, Clark said, because Hale is so riddled with the region's contradictions.

"He was born to culturally obsessed Brahmin parents, went to tweedy schools like the country squire. So you would assume he goes down on weekends to sail from Newburyport, right? Wrong. His favorite vacation is driving a big powerboat around Lake Winnipesaukee," said Clark. "Just when you think you have him figured out, he thwarts it.

"If there were no Jud Hale, we'd have to invent one. He represents more pieces of New England than anyone we know."

In much the same way, Clark said, *Yankee* under Hale's direction has learned how to surprise readers who have come to expect a certain traditionalist package from the magazine. There have been stories about poverty in Vermont's Northeast Kingdom, and attempts to revitalize troubled towns like Gloucester and New Bedford, Massachusetts.

"We've done AIDS in Vermont," noted Hale, challenging the magazine's reputation for quaintness.

Clark also pointed to a story in the December 1998 issue on a gay man in Lewiston, Maine, whose fortunes spiraled downward after he won the lottery, ending with his murder in a motel room.

Others might dispute Clark and Hale's characterization of the magazine's realism; the most common criticism of the magazine remains that it portrays a prettified version of the region. Indeed, the editor's note in the December 1998 issue included a warning of sorts about the Lewiston story, as if acknowledging it fell outside the magazine's boundaries. "Many readers may be offended by 'Fortune's Fool,'" the note read.

Many of the magazine's mainstays have changed little over time: There's plenty of fix-it advice, regional recipes, profiles of artisans (wooden boatbuilders, basketmakers, coopers), features on favored destinations like the Cape, the Maine coast, and the White Mountains.

To some extent, Clark said, relying on the old standbys is unavoidable. The fact is, he said, many remnants of old New England survive, and most subscribers do not tire of reading about them. Referring to a cover story on a family of maple syrupers, Clark said, "Every once in a while you just have to do the icon. With that one, we figured enough time had gone by, that it was safe to come back to the icon. It's what we do to respond to those who say there is no region anymore."

Hale agreed. Contrary to what the doomsayers argue, he said, New England is doing better as a region than it was twenty years ago, thanks to its strong new technology sector and to people moving into the region who are committed to preserving its customs. That so many towns are working to spruce up their main streets and refurbish landmarks is proof, he said, that the region's identity is not moribund.

"One of the things I tell people is that the image is real: Come with me, and I'll show it to you. Do you think the image is white churches in the middle of town? Well, we have hundreds of those," he said.

A recent encounter in western Maine only reinforced this for Hale, he said. He stopped by a general store for some antacid tablet and was dismayed to learn that the store offered only the basic kind, not any flavored ones. As he left with his purchase, an old man sitting in a rocking chair by the door muttered to him, "Well, it looks like you're going to have to rough it, doesn't it?"

"At that point, I said to myself, 'If only the cynics could be here now!'" Hale recalled.

There was nothing new about the declarations of New England's demise as a distinct region, Hale said, as a line of Sagendorph's in the debut 1935 issue indicates: "For the Yankee, this is the age of bewilderment. He sees individuality, initiative, natural ingenuity, the things his father and their fathers fought for—about to be sold, to be 'swallered inter a sea of chainstores, national releases, and nationwide hookups.'"

With so many New Englanders, or ex-New Englanders, as readers, the magazine is no stranger to similar crusty laments. One reader bemoaned a feature on the furthest reaches of the Maine coast, predicting the article would lead to a land rush on the area. A Florida subscriber had this to say about a cover story on the "real Cape Cod": "The real Cape Cod is still there, but if you can't find it then I guess it should be left to those of us who know exactly where it is!"

If there is any regional trend that does worry him, Hale said, it is what he sees as an overindulgence by some residents in the Yankee virtue of self-reliance. More and more people, it seems, are isolating themselves out in the country in their big homes and big cars, undermining the village unit.

"Not as many people find entertainment in being together. Sure, you need to be self-sufficient and feel satisfied unto yourself, but maybe it's gone too far," he said.

Such concerns, though, don't keep Hale from feeling confident about the magazine's future. Realizing that its readership is aging, Hale said, the magazine is making an effort to include more "service-oriented" features for younger families. Within the ninety-employee company, the younger generation is already well involved: Helping run the business side of things out of *Yankee*'s Boston office is Jud Hale Jr.

Whatever the coming years hold for the region, Hale said, the magazine will forever be able to appeal to the national ideal of what New England was, and what it may or may not still be.

"I'm always amazed, on my tours, how in Houston, say, you see New England scenes on Christmas cards. I know I haven't seen a Texas scene on a Christmas card here. In St. Louis they have a New England Club. Do we have a St. Louis club here?" he said.

"Am I being a little snobbish? Maybe a little bit. But every person who loves their region has been accused of being a snob."

J. D. Salinger

His fictional creation, Holden Caulfield, remains a voice for teenagers everywhere.

BY JIM GRAHAM

J. D. Salinger hasn't shown his face much outside his remote country estate for more than forty years now. He does not grant interviews. He hates having his picture taken. Yet his work remains in the spotlight because his 1951 creation, Holden Caulfield, is still raising hell in public schools the world over.

Caulfield, the main character in Salinger's novel, *The Catcher in the Rye,* is a seventeen-year-old with a serious attitude problem. He says most adults are phonies. He thinks the most popular kids in school are, too. He swears too much. He daydreams about sex. He is easily bored and constantly critical. He

Salinger as a young man.
AP/ Wide World Photos.

blows off homework assignments, skips classes, and gets drunk on occasion. And he struggles mightily to find his way in a world full of hypocrisy.

Kids love Caulfield. Even today, they identify with him or, at least, with aspects of his adolescent angst, making him one of the most talked-about, enduring characters in literature.

"You either were like him when you were growing up, or you knew somebody who was," said Mark Phelps, an English teacher in Concord. "The reality of Holden Caulfield is something kids are able to look at clearly."

That scares some adults, and conservative groups want nothing to do with him. *The Catcher in the Rye* remains one of the most frequently banned books in public schools. As recently as 1994, it was removed as mandatory reading from Goffstown schools because parents charged it contained "vulgar words" and presented several characters' "sexual exploits."

So while Salinger remains a mystery man in his New Hampshire surroundings, his legacy—Caulfield—remains an open book.

"Until Holden Caulfield came along, there was no other voice of that age in literature that was so immediate and genuine sounding," said Robert Pingree, an English teacher at Concord High School.

On its face, Caulfield's story is simple enough. From the confines of a mental institution, he delivers a monologue recounting his progression from confused adolescent to clinically disturbed young man. The story begins when Caulfield is kicked out of his fourth private school, Pencey Prep, for bad grades and a bad attitude. It concludes with Caulfield's painful realization, and grudging acceptance, that he can no longer escape the realities of growing up.

Written in rapid-fire, stream-of-consciousness prose, the book reads as if Salinger crawled inside a teenager's head and looked out at his school and the greater world.

> You ought to go to a boys' school sometime. Try it sometime. It's full of phonies, and all you do is study so that you can learn enough to be smart enough to be able to buy a goddam Cadillac someday, and you have to keep making believe you give a damn if the football team loses, and all you do is talk about girls and liquor and sex all day, and everybody sticks together in these dirty little cliques. The guys that are on the basketball team stick together, the Catholics stick together, the goddam intellectuals stick together, the guys that play bridge stick together. Even the guys that belong to the goddam Book-of-the-Month Club stick together.

Reading *The Catcher in the Rye*, teenagers trying to make sense of the confusing cliques in their own schools find a certain truth. With Caulfield, even the outcasts discover they are not alone.

"What Salinger leaves us is a new image of the adolescent hero," said William Cook, an English professor at Dartmouth College, who taught the book as a high school teacher in Princeton, New Jersey, for twenty-one years.

Caulfield, he said, was the first teenage hero in literature who blatantly rejected, even ridiculed, society's conventions. There had been teenage heroes before, of course, but none that so openly rebelled against the pressures to conform.

"Holden Caulfield is a far different kind of adolescent hero than someone like Huck Finn, in that Salinger's depiction of American culture is far darker and more hopeless than that of (Mark) Twain," Cook said.

Caulfield hit the bookshelves four years before strikingly similar themes were played out in the James Dean movie *Rebel Without a Cause,* and a full decade before the nation's youth staged a cultural revolution marked by sex, drugs, rock 'n' roll, long hair, and anti-war protests. What's historically surprising is that Salinger's masterpiece actually began shocking public sentiments in 1945 and 1946, when portions were published in *Collier's* and *The New Yorker.* This was just after World War II, when conformity and unfailing respect for adult authority were demanded of the nation's youth. So when Caulfield came along and labeled conventional wisdom "phony," it created a furor that still hasn't abated.

"It stabs at the basic assumptions of the culture, which represents our whole myth of what America is all about," Cook said. For the same reason, rebellious youths of the 1960s also gravitated to another of society's famous literary dropouts, Henry David Thoreau, and his book, *Walden.*

Between being kicked out of school and heading home to New York City for Christmas vacation, Caulfield spends several days roaming aimlessly about the city on his own, sinking deeper into his self-absorbed world of confusion, cynicism, depression, and debauchery. He has a frustrating encounter with a prostitute. He tries, and fails, to impress other women his own age. He desperately reaches out to old acquaintances, most of whom reject him. He brags about his ability to hold liquor, then acts like a fool when he gets drunk.

It is not comforting reading.

But Caulfield also comes to an enlightened realization during his gloomy bender. On a visit to his ten-year-old sister's nearby elementary school, Caulfield is enraged when he discovers an epithet scrawled on the stairwell wall, right where all the impressionable children will see it.

"It drove me damn near crazy. . . . I kept wanting to kill whoever'd written it," Caulfield says.

But after erasing it, he discovers a similar swear scratched on a separate stairwell. He concludes he can't erase all the swears and that it is naive to think that children can be sheltered from the worst of growing up.

> If you had a million years to do it in, you couldn't rub out even half the 'f—— you' signs in the world. It's impossible. . . . That's the whole trouble. You can't ever find a place that's nice and peaceful, because there isn't any. You may think there is, but once you get there, when you're not looking, somebody'll sneak up and write 'F—— you' right under your nose.

In a way, this realization is liberating for Caulfield. Not long after, he watches and begins to worry about his little sister's safety as she rides a revolving carrousel in Central Park. Leaning out far from the wooden horse she is riding to grab the gold ring, she appears in danger of falling. Yet Caulfield suppresses his urge to reach out and protect her.

"The thing with kids is, if they want to grab for the gold ring, you have to let them do it, and not say anything," Caulfield says. "If they fall off, they fall off, but it's bad if you say anything to them."

Salinger's book has lasting, broad appeal to both the famous and infamous who, at one time in their lives, struggled with how they would fit into the mainstream. Microsoft founder and billionaire Bill Gates and movie actress Winona Ryder both say it is their favorite book. Mark Chapman carried it with him when he gunned down former Beatles star John Lennon on a New York City street.

Born Jerome David Salinger, the author knew of what he wrote. He lived in New York City most of his life. He was educated at Valley Forge Military Academy (the model for Pencey Prep) and New York and Columbia universities. He served in the infantry in World War II.

Although he shunned publicity, Salinger did not vanish from the literary world after *The Catcher in the Rye*. He also published *Nine Stories* in 1953 and *Franny and Zooey* in 1961 and continued writing for *The New Yorker*.

Today, he lives in Cornish, a quiet town of 1,600 along the Vermont border. He reportedly still writes from his hilltop home, tucked away at the end of a seldom-traveled dirt road and surrounded by woods—but he resists publishing his newer works because of the invasion of privacy it would invite.

Salinger has two grown children from his marriage to Clair Douglas, which ended in 1967. He is reported to have remarried in the early 1990s, though details of the relationship have not been published.

Most recently, he is known for a book he did not write, or invite. Joyce Maynard, a nationally syndicated columnist, single mother and native of Hillsboro, wrote a tell-all book in 1998 about her affair with the reclusive author three decades earlier.

Maynard's *At Home in the World* details how, as an eighteen-year-old writer and student at Yale, she received a letter of praise from Salinger, who was then fifty-three. Their correspondence led to an affair that fizzled less than a year after Maynard moved in with Salinger.

The book received a lukewarm reception, and Maynard was roundly criticized for profiteering on her relationship with the intensely private Salinger so many years ago.

Salinger offered no public comment on the Maynard book. His neighbors went out of their way to protect his privacy when reporters began arriving in anticipation of the book's publication.

Perhaps Salinger is content with his legacy and with letting Caulfield do his talking. Perhaps, as Caulfield says, Salinger's most dedicated readers feel they already know him as an old friend.

"What really knocks me out," Caulfield says, "is a book that, when you're all done reading it, you wish the author that wrote it was a terrific friend of yours and you could call him up on the phone whenever you felt like it. That doesn't happen much, though."

Contributors

Mary Allen is a local editor at the *Concord Monitor*.

Felice Belman, the former city editor of the *Concord Monitor*, is an editor at the *Washington Post*.

Michael J. Birkner, a former *Concord Monitor* editorial page editor, is the chairman of the history department at Gettysburg College.

Aaron Bowden is a reporter for the *Concord Monitor*.

Scott Calvert is a reporter for the *Baltimore Sun*.

Sarah M. Earle is a reporter for the *Concord Monitor*.

Jonathan Fahey is a reporter for *Forbes* magazine.

Gwen Filosa is a reporter for the New Orleans *Times-Picayune*.

Jim Graham is a reporter for the *Concord Monitor*.

Katie Helm is a former reporter for the *Concord Monitor*.

Burton Hersh is an author who lives in Bradford.

Sarah Koenig is a reporter for the *Baltimore Sun*.

Alec MacGillis is a reporter for the *Baltimore Sun*.

Amy McConnell is a reporter for the *Concord Monitor*.

Tim McLaughlin is a reporter for the Reuters news service.

Chris Morris is the news editor of the *Concord Monitor*.

Mike Pride is the editor of the *Concord Monitor*.

Sandy Smith is the sports editor of the *Concord Monitor*.

Nancie Stone is a reporter for the *Concord Monitor*.

Carrie Sturrock is a reporter for the *Charlotte Observer*.

Annmarie Timmins is a local editor at the *Concord Monitor*.

Mark Travis is the editorial page editor of the *Concord Monitor*.

Steve Varnum is a reporter for the *Concord Monitor*.

Index